# HAND ON THE SHOULDER

## FINDING *FREEDOM* IN THE *CONFLUENCE* OF *LOVE* & *CAREER*

# Hand on the Shoulder

## Finding Freedom in the Confluence of Love & Career

**GRANT TATE**

HOLON
PUBLISHING

www.Holon.co

ISBN#: 978-1-955342-51-3 (Hardback)
ISBN#: 978-1-955342-52-0 (Paperback)
ISBN#: 978-1-955342-53-7 (eBook)

Published by:

Holon Publishing & Collective Press
A Storytelling Company
www.Holon.co

*This book is dedicated to my brother,
Warren S. Tate, who has given me and so many
other people a much-needed hand on the shoulder.*

*—GT*

# CONTENTS

| | |
|---|---|
| *Introduction* | *xi* |
| *I. Hand on the Shoulder* | *1* |
| 1. It Started with a Phone Call | 3 |
| 2. Albuquerque | 4 |
| 3. Sabbatical | 5 |
| 4. Dad | 7 |
| 5. As White as Silk | 9 |
| 6. Black Kid | 11 |
| 7. Trains | 12 |
| 8. The War | 14 |
| 9. Picking Peaches | 17 |
| 10. Small Kid | 19 |
| 11. Plane Schedule | 20 |
| 12. Home Town Mentor | 21 |
| 13. Haywood Johnson | 25 |
| 14. Managing the Store | 28 |
| 15. On the Plane | 29 |
| 16. Mom | 31 |
| 17. Cemetery | 32 |
| 18. The Workshop | 35 |
| *II. A Kid Enters Big Blue* | *37* |
| 19. Engineering School: A Struggle | 39 |
| 20. First Days at IBM | 41 |
| 21. Joyce | 43 |
| 22. College or Not? | 45 |
| 23. Endicott | 47 |
| 24. Mrs. LaShier | 48 |
| 25. After Jenkins | 49 |
| 26. Manufacturing People | 51 |
| 27. The Wedding | 54 |

28. Real Work     56

*III. Getting on the Fast Track*     **61**

29. Lt. Tate     63
30. Capt. Luebbert     67
31. Compelo Tech     70
32. A Step Up     77
33. JFK     82
34. Five-Year Reflection     84
35. Big Changes     86

*IV. In the Shadow of the Rockies*     **91**

36. Boulder     93
37. Eutaw Drive     94
38. Crisis     96
39. Mountain Air     104
40. An Executive Arrives     106
41. Happy in Boulder     112
42. A New Adventure     114
43. Surprise Party     117
44. Stanford     119
45. Boulder After Stanford     124
46. The Board of Directors     125
47. Reflections On Colorado     128

*V. Entering the Corporate Jungle*     **131**

48. Headquarters     133
49. Go Out There and Fix it!     139
50. Mary Lou     144
51. The Announcement     148
52. My Contract     157
53. Darlene     158
54. Trustworthy Tony     159
55. Organizational Change     161
56. Porsche     164
57. Secretarial Centers!     166
58. The Geyser     168
59. Cary Again     170
60. Judge Dixon     176
61. Turnaround Completed     178
62. Bad Move     181

63. International Division 184
64. Southern Sheriff 189
65. Innersanctum 191
66. New Mexico 196
**VI. Where the Heck am I?** **203**
67. Back to IBM 205
68. Adrift 208
69. Jim Morgan 210
70. Sally 211
71. The Graduation 213
72. White Plains Y 215
73. Moving in 217
74. The Personal Computer 219
75. Therapy 227
76. A Calmer Assignment 233
77. Esther 237
78. Retirement 246
79. The University 249
80. Hawaii 252
81. Sticking a Toe in Politics 256
82. Prague in 1991 259
**VII. Reconstructing a Life** **267**
83. Weimer's Call 269
84. Montesson 270
85. The Voice 271
86. Ancolien 272
87. Bastille Day 276
88. Losing Leo 278
89. Never Bike in Paris 280
90. Maisons-Lafitte 283
91. Sad Jane 286
92. Leaving Paris 289
93. Hello, Netherlands 290
94. Meerssen 292
95. Valkenburg 295
96. Soren 299
97. In the Shadow of the Castle 300
98. Crazy Wedding 302

99. Life in the Netherlands     306
100. Florence     307
101. Happy Dutch Wedding     311
102. Our New Company     313
**VIII. Closing the Circle**     **319**
103. To the USA     321
104. Jerome     324
105. The Light     326
106. Mom Drifting Away     327
107. A New Century     329
108. Return to New Mexico     332
**Epilogue**     **337**
**About the Author: Grant Tate**     **341**

# INTRODUCTION

It was a cold day in June when I arrived at the Susquehanna River. The town of Endicott lay across the river, still shrouded in a morning mist and looking like a place from another era. Getting here from Virginia was the longest distance I had ever driven alone and the first trip of any kind in my new 1957 Plymouth, the model with the huge tail fins and push-button automatic transmission.

An engineering degree in hand, I was taking my first step into the unknown world of big business, technology, real Italian spaghetti, and northern American culture. IBM's vast production plants with 6,000 workers lay just across the river. On Monday morning, I was to report to their personnel department and begin finding my way in the complex labyrinth of the corporate world.

In four weeks, I would return to my small town, Orange, Virginia, to marry my high-school sweetheart and, a few days later, have her join me in this venture into the unknown. If she had been sitting with me looking across the Susquehanna Bridge, I could never have explained the future we would experience; two small town kids on an uncharted road, infused with the culture, expectations, and values of the South.

In my childhood, there was a large open space called Wynn's Field behind the back fence that bordered our house. I sometimes stared over the fence curious to see what went on back there. A small creek, scrubby bushes, a few trees, and some unidentifiable pieces of metal sparked my interest.

"Play all you want in the backyard, but don't go into Wynn's Field," Mom said.

As a child, I never crossed the fence into Wynn's Field, but I have been searching for that place ever since. I like change, meeting new people, seeing new places, having new experiences, and learning new things. I like to explore.

But taking risks and entrepreneurship were not the legacies of my clan. They were more likely to be dirt farmers than estate owners. And I don't know any relative who was willing to risk other people's money to start or grow a business. That would have been contrary to the family's ethics. The family ethic demanded good behavior: attend church, love each other, help other people, work hard, raise your family, avoid conflict, take responsibility, obey the rules, and be self-sufficient.

That legacy was fine until it wasn't. My self-sufficiency folded under the weight of carrying too much responsibility alone. When I faced difficulties, I was embarrassed to admit them to my family and friends. I found myself alone on the prow of the ship with the cold wind blowing in my face, blinding me to the need to reach out to my shipmates.

When I needed to reach out, I turned inward, but finding no one there, swirled around in the miasma. I was drifting. I had stopped exploring. I was estranged from my wife, my extended family, my friends. I had failed to build a personal support system.

When I finally learned to reach out, to give and receive love and support, the path became clear, but it ultimately took moving to a new continent to find the way.

The stories in this book are the stepping stones—some leading to new adventures, others to slippery convolutions. And, at the foundation of each step lay decisions and assumptions resulting in unanticipated consequences. Those decisions were made in the context of the intersecting tides of personal drive, southern culture, company norms, and family needs. Tides I sometimes failed to understand while moving through life.

As with all memoirs, this is the way I remember things. I have changed some names to protect people's privacy, but used the real names of prominent business leaders, who do not deserve to hide.

Writing this book has been part of the healing process, an opportunity to reexamine turning points, to reconsider old decisions, and to take a fresh look at times and relationships from my upbringing in my small town in Virginia to my stepping into a transformed life at the turn of the new century.

Yes, there is much to say about my life since January 1, 2000, when this book ends: the flowering of a new relationship, the exploration of a new profession in consulting, the new stories, the new characters. But that book will have to wait.

I write this with deep apologies to my three children, David, Lynn, and Laura for the missed opportunities of time together and for my absences in time of need. But I am thankful for them, my wife, Ancolien, and my brother, Warren, for their love and support during my exploration of life.

I thank my editor, Rebekah Spivey for her expertise and inspiration in preparing the text. Her wisdom, insight and good humor have been guiding lights. Also, thanks members of the Holon team, Grace Beck, Leslie Cao, and Victoria Stingo for their support and guidance, and Leslie, in particular, for our many conversations in formulating this book. And special thanks to my physical therapist, Rebecca Brown, who helped me keep a gimpy hip under control during the writing period.

And thanks to my many friends and colleagues who encouraged me to take on this project. "I'd like to know how you came to be who you are," was a frequent comment. This book helps answer that.

# *HAND* ON THE *SHOULDER*

# IT STARTED WITH A PHONE CALL

It is left to me now to untangle the intricate web of events that set me on my slow downward slide. At the time, I was completely unaware that my support system was rotting from within and without. I did not feel the first molecule of rust that formed on my girders. I knew that something was missing and had searched for it in forbidden places; but had no idea what was driving me, no idea of my growing thirst for intimacy, no idea that my path was anything but the right one.

# ALBUQUERQUE

A hand on the shoulder interrupts my train of thought. Turning, I look into the eyes of Jerry Jordan, my friend, and Dean of the Anderson School of Business at the University of New Mexico.

"Your wife is on the phone in my office and needs to speak to you," he says quietly.

Oh my God, what is this? Joyce has never interrupted a meeting before. Someone—maybe one of the children—must have been hurt.

I pick up the phone to hear her crying.

"What's wrong?" I say. "What is it?"

"It's your dad," she says among the sobs. "He died this morning during his test at the hospital."

"No! No! No!" I sob, sinking into the chair. "He was only taking a stress test. How could this be? I just saw him two days ago and he seemed fine."

I sink into Jerry's chair, stunned, trying to process the news.

Jerry Jordan steps in the room. "I'm so sorry," he says. "You can stay right here if you want."

"I need to get to Virginia," I say.

"Bill Gross's team over at Engineering is already looking at plane schedules," Jerry replies. We didn't know whether you wanted to go to Connecticut or Virginia. I'll get you some coffee, and you can stay here until we get the reservations pinned down."

# SABBATICAL

After almost five years as Director of Planning and Technical Services at IBM's General Business Group, International division (GBG/I), I was ready for a change. I had never been in a job that long, and it was beginning to feel like a drag. I'd lost track of how many divisional strategic and operational plans we had completed. Lately, every plan seemed the same. I'm a turnaround guy, not a crank-turner. It was 1979 and there were no immediate prospects for a new opportunity at the company. That year, *Business Week* had asked, "Is IBM just another mature company?" We'd been losing market share, stock prices were down, and our growth rate had stalled.

Some would have said the job was exciting. Our division covered Canada, Europe, Asia, and Latin America. There were 11 manufacturing plants in ten different countries for which my unit ran the strategic planning processes. In addition, we designated where each product would be manufactured; a critically important decision process that often involved IBM's top management. 50 people from across ten different countries were on my team.

I was constantly traveling. Almost 40 percent of my days were spent in travel, often including weekends. Paris, Berlin, Amsterdam, Bogota, Guadalajara, Madrid became regular destinations. Exciting, yes, but tiring, to me and the family. During one period of six months, I asked for a travel moratorium because my son, David, was having trouble in school, requiring at-home tutoring for a whole semester.

Yes, it was time for a change. So, I applied for the "faculty loan program," where the company provided an employee to help a college or university implement its minority program, requesting an assignment in the West. At about the same time, headquarters received a letter from Dean William Gross at the University of New Mexico, asking for help. Two weeks later, I flew to Albuquerque for an interview, and within a month my wife, Joyce, and our daughter, Laura, and I moved to New Mexico to begin a new adventure while our daughter, Lynn, and son, David, stayed behind in college.

\* \* \*

I look at my watch. 11:00 am Albuquerque time, 1:00 pm in the East. They'll be lucky to find me a plane today. Just as well get comfortable here. My mind turns back to Dad.

# DAD

Dad frequently complained of indigestion and tried numerous antacids and other remedies over the years. He also once had rheumatic fever, a disease that can damage a heart. Perhaps, the chest discomfort had been due to an underlying heart condition.

As far as I know, Dad never had a day of formal management training in his life. He used sound human relations and family values. He never gave me much specific career advice except "go to college and stay out of the textile industry."

I've often wondered how to measure his influence on my working life. Unlike him, I've had years of business and management training. Yet the early lessons from Dad and another mentor, Goree Waugh, seem to be the most enduring.

There is no graduate business school named the "G. Wesley Tate School of Management." Nor is there a professorship named after him. But that is not what he would have wanted. Helping people was his legacy; not making a name for himself, not making money.

When I was growing up, Dad worked at American Silk Mills in Orange. He was the supervisor of the department that turned raw threads into the yarn used by the hundreds of looms that wove special textiles for the fashion industry. I remember visiting the mill, hearing hundreds of redrawing and quilling machines, and seeing people hurrying around to load the monsters with nylon, rayon, and other synthetics. Dad was proud to introduce visitors to the people he worked with and to explain how the complicated machines worked. "Our fibers make our textiles different," he'd say. "The texture of the final product depends on us."

When he began his job at the mill, he worked 12 hours a day, six days a week without overtime pay. The factory closed down one week a year so that people could have a short vacation. As far as I remember, that was the only benefit; no medical plan, no retirement—just work your hours and get your pay.

I remember the whine and roar of the machines in Dad's department and the strange odor of oil, ozone, and raw textiles they generated. That noise was multiplied in the other major department, weaving, where hundreds of looms sent shuttles flying back and forth at high speeds. No one in the company apparently had thought of providing ear protection for the operators.

Dad was a good manager. Many of our dinner conversations revolved around tales of the people in his department, many of whom had grown up in poverty and were thankful for having a paying job. A young woman passed out on the job one day. While helping her, Dad learned she hadn't eaten in days. He took her to the store across the street and bought her some food to help her get on the track to better health.

Yes, Dad cared about his people but had little good to say about the mill owner, Milton Rubin, who showed up occasionally, using abusive language to berate mill management for not producing enough. Dinners at home after one of Rubin's visits did not generate good memories. Rubin, from New Jersey, started the mill in Orange to take advantage of cheap labor, and he wanted to keep it that way.

After 25 years, Rubin gave Dad a Swiss watch—a meager reward for years of dedicated work. That watch is still in my mother's memory box—a symbol of years of sweat and toil.

Soon after receiving the watch, Dad finally had his fill. He was sick of the working conditions and the way that the upper management treated people.

"I really have to leave the silk mill," he told me as we walked the long hill toward our house, "Don't know what I'll do for a job. I want you to stay in college. You're only in your second year."

"I'll be okay," I said. "Scholarships and part-time jobs will see me through."

Soon, Dad enrolled in accounting classes and began a new career. But his legacy as a manager lived on. I ran into people who said, "Wesley was the best manager I ever had. He was tough, but he cared about us."

# AS WHITE AS SILK

But there were limited types of employees. There were no Black people working in the American Silk Mill, unless they were doing janitorial work. In Orange, Virginia then, there were two different societies, Black and White. There were separate water fountains, separate doctors, separate schools, separate churches, even a separate taxi service owned by Simon Coleman for Black people. Retail and other businesses served both, but of course, Black Americans were afforded a lower level of service. Getting loans or credit was a challenge. Dad had quite a few Black friends, including Rosa Graves, a lifelong friend of the family. Mom and Dad never said anything sounding outright racist or prejudicial, but there was always an undertone that the Black Americans were lower class. I interpreted that as, "Black people are good as individuals, but, as a group, keep them in their place." At an early age, that confused me. As time went on, the idea became abhorrent.

In school, no one ever said Black people were inferior, it was simply a societal assumption. There was slight mention of slavery in history classes, but cruelty or oppression was never mentioned. Pictures, stories, or books about slaves showed only kind Aunt Jamimas or Uncle Toms going about their duties with warm, happy smiles. Those myths helped define the relationship between Black and White people. Treat Black people with kindness and they will reward you with a smile. Don't tolerate any backtalk or sass. Always encourage subservience.

In the South, the Civil War was called "The War Between the States," fought, not about slavery, but about states' rights. The periods of Reconstruction, and afterwards, Jim Crow, were given one chapter in the Virginia History book with perhaps one hour of discussion in the classroom. Robert E. Lee was the greatest general in the war. He and all his compatriots fought valiantly for a cause that was pure but turned out to be futile. But remember, the South will rise again. Remember that as we all sing "Dixie."

Confederate flags were flying in public places. A statue of a Confederate soldier still stands on a high pedestal in front of the Orange County Courthouse. The local Lion's Club sponsored a yearly minstrel show in the high school auditorium. The high school chorus repertoire included spirituals promoting the idea of the "dear old darkie."

Public schools were separate, but far from equal. Elementary and middle schools for Black kids were significantly run down with little investment. Black high schoolers attended a relatively new, but distant, George Washington Carver High School.

The most prestigious club in the community for women was the United Daughters of the Confederacy. Members had to show evidence of descendancy from a Civil War veteran or have some documented tie to one. To my knowledge, none of my relatives ever qualified.

# BLACK KID

At the age of six or eight, I liked to play with toy soldiers. World War II was raging in Europe and the far East, so I tried to simulate some of the small battles. One morning, sitting in our front yard on Main Street, I assembled a fight between two toy platoons.

A Black kid, slightly larger than I, approached from down the street. I started feeling a bit nervous. I knew Black and White people didn't mix, and I'd heard Black people stole things. I looked at my toys, wondering if I should pick them up and run inside.

The kid came close and said, "Can I play, too?"

I looked up at his smiling face and said, "Sure. Which side do you want?"

For the next 30 minutes or so, we played shoot 'em with the soldiers, making our sounds of pow, aaarg, and boom.

After a while, Dad's car pulled up to the curb. He was coming home for lunch. My heart flipped, wondering what he would say. He stepped out of the car and looked over at us sitting in the yard, toy soldiers scattered around.

"This is my friend," I said hesitantly, even though I didn't know the kid's name.

"Hi," Dad said, stepping up to the porch.

My young friend jumped up and ran down the street, leaving me to gather up the toy soldiers.

I went inside, head bowed, just as Dad was ready to sit down with Mom for lunch.

"I… I'm sorry," I said.

"Did you have fun?" Dad asked, never addressing my comment.

"Well… yes," I replied.

The next day and for several days after, I returned to the same spot with my toy soldiers, hoping my friend would show up, but I never saw him again.

# TRAINS

In those days, Orange was a railroad town, a dangerous little town. Two tracks, one owned by Southern Railways and the other by the Chesapeake and Ohio split the town right down the middle, cutting through Main Street with the power and authority of black, smoke-breathing dragons. The townspeople could set their watches by the train whistles. "There comes the 9:07," Mr. Watts would say, pulling his watch out of his pants pocket to check it. After all, railroad time was as official as the great ball in Greenwich. There was a time when the trains passed through without the warning whistles, but the wreck of old '97 changed all that. After the monster jumped the tracks on the curve just a mile out of town, people demanded not just a toot, but a long blast from every approaching train.

Even at that, getting run over by a train was a worry for every mother in town. They warned their children, "Listen for the train whistle, and don't get too close to the train, the wind will suck you under the wheels and cut you in half." Every time Mom and I waited for a train to pass, the slightest puff of wind in my face was a sure sign the passing freight was ready to suck me into its grinding wheels.

There were also other hazards. The engines belched not just smoke, but soot. After each passing coal-burning steam engine, small black particles with tiny edges like cut diamonds filled the air, penetrating people's lungs, pores, and eyes. Almost every time we went downtown, a cinder seemed to light in my eye. Mom would pull a clean, crocheted handkerchief out of her purse, say, "Open your eye, now and look up." She'd gently extract the black boulder while I screamed in teary pain.

We lived on the East side of the tracks in one of the brick houses up on Standpipe Hill. Waugh Furniture, the Orange Hotel, Gill's Hardware, Dr. Hankins office, Thompsons Food Market, and Gryme's Drug Store were along Main Street on our side of the tracks. Yet, a typical shopping day downtown would take us all the way up Main Street to Legget's Department Store, Sparks Grocery, Page's Drug Store, Lerner's Store, the 5 and 10, or the Western Auto. The movie theatre and the churches lay toward the far end of Main Street. I liked to look at the bicycles in the Western Auto and the cap pistols in the 5 and 10, hoping someday, I'd save enough from my ten cents a week allowance to buy one of them.

One day, as we walked along Main Street in front of Legget's, I heard the loud and familiar wail of the mid-morning passenger train approaching the crossing. The ground shook beneath our feet as the engine reached the edge of town. Suddenly, the roar of the passing train was punctuated by a bone-chilling scream. I clutched Mom's hand as we turned toward the tracks while men ran to the crossing. Instead of continuing toward Washington, the train slowed and eventually came to a stop. We could see a crowd gather around something lying next to the tracks. Mom's face was pale and grim.

"What is it?" I said.

"Someone got hit by the train," she said.

"How could that be?" I asked. "We heard the whistle blow. Did they get sucked under?"

"Don't know. Don't know," she said quietly.

We went into Legget's where she shopped for some new material for two shirts she was going to make for me. I had a hard time thinking about anything else but the screaming person who got sucked into the train. We had to cross the tracks to get home, and I never wanted to walk over the crossing again.

That night, Mom told Dad the story.

"I heard about it," he said. "It was somebody from Madison."

"Didn't they know about the trains?" I asked.

"Don't know. Don't know. Stay away from those trains," Dad said to me.

He really didn't have to tell me that.

# THE WAR

Racial issues were not high on anyone's mind in the forties. We were in the midst of a world war. The draft had taken most of the eligible men, Black and White, from our small town of Orange. Dad was exempt because he had contracted rheumatic fever a few years earlier, and his job at the silk mill was important because they were making parachutes for the war effort.

When the war started, my cousin, Bobby, and I were playing hide and seek among the fifty-year-old boxwoods on my grandparents' front lawn down in Louisa County. Although it was December, the grass was still green, and the bright Virginia sunshine warmed our bodies with a spring-like glow. Dad sat on a wooden lawn chair reading the Sunday paper we'd picked up on the way down from Orange.

It wasn't unusual for us to spend Sunday in Fredericks Hall, a tiny train stop where my grandparents lived in a big clapboard farmhouse. The visits were joyous occasions. I loved the fields, the barnyard, the woods that seemed to go on forever, the freedom of exploration, and the opportunity of playing with my cousins, who always seemed to be there, and Grandma Tate's home cooking.

Grandma Tate, a Sunday School teacher at Bethpage Church, didn't want us to play "guns" on Sunday, but cops and robbers—or more accurately, cowboys and Indians—were our favorite games. We'd run around with our shiny cap pistols pretending to be Gene Autry, Roy Rogers, or Hopalong Cassidy. We whooped and galloped around the house and the fields and routed our imaginary enemies with overwhelming firepower and verve.

But that Sunday was different. Granddad Tate came out of the back porch and into the yard, almost running to where Dad was sitting.

"Pearl Harbor has been bombed, and the war has started!" Dad jumped out of his chair. The two of them talked in quiet voices while Bobby and I stopped our game, wondering what was going on. We heard the word "war," but had no idea what it meant. Grandad and Dad's fearful and confused faces told us it was serious.

\* \* \*

In a few months, my uncle would visit us in his uniform, kiss me goodbye, and leave for the 8th Air Force. Gasoline and food would be rationed and the speed limits set to 35 miles per hour. Military convoys would become common sights on Virginia roads, and all of us, no matter how young, would learn to recognize German and Japanese planes from their profiles. We'd hear stories of the killed, the missing in action, the downed planes. Stars would be displayed in the windows of parents or wives and children who were never to see a loved one again.

Visits to my grandparents became less frequent as we strived to save gasoline. My grandfather seemed to spend every evening listening to his old battery radio, listening to Lowell Thomas's report on the battles of the day.

Yes, life changed on the 7th day of December 1941. The world would never be the same; I would never be the same. Our cops and robbers games turned to war games, played with miniature soldiers in grass and sand, but we were darkly aware that somewhere real life was being played out with gut-tearing bullets and blockbuster bombs. We lost our innocence after a radio broadcast.

Yet, for me, life went on. My family was not living in fear, although perhaps we should have been. Life was restricted, though. The town air raid siren often blasted a warning to turn off all lights unless your house was equipped with special opaque window shades. We never knew, of course, if there was a real danger of air raids or if these were only exercises. Nevertheless, everyone in town took it seriously. Having studied the profiles and silhouettes of German aircraft like most kids my age, I knew none of their bombers could fly from Germany to our town, so I can't remember ever feeling fear during the exercises.

"Strangely, toward the end of the war, Mom and Dad decided to have a house built in Marshall Heights, a neighborhood in Orange. In the process of it being built, we moved in with Mom's parents just outside town, and soon, somehow, I learned that Mom was "expecting." In late 1945, I helped welcome my brother, Warren, to the family, followed almost immediately by a move into a new place on a hill in Orange.

* * *

From that spot on the hill, we could still hear the train whistles blow, the trains marking changes in America at large. During the war, we often saw a long line of cars carrying brown jeeps, trucks, howitzers, and tanks pass slowly through our quiet town while we, who were either too young, women, or ineligible for the draft, watched in awe. Once in a while, a passenger train filled with waving soldiers and sailors made us wonder what exotic places would find them next. My uncle, Freddie, had boarded one of those trains. As had our family friend, Buck Carpenter, Mrs. Gill's son, Buck, and a lot of others I didn't know.

Late in the war, one of the trains with green cars came through bearing the body of President Roosevelt, who died at Hot Springs, Georgia. Our leader was gone.

# PICKING PEACHES

The summer of my 14th year, I joined a group of teenagers to work in the Mooremont Peach Orchard. We met a flatbed truck in downtown Orange, jumped in the back, and rode windswept to the orchard about ten miles away, where the field boss directed us to our crew for the day.

We got a quick lesson about how to select the peaches, handle them without bruising, and place them in boxes for transportation to the packing shed. I was more interested in keeping away from the poison ivy that formed a carpet among the trees. Soon, however, I was so covered with sweat and peach fuzz that I doubted the poison oil could penetrate it. At the end of the first day, I was completely covered, head to toe, with itchy, scratchy fuzz. I had the shower of a lifetime that night.

By weekend, I'd picked thousands of peaches and had eaten probably a bushel of them. Most of us knew how much we'd get paid, but rumors said that the man who owned the place sometimes gave bonuses. On Friday afternoon, we assembled around the packing shed where old man Moore sat on an upside-down basket on top of a small knoll. About 30 of us formed a line that snaked its way to his feet. He wore a rumbled cowboy hat and looked like an overseer from the old movies. We stared bug eyed as he stood up and pulled a fat roll of bills out of his pocket.

The first worker stepped forward. We could hear soft murmurs between the man and the first worker, followed by the old man peeling off some bills and handing them to the worker. The process was repeated 20 times until my turn came.

"What did you do this week?" asked the man in his gravelly drawl.

"I picked about a thousand bushels," I blurted, not having any idea how many I actually picked.

A slight grin across the wrinkled face as he peeled off five crisp new bills, handing them to me. I didn't look down to see what kind of bills he'd given me, but it seemed like a lot.

"See you next week," he said.

Walking away, I looked at my hand to see five twenty-dollar bills, an amazing amount for my week's work.

In the middle of the next week, a field boss showed up in a pickup truck near where I was picking.

"Hey you," he said. "We need you in the packing house."

Soon, I was in the production line sorting and arranging, and packing the peaches for shipping to distant markets. I had received my first promotion, but I never found out why. I wasn't a better picker than my crewmates. Maybe the old man liked my looks or my smarty comment.

# SMALL KID

I was a little kid for my grade. Left-handed, with a birthday in November (a Scorpio for those who are interested). Because of my age, my parents decided to put me in Ms. Honor Hamilton's private school rather than delaying my schooling for another year, which my birth month would have meant. Ms. Hamilton provided a small class with attention to handwriting, reading, and other basic skills.

But consequently, I was almost a year younger than my classmates in regular school. And, I was also smaller—a skinny little guy, unaccustomed to dealing with bullies on the playground. I soon learned that strategy and guile were my way to excel—well heck, even survive.

One guy in my neighborhood, Andy Bierne, younger but bigger than I, continually gave me a hard time. One day, I strung a rope across a path through some woods that were down the hill from my house. After school, I taunted Andy by throwing a rock at his feet, then turned to run down the path. I knew, of course, when to jump the rope, but Andy hit it, falling on his face—not hurt, but frustrated.

The next year, I made friends with Alton Breeden, a tough guy, and asked him to teach me some tricks. Every day during recess, we met at the sawdust pit that was made for high jumping exercises, where he taught me some basic jiu jitsu. It magically transformed my confidence on the playground; I almost broke a bully's arm after he took a swing at me.

Those lessons informed my work life, where I learned that applied knowledge and strategy were not just requirements for success, but basic survival tools.

# PLANE SCHEDULE

"Mary just called over from Dean Gross's office, and you're scheduled for a 4:15 flight. You'll have to make a few stops and get into DC really late, but you'll save almost a day this way," Jerry says.

"I'll get a taxi over to the airport, wait there, and get something to eat," I reply. "Thanks so much for your help."

\* \* \*

At the airport, I force down an enchilada with beans and find a comfortable place to sit. I think about Dad's mentoring, but also remember another mentor, Goree Waugh.

# HOME TOWN
# MENTOR

In the summer after my junior year of high school, I found a summer job at the G. A. Waugh Furniture store on Main Street, owned by Goree Waugh, whom everyone in town seemed to know.

Joe Minor entered through the door with his head down. It had been a rough night, and Joe's head pounded with the aftermath of cheap whiskey—and the jailhouse bunk had no mattress. Goree met him halfway down the aisle, between the rows of refrigerators and stoves.

"What happened, Joe"

"I done had a little too much to drink and Sher'f Myers throwed me in jail after I swung at Tom Johnson. I'm cain't go home... I jus don know wha da do."

"Let's go sit by the stove, Joe... and talk."

An hour later, Joe Minor walked out of the G. A. Waugh Furniture Co. with a short-term loan, aspirin for his headache, and some hard advice about the responsibilities of a family man. The next week, a cold sober Joe returned to the store to pay five dollars toward his new loan and another five on the stove he bought last year for credit at no interest. Joe was one of many who made their weekly visit to the small-town furniture store to pay some small amount on their account and pass the time of day with Goree.

The Waugh family went back generations in Orange County. Goree still owned the family farm, "Bushy Mountain," close to the peach orchard where I'd worked, although he spent most of his time at his house on Madison Street—just three blocks from the store.

Roy Perkins, Joe Minor's father-in-law and patriarch of a large Black family ran the farm for Goree and watched over the cows and horses. Roy successfully farmed the rugged mountain terrain of Bushy Mountain and earned enough to provide a comfortable living and educate his many children. Roy's face was a photographer's dream, with lines that reflected wisdom and a kind heart. When Roy shook hands, he gave you the feeling of being embraced by a strong, sensitive father.

Roy came into the furniture store almost every Saturday in his bib overalls and rumpled hat. Roy would saunter up to the mezzanine, where he and Goree greeted each other as if they'd been apart for months. Then they'd launch into an hour or more of quiet conversation, chatting about crops, the newest calves, or life in general. Roy and Goree made a colorful pair—the gentle farmer and the country gentleman.

"There can't be a business without customers," Goree would say, "and in a small town like this, we need customers for life. We have to make them feel special, and we'll give them top quality, the best service, and a fair price."

Goree stood a stately 6'2". Most people in town couldn't see the top of his bald head. What they saw most was his ready smile. He was a man you could talk to and someone you could trust. "A friend is the most precious thing a person can have, and integrity is the foundation of friendship," he said.

Underneath the tweed coat and quiet sophistication lived a cowboy. Spring was roundup time on Bushy Mountain. That's when Goree's special friends and I learned a new meaning of a day's work: Rise at 3:30 am, drive to the farm, catch the horses, ride to the top of the mountain, search for new calves, herd them back down the rock paths, run them into pens, inspect and tag the calves, and finally… eat a well-deserved meal. That was companionship, Waugh style.

G. A. Waugh Furniture Company occupied a prominent building with a multi-bay storefront on Main Street. There were three long rooms displaying furniture, heating stoves, refrigerators and other large appliances, mattresses, and many varieties of flooring. An upstairs warehouse held furniture, much of it purchased at yearly furniture marts in North Carolina, waiting to be moved to the main floor where it could be sold.

I was the fourth member of the team that consisted of Goree, Winfrey Jacobs, and Haywood Johnson. A few minutes after my arrival, Goree handed me a broom and said, "We all start the day by sweeping up the place." The place was vast with multiple aisles and nooks among various displays of furniture and other odds and ends. The brown wooden floor seemingly went on forever. Nevertheless, we all picked our places and went to work.

Sweeping the floor was one of many routines required to maintain and run the store. For instance, dusting and polishing the fine furniture, cleaning the large display windows—the list was long. But on that list was a task I learned to hate: measuring and coiling the material to repair split-bottom chairs. Those chairs, with seats of woven "splits," half-inch wide strips of fiber, were quite popular in those days. But the woven bottoms tended to wear out in a few years. Customers often brought their chairs to Waugh Furniture for repair, where we would remove the worn seating and replace it with new, freshly woven material. On the other hand, a customer could weave a chair bottom themselves, with a roll of fiber material, which we sold in lengths exactly long enough to repair one typical chair.

So, preparing those rolls to sell was part of our routine. That involved measuring 25 yards of the material, rolling the material round and round into a spiral disc, and tying it into a neat platter. This process would take 15 to 30 minutes even if one had the skill to do it. It was extremely labor-intensive—and boring. So, after doing that for a few weeks, I went into my dad's shop and made a simple device that would automatically measure the tape material and generate the spiral. We used that device for years after.

After I mastered the daily chores, Goree set out to teach me how to greet and work with customers, how to find out their needs, and how to help them select furniture or appliances to meet those needs. Goree and Winfrey Jacobs took me under their wings, leading me into the world of retail sales.

At first, I only shadowed each of them as they met and worked with a customer. Most of the time, they knew the person before even saying hello. Winfrey Jacobs had prominent white hair and a gentle manner. He spoke to each person as if they were a long-lost friend. "Hi, Mrs. Jones, how is your son, Harry? I heard he broke his arm last week." After getting up-to-date on the family, Winfrey would quietly ask a few questions to find out what Mrs. Jones needed. As I followed him around, listening quietly, he'd introduce me to each person as a new member of the team. After Mrs. Jones left, whether she bought anything or not, we'd talk about the interaction and how Winfrey's approach worked.

After Goree observed my sweeping for a week or so, he stopped me one morning and said, "You're the worst sweeper I've ever seen. How would you like to be our bookkeeper?" With that, Goree taught me to keep the books for the company, entering sales data, keeping customer accounts updated, recording payments. Goree handled the checkbook and the financial records but depended on me—just sixteen—to keep accurate records of all transactions. We had no computers in those days; everything was entered by hand in big journals.

Goree and I sat at side-by-side desks on the mezzanine, overlooking the entire first floor of the store. When a potential customer came into the front door, one of us went down the mezzanine's five steps to greet the person. But before that, however, Goree would challenge me: What is that person's name? What did she buy last in the store? Where does she live? Is she in a hurry or is she relaxed and interested in just looking around? Or what might she need to buy today?

By the time Goree made contact with the person, he had a conversation ready to go. At first, I watched and listened in awe of this amazing salesman and manager, but later, I too learned to glide into easy conversation. Whether it be sales, leadership, or personal relations, Goree was the master. He taught with quiet coaching and by strong example.

Once, a woman I knew as Gladys Eldridge entered the store and headed right for the living room furniture in the next room. I followed her, greeted her by name, and asked if I could help her. "Do you have any of those new sexual sofas," she said.

"Yes, Ma'am," I replied, suppressing my laugh and moving toward the sectional sofas that had become popular in the last year. I sold her a sofa, but never knew if she used it for sexual purposes.

Mrs. Eldridge had the money to buy the sofa, but many of Goree's customers had big needs and little means. Goree let people buy what they needed on credit with no interest. He'd only ask them to commit to a regular payment every week or every month until the item was paid off. We had dozens of customers, who came in every week to pay $1 to $10 on their account. And most of them looked at it as a visit, not an obligation thanks to the warm response they got from all of us in the store. At first, I wondered if Goree might be jacking up the prices to cover the lack of interest income; but, when I became the bookkeeper, I found he marked up the prices no more than the norm in our town.

The last time I saw Goree was at the Piedmont Nursing Home. Partially crippled by a stroke, he still seemed tall and stately in his wheelchair. Surprisingly, he remembered me, the store clerk from 40 years ago, and he missed the store, the farm, and his friends.

"Roy Perkins is gone now," he said with tears in his eyes. "Roy was my best friend."

"Yes, I loved Roy, too." I said, and I thought how few White men could call a Black man their best friend. But then, Goree was someone special.

# HAYWOOD JOHNSON

In the back of the store, beside the steps to the mezzanine, lay a small shop with a workbench filled with tools for installing stoves, laying linoleum, re-caning chairs, and repairing everything we sold. The workshop's maven was Haywood Johnson, a tall, strong Black man with a winning smile and a hearty laugh. A veteran of World War II, Haywood seemed to be an expert at everything. He could flawlessly cut linoleum to fit any irregular floor, he could install oil stoves with intricate piping and connecting hoses, he could make a furniture scratch disappear like magic.

Haywood was the store's master craftsman. His skills were unmatched by anyone else in town. I soon became his apprentice. But being half his strength, I learned to use my head rather than my muscles to get things done. Linoleum was delivered to us in 12-foot-wide rolls that weighed well over 300 pounds. Haywood could lift each end of the roll with little trouble, placing each on a dolly so we could roll the monster to the display room. I was good at pushing but not at lifting. One day, I amazed Haywood by using the leverage of our hand-operated floor-to-floor elevator to lift the roll ends, then slide the dollies underneath. Same result, no lifting.

As the smallest of our team, I was the one designated to crawl under old houses to wind copper tubing from the oil tank to the new stove we came to install. But it wasn't the tubing that set my nerves on end, it was the possibility of copperheads, the most common snake in Virginia. Luckily, I never encountered one. Haywood would say, "Now you look around with the flashlight before you move forward."

Haywood and I formed the delivery and installation department of G. A. Waugh Furniture Company. Together, we loaded furniture, stoves, and other goods on the rattling, Dodge five-speed truck for delivery out in the countryside. We hauled dressers, mattresses, and chairs all over Orange and the surrounding counties. We saw a closeup image of life among the rural people of Virginia. Haywood knew the territory like the back of his hand. We saw houses decorated with fine antiques, and we saw small places with only a few sticks of furniture.

One day, Hayward said, "I really didn't know it was that bad," after visiting some people in severely rundown housing.

Sometimes, bill collecting became an added task. The furniture store had amazingly few delinquent accounts, but sometimes people would leave town without paying.

Once we knocked on the door of an unpainted rural house, looking for a young man named Tom who hadn't paid anything on his account for several months. There were three relatively new cars parked in the driveway when we arrived.

A short, dark woman wiping her hands on a dishtowel came to the screen door looking puzzled.

"Hello there, Mrs. Thompson. Can we speak to Tom," said Haywood.

"Well, lordy, man, I haven't seen Tom for a month or more. Last I seen him, he was headed for Washington. I'm so worried about him."

"Ma'am, whose car is that out there in the driveway? Did he leave without his new car?"

"Naw. That isn't his car. That belongs to my brother, Tom's uncle. Tom went away with some friends last week."

"How come it has Tom's license plate on it," Haywood bluffed.

The woman shuffled in place, turning the dish towel over and over as if kneading it. Her brown eyes darted from side to side.

"I… I… don't know."

"Come on, Ma'am, can we speak to Tom."

"I've told you. He isn't here."

"Well, you tell him to come see us on Saturday. He owes us some money on his account," Haywood said loudly.

"If I hear from him, I'll tell him," she stuttered.

"Where do you think he was?" I asked Haywood as we got in the truck.

"Probably hiding in an upstairs bedroom and hearing every word. That's why I was talking so loud."

"Do you think he'll show up?"

"I doubt it. He drinks a lot and doesn't work much. Not like his mamma or his daddy. They're good folks."

Every week thereafter, when I posted receipts into the company journal by hand, I watched to see if Tom ever paid anything on his bill, but the account moved toward write-off—that never-never accounting land for uncollectible accounts. Tom became one of a tiny band of people who didn't pay their bills to the furniture store.

Sometimes we'd spend most of a day installing tile or linoleum on someone's kitchen floor. For that job, I was Haywood's assistant—handing him tools and doing the low-skill tasks: helping carry heavy rolls of linoleum, spreading paste, cleaning up after the job. If we had a full day's job, we usually carried our lunches in brown paper bags, knowing we'd be in some remote place.

One day we went to a store in Mine Run, a small crossroads in the northern part of the county, to install linoleum on a large kitchen. The store supplied bread, light groceries, miscellaneous supplies, soft drinks, and snacks to the locals. The owners lived in the back, which was surprisingly spacious considering a large portion of the building was devoted to commerce.

Haywood and I arrived at 8:30, greeted the owners, and went immediately to work, stripping the old floor and preparing to install the new one. By lunch, we were just over halfway through.

At noon, the wife leaned through the door and said, "Would you all like some hot lunch?"

I wasn't sure where she could have cooked a warm meal since we were working in the kitchen, but a vision of hot biscuits and country ham filled my head. "Sure," I said, smiling at Haywood. "Sounds like a good idea."

We washed the glue off our hands in the kitchen sink and headed for the dining room. There, she had set a table for three. The Mr. was standing at his place, Mrs. standing at hers, and she motioned me toward the third seat.

"Haywood, we've fixed a place for you on the porch," she said nonchalantly.

I must have turned pale. Haywood must have been shocked, but his face showed almost no emotion. I looked at him, back at Mrs., while struggling for words. The silence went on for what seemed like hours. What should I do? I don't want to insult some of the furniture store's best customers. Yet, I can't let them treat Haywood this way. What should I do? What should I do?

Finally, I blurted out, "Thanks so much, but Haywood and I eat together."

The two of us went to the porch. Soon the silent Mrs. brought my plate and place setting to the small table where Haywood's had already been set. I wanted to know what Haywood was thinking, but I was afraid to ask. Instead, we ate our lunch without a word, each staring down at our food, Haywood with his feelings, me with mine.

# MANAGING
# THE STORE

During my second summer at the store, as Goree and I were working at our desks on the mezzanine, he turned to me and said, "You know I'm going to Scout Camp for the month of July?"

"Yes," I replied.

"Well, I'd like for you to manage the store for me."

"OK," I said, "but what will the other guys think?"

"I'm sure they'll agree," he said.

"What about the bills and checks?"

"Well, you can process the payments, write the checks, and my wife, Dot, can sign them. We can go over any other loose ends before I leave," Goree said.

Managing the store during July wasn't such a big deal. Winfrey, Haywood, and I always operated as a team. We worked together on sales, scheduled our deliveries, and compared notes at the beginning of every day. But, Goree assigning me that responsibility at my age boosted my confidence more than any other words of praise. He had no doubt we could take care of things, while he helped mentor a group of young men at Scout Camp.

I worked at Waugh Furniture every summer and almost every weekend while I attended the University of Virginia. The skills I learned from my colleagues there, Goree Waugh, Winfrey Jacobs, and Haywood Johnson probably helped me more than all the engineering courses University of Virginia had to offer. I graduated high school with several marketable skills: sales, bookkeeping, delivery, store management, drafting, and human relations. After that experience, I knew how to make a path in the world.

# ON THE PLANE

*The New York Times* lays wilting in my hands. How could I imagine reading it? I was surprised to find today's issue, October 10, 1980. When we first came to Albuquerque, the *Sunday Times* arrived the following Tuesday. The presidential election is coming up and Reagan seems to be in the lead. Carter is a good man, but he seems to be in over his head. Anderson, the third-party candidate, speaks truth but has no chance in our system.

My head is pasted against the plane window, watching the plains of Texas roll by. Changing planes in Dallas is a pain in the neck but is necessary to get me to Virginia before tomorrow. My university colleagues worked hard to get these reservations.

I pull *The One Minute Manager* from my briefcase, but I can't concentrate. Nothing seems to get through my fog.

How will Joyce and the children get to Virginia? I wonder. Will she be willing to drive the 400 miles? She's never been big on family events.

I'm still wondering what happened to Dad. He was just 69 years old, for god's sake. A couple of days ago, I dropped by Virginia on a business trip that was taking me to Washington, Albuquerque, and back to New York. He had been to the doctor, who scheduled a heart stress test at the University of Virginia hospital in the nearby city of Charlottesville.

Dad seemed fine at the time, but he told me he'd experienced a couple of dizzy spells. He didn't give me a lot of details about the situation. I should have asked more. I remember our meeting.

Dad greets me at the door as if he knew the exact moment I would arrive from National Airport. I knew he'd have calculated my driving time for the hundred-mile track.

"Hey. How are you doing?" he says.

"Great, how are you?"

"OK. OK come on in."

I throw my suit jacket over a chair as we walk into the living room.

"I shouldn't sit down yet—I ripped my pants. Here, look at this." I say turning for him to see.

"Are you getting too big for your britches?" he asks.

"Nope, just move around too much," I smile.

"Come on, we'll fix it," he says, leading upstairs to the sewing room.

We enter Mom's sewing room—usually a woman's domain—which is the size of a small dressing room. Swatches of cotton, nylon, and rayon are stacked in columns on a workbench Dad made from a door, which also holds mom's prized Singer sewing machine.

A shoebox full of threads rests beside the machine. The room's odor reminds me of the textile mill where Dad used to work; an oily, synthetic odor punctuated by the aroma of a clean cotton shirt.

"Takeoff your pants. I'll show you how to run this machine," he says.

I complied, handing him my Brooks Brothers trousers.

Teaching. He was always teaching.

"This little thing is a bobbin. Make sure it has threads. Put the head down like this. Choose your stitch with this cam," he tells me, showing me the parts.

In 10 minutes, I was sitting at the sewing machine, stepping on the pedal.

"See. Now you'll be independent from now on," Dad says.

* * *

I think of all the things we didn't talk about, or actually never have talked about: What it's really been like to work in a big company, the stresses of doing big organization changes, my growing loneliness, a wife who seems to resent my job and my ambitions. Could he have had ways to solve these problems? What would he have said if I had let it all pour out? What if I had actually been able to describe what's going on? It's gnawing at me, but I have no idea how to say it or who to say it to. All I know now is that I am completely alone—on the prow of the ship with the cold wind in my face. How could I have been so stupid not to ask Dad for his perspective, his advice? Maybe I thought he would have criticized me for my bad choices, for not visiting enough, for not caring about the family, for marrying someone he didn't approve of. I don't know. I don't know what he would have thought. It's too late.

# MOM

I wonder how Mom will cope. Shy, she's always depended on Dad to be the face of the family, to make the difficult decisions. The only girl and youngest in a family of five, she was protected—even pampered—by her parents and older brothers while growing up in rural Louisa County. She met Dad at an early age and, with her mom and dad, moved to Orange soon after Dad began working at the silk mill. Whether Dad was the motivation for the family's move or not, is a mystery to my brother and me.

Her mother, Grandma Luck, was a wiry, strong-minded, skilled woman who seemed to always have things in control. Addie Luck was an expert seamstress, household and garden manager, with hands always crocheting during down times. She passed on those skills to Mom, but Mom preferred the quiet background rather than being out front in the family. Yet, she had the willpower and determination to do whatever necessary to support the family, and that meant being a good wife and mother to her two boys. When Dad became sick with rheumatic fever, she went to work in the local hosiery mill to bring in money.

Later in life, when Warren needed money for college, Mom went to work for and eventually bought Green Stationers, a retail outlet selling office supplies in Orange, turning it into a profitable venture. She became an effective store manager and a popular fixture among the retail trade in the town. Dad became her employee, but Carrie was clearly in charge. Though she was quiet, she knew how she wanted things to be done and made sure it was done her way. She apparently inherited her mother's grit and determination.

"This business's main goal is to take care of our customers," she said.

"Have you ever read Peter Drucker?" I once asked her, referring to one of the prominent business philosophers.

"Who is that?" she answered. She didn't have to read about business to know how to run the store.

# CEMETERY

We are gathered on the hillside at Graham Cemetery, just outside Orange and less than a mile from the site of a famous train wreck, "The Fat Nancy," in 1888. The train tracks about a quarter of a mile away in the valley are plainly visible from our position. Because of that, this seems to be a strange place for a cemetery.

Family and people from the town wait for the Methodist minister, Mr. Harry Spear, to speak the final words over Dad's casket. We'd met Spear for the first time when he came by to visit Mom a few days ago. I grew up in Trinity Methodist Church and knew every minister until the last 20 years. Mr. Kelley, the first minister I ever met, was probably the reason Mom and Dad selected the church, which had quite different beliefs and rituals than the country churches in Louisa County.

Spear is speaking now. I recognize the words as coming out of the Methodist ritual, common, not memorable. Head bowed, a tear rolls down my cheek as I suppress a sob demanding to get out.

"This is so silly," says Joyce, who is standing at my side.

She does not explain, nor do I ask what she means.

I am alone in my grief.

Critical of my family up to the very end, I think. It seems like a culmination of the years she's resented my family—a resentment I never understood, but that manifested itself in not-so-subtle ways.

We lived 400 miles away from Orange, but when we visited, allocating family time between her family and mine and deciding where we slept were constant struggles. The conflicts over the children's time were particularly acute.

Over the years, our trips to Virginia became less frequent, probably because I wanted to avoid the inevitable conflict with Joyce. David, however, occasionally spent time in Virginia, developing a close relationship with Dad, in particular. The girls, Lynn and Laura, never had the chance to develop a close relationship with their grandparents—the loss of an important opportunity.

My own inadequacies certainly were a factor. I had no idea how to understand Joyce's concerns or how to express mine. Our discussions were arguments, not discussions. I suspect Joyce must have sensed Mom and

Dad's cautions about our early relationship. They were determined that I should go to college and feared that a high-school romance would derail it.

"They just don't like me," Joyce once said.

"No. That's not true," I answered. "They just wanted me to finish college."

But Joyce and I never resolved that different viewpoint. Her resentment took a different turn in our relationship. She never understood my drive to get more education, such as the doctorate of which I am in the final phases and will complete next year. Snide remarks are her typical responses.

"Oh, your dad just brought home another "A." Whoopee!" she announced to the children at our dinner table a couple of years ago.

"You've got all these degrees, and I have none," was so common I lost count over the years.

My typical response was, "We've lived in the shadow of colleges in every town we've lived, and I've encouraged you to go, if a degree is what you want." But she never took a step in that direction.

Joyce and I started dating when I was just sixteen—a senior in high school, and she was a junior. We immediately hit it off and we started spending every opportunity together, not just dates, but family events, such as visits to relatives. At first, Mom and Dad welcomed her, but as time passed, they, especially Dad, became concerned about the intensity of our relationship and about the lack of exclusive family time together.

"You're too young to be so serious," Dad said.

A date with Joyce required a drive to her home in Rapidan, seven miles away down a relatively narrow road. That meant using the family car, for which I had to ask permission. In retrospect, Dad was tolerant of my use of the car, even though at age 16 and a half, I had been driving for just over a year.

In spite of Dad's concern, my relationship with Joyce became intense. I wanted to be with her every day. She invaded every thought. We became a "thing" in the eyes of friends and acquaintances. We did everything together and were the epitome of passion-driven teenage love. We were blindly playing out the story, the story played by so many young couples in our high school: date, get married, get a job, have kids, buy a small house in Orange. That's what couples do.

Dad saw a different vision for me: go to college, get a profession, explore the world; opportunities he never had. Goree Waugh and Mr. Stowitts reinforced Dad's viewpoint. Each had a slightly different scenario of my future, but all strongly encouraged the college route.

"You're good with science and math, and you have a great scholastic record. You can get into any school you want," Mr. Stowitts said. "You have a lot of talent."

And, Grandmother Tate has been telling me since an early age, "If you have talent and you're not using it, that's a sin."

I accepted their advice and set my path for college, knowing at some level that path and my passion were at conflict. But I was blindly moving ahead, damn the consequences.

# THE WORKSHOP

All the family is here: brother Warren, his wife, Judy, cousins too numerous to mention, aunts Ruth and Lucille, Uncle Ed, and some other people I hardly recognize—all jam-packed into our small house on South Almond Street. They brought fried chicken, casseroles, homemade rolls, cake, and pies—all in the tradition of Southern protestant funerals. Mom sits quietly in the living room while each person stops by one-after-one, not knowing exactly what to say: Wesley was a good man. We'll miss him so much. I'm so sorry. I was shocked.

I mill around the group, speaking to each person, trying to be civil. The numbness endures, too shocked to cry, too many questions unanswered. What happened? How could he have died in a hospital while on a treadmill? Why couldn't they save him? "I feel woozie," were his last words before passing out.

Slipping out of the living room, I go to the door leading to the basement, down the creaking steps, past the aging Lennox furnace, and to the workshop, the place where Dad taught me the basics of woodworking and building. The sobs started even before the door opened. The odors of wood and oil, interlaced with basement dampness, pried open my door to grief. But this time, the odor of Aqua Velva, Dad's shaving lotion, was absent.

My knees almost buckle as I lean against the doorframe.

Dad was probably down here last week. A slightly disassembled toaster sits on the workbench, still strewn with screwdrivers, pliers, and pieces of wire, screws, and tabs. "Never throw away anything until you understand why it stopped working," he told me. "Even if we can't fix it, we can learn how it works." What had he learned about this toaster? Could he have fixed it if he had more time?

I grew up knowing Dad could fix anything. If something didn't work, don't call a repair person, take it apart and figure out what's wrong. He was referring, of course, to mechanical and electrical stuff, but I later realized that he was just as good with other problem-solving. First understand the problem, then find ways to solve it.

I spy Dad's hammer on the workbench. Dad used it in his early days as a carpenter's assistant to his father, who built houses and barns, many of which are still standing all over Louisa and Hanover counties.

I remember the image of Dad's strong fingers gripping the wooden handle while driving a nail with expert precision, his gold ring with a ruby setting flashing an arc in the fluorescently lit room.

Dad used the building process to pass on the family's homespun philosophy to his sons.

"Never hold a nail for someone else to hammer. Do your own work." he said. "Besides, they may mash your finger."

"A bent nail means your penis is not fully grown."

\* \* \*

Tiny unlabeled boxes of nails, screws, and other parts sit on shelves above the workbench. I was never able to find anything except by looking in each box, but Dad seemed to have it all in his head. He never threw away anything. All those parts and screws were salvaged from things we took apart. "You never know when you might need one of these," he'd say, holding up some weirdly shaped component.

Cans of used paint are stacked against the cinderblock wall just below the never-opened, metal-framed basement window so common in 1940's basements. The table saw stands in the corner next to the lathe he always wanted but never seemed to use, jammed up against it.

I glanced up at the bare joists lining the ceiling, a place my eyes had seldom traveled when he and I were working here. I pull down two three-year-old Playboy magazines, safely hidden in a crossbeam. Finally, something to smile about here. These were his private secrets, never shared with me, but these make me love him more. A man who always stood for good, for doing the right thing, still had a private side, and I wonder what else I never knew.

Racks on the wall to my right hold various sizes and shapes of wood. As with parts, never throw away a piece of lumber. We will someday need it.

Two spinning rods hang on other hooks. Opening the tackle box underneath, there are all the familiar lures Dad and I used while fishing the Rapidan River: jitterbugs, plastic minnow replicas, an old bottle of fish eggs—once red, now turned a dull gray. Will I ever be able to go fishing again without my heart breaking?

Some guy upstairs had said, "It seemed like the lights went out on Main Street when I heard the news."

My light just went out.

# A *KID* ENTERS *BIG BLUE*

# ENGINEERING SCHOOL: A STRUGGLE

The box teetered on the shelf's edge as if wondering how it should respond to my tugs and pokes. I stood stretched over the unopened boxes, trying to assemble all the memorabilia into one box. Suddenly nature decided, and the box crashed to my feet, scattering letters, high school pins, flattened baseball gloves and souvenirs from our class trip to Washington, all over the floor. Damn, it doesn't pay to be in a hurry.

Two paperbacks caught my eye. I picked them up, one in each hand. *Your Career in Engineering* was one title, *Your Career in Journalism* was the other.

I remember the decision. I'd been the editor for the school paper and loved it. Standing on my teenage bully pulpit, lobbying the school administration for a better study hall, pushing the town fathers to build a youth center. I was launching an early path in journalism.

Everyone seemed to assume that was my direction. Everyone but my best friend, Randolph Simpson, and also, Mr. Stowitts.

"But you're good in science and math," they said. "Journalism would be a waste of that talent. You should go to MIT or Caltech.'

"What a joke," I thought. "I'd never make it into MIT. Besides, that takes money."

A year later, scholarship in hand, I was on my way to UVA's school of engineering with my brain engaged, but I was leaving my heart at the local paper.

The four years of engineering school were a struggle. Math and science came easy in high school, but the additional rigor of university-level courses pushed me to the limit. Most nights saw me staying up until 2:00 am doing homework and class exercises with a short break at midnight for a hamburger at the Castle, a snack bar in our dorm.

A scholarship covered my tuition and some of my dorm expenses. Yet, I needed other jobs to pay for food, books, clothing, and other expenses. I continued my work at the furniture company every weekend since the university was only 30 miles away, plus I landed a teaching assistant job in the mechanical drawing lab for which my high school courses prepared me. ROTC provided a supplemental monthly stipend, and other jobs such as lab assistant and dorm counselor provided additional income.

I graduated from the university with $100 in my checking account.

* * *

All sectors were trying to recruit engineers in my final year. My paper on inertial guidance systems, published in the *Virginia Engineering Review*, attracted offers even from companies I'd never visited. However, I visited companies in New York, Maryland, Pennsylvania, and New Mexico. I'll always remember the looks on Mom and Dad's faces when they dropped me off in Washington, DC for an interview with Sandia Labs in New Mexico. That was a long way from Orange, Virginia.

In spite of the many interviews revolving around my published paper, which involved a technology used in missile guidance systems, I accepted IBM's offer in Endicott, NY. Unlike my classmates, I chose a job in manufacturing, testing data processing machines, as compared to a design job in a laboratory. A couple of my buddies, Bob Leavenworth and Fred Eichelman, thought I was crazy. "Engineers have no opportunities in manufacturing," Fred said. "You'll get stuck in a routine."

# FIRST DAYS AT IBM

"What do you mean that you want to take off two days in the middle of the training class?" Carrot-head Tom Jenkins, my new manager, says. He glares at me as if I'm some sort of disloyal nut for asking. He is standing in the door to his green manager's cubicle, one of those 6"x 8", half-partition structures, placed in the middle of the manufacturing floor—contraptions once manufactured by Virginia Metal Products in my hometown of Orange, VA. He stands there, hands on hips, sleeves rolled up two turns halfway to the elbows, wearing a button-down-collar white shirt with striped tie tucked just below the third button. He looks traditional IBM, but I figure this is a guy who scratched his way up from the bottom of the manufacturing rung. I know the type. They've worked their way into a little king's position and want to flaunt their power—the kind of guy who hates people with college degrees.

Since this was my first day on the job, I thought it important to let my manager know about the agreement made when I was hired. It was the first confrontation in my corporate career.

"I told Dale Learn, the recruiter, when he hired me, I was going back to Virginia in July to get married. Hey, it's only Thursday and Friday—two days," I say, humbly.

"Yeah, two days at the most critical part of the six weeks class! You may never catch up."

"I'll be back on the following Monday. I'll catch up."

Tom stares into my eyes and shuffles around as if contemplating how to punch me in the face without getting in trouble. I watch his pale blue eyes, wondering what he's thinking.

"I'll have to think about it," he says. The right side of his lip is twitching. His forehead furrowed like my grandfather's cornfield. "Check with me in a couple of days."

On my first day on the job, I antagonized my manager and found out I might either postpone my wedding or fall behind my fellow workers in the class. Great! I've been enthusiastic about joining IBM. The recruiter convinced me it was a great company with good benefits, and their salary offer was as good as the other 15 or 20 offers. And besides, they said this company cares about its people.

But Jenkins' attitude casts a pall over my spirit. Maybe my classmates at UVA were right. Manufacturing people focus on one thing, get the products shipped on time at the right cost. They don't give a damn about anything else. The recruiter said IBM was different. "The customer is king, and we care about quality," he'd said. Jenkins makes me wonder if down under, this is just another company. And I'm not sure I'll fit into manufacturing. I've never paid much attention to schedules, hate getting up early, barely made it by 7:30 this morning, and forgot about the half mile walk from the parking lot.

This first day reminds me of my summer job in the peach orchard—keep your head down and don't ask questions. Just do what the boss tells you. There's no place for intellectual or sophisticated conversation.

# JOYCE

Joyce grew up in the riverside village of Rapidan, Virginia, seven miles north of Orange. The Rapidan Milling Company, powered by water from the river, formed the center of the berg, where farm trucks loaded with grain lined up to sell the spoils of their crops. Sunday found the two churches—Episcopal, for the well-off, and Baptist, for the ordinary—filled almost to capacity with villagers and families from the surrounding countryside.

Joyce's father worked for the railroad, considered a secure employer in the 1950s, when benefits like pension plans were rare in Virginia. Her mother, following tradition, worked at home, caring for Joyce and her older siblings—two brothers, and a sister. Yet, by the time I met Joyce, her siblings were in their independent adult life.

We first met during our summer jobs at Mormont Peach Orchard, located on a mountain road a few miles from Rapidan. In the 1950s, picking peaches was a lucrative job for teenagers. Joyce was part of the Rapidan contingent, who lived relatively close to the orchard.

Joyce attracted me because she was smart, cute, had soft brown eyes, a heart-shaped face with high cheekbones, and short-cropped brown hair. She had an unusual walk, smooth and confident, reminding me of a cat. Unlike my role of picking peaches in the orchard, she worked in the packing shed, which required the skills to cull faulty peaches and pack bushel baskets with a top ring of top-quality fruit. At the end of my shift one day, I watched her lithe movements smoothly executing her tasks.

I got to know Joyce in high school. A year behind me, she was a leader among her class group, president of several school clubs, vice president of the student council, sang alto in the chorus—if it involved smarts and personal relations, she was part of it. Her friends were more likely to be valedictorians than jocks.

Joyce was a junior, I a senior, just sixteen, when we first dated in 1952. Driving the seven miles to Rapidan to pick her up for the movies was a route well-practiced for me, with over a year of driving experience over a road to the river often fished by Dad and me. She described her house as the original schoolhouse that was now a dwelling. That building was familiar to me, having passed it many times. It was distinctive because of its tall columns supporting a two-story porch ceiling and four oversized front windows. She met me with a big smile, and we were off to the Madison Theatre in Orange.

Several dates later, I learned her grandparents lived in the schoolhouse while she and her parents occupied another historic place closer to the river. She was embarrassed because her own home was too old.

# COLLEGE OR NOT?

I graduated high school at 16 and decided to spend another year in a post-graduate program at the high school, working in the physics lab, taking typing and monitoring math classes. The year provided more maturity before going to college, while giving me time to save money by working at the furniture store. Joyce graduated as I was completing that year.

Joyce and I continued dating through my four years of college. She, however, opted out of college, although her grades and aptitudes were greater than mine. She, too, could have received scholarships but chose to work in a local insurance agency instead.

I did not understand her decision. She was a leader in clubs, the chorus, and the school newspaper. Mr. Stowitts could have found scholarships for her just as he had for me.

"We could still date if you go to college. Madison and Longwood are all within driving distance of UVA," I said.

Yet, she would not budge. I saw no reason why she wanted to stay in Orange. Did she need to make money to support her parents? Was she depending on our relationship while I went to college? "I'll just stay in Orange and work," she said.

I never directly asked her if she was staying behind to wait for me, like some war bride, but I should have asked because I carried some sense of obligation during all my years in college. She was playing the role of a dedicated wife while I was acting the good Christian Southern boy. So, keep your head down, meet your responsibilities, follow the rules. I wanted us to be together, and I held a fear I might lose her. I loved her, loved being with her, but not sure what all this meant.

There were chances for me to explore other relationships. A classmate at UVA asked me to go on a double date with him and two young women from Sweetbriar College about 50 miles from Charlottesville, but I declined, saying I had to work on Saturday. That was true, but it would have been easy to wrangle a day off to go on the date.

Later, on the way to an interview, I sat by a young woman on a plane to Rochester, NY. We had a lively conversation, covering everything from science to the politics of the day. We exchanged phone numbers, but neither one of us ever called.

I loved Joyce and did not want to risk losing her. My sense of obligation dulled my sense of exploration.

# ENDICOTT

Endicott is a mill town on the Susquehanna River. Immigrants from Ellis Island are said to have found the town with their first sentence in English: "Which way E-J?" referring to the Endicott-Johnson Shoe Factory just down the street from the IBM plant. Every morning, the pungent odor of hundreds of cowhides being cured in E-J's tannery shrouds the town. The Endicott-Johnson factory, founded in 1899, with history back to 1854, is the epitome of old-style manufacturing. Dark and dank, with red brick walls and steel window frames, the buildings have probably been there since the company's founding. In stark contrast, the IBM buildings down the street gleam with white concrete and glass brick windows, looking more like a hospital than a manufacturing plant. A smart American flag flies from each of the towers that accentuate each building module. The adjoining sidewalks and streets show not a sign of dirt or paper. IBM's maintenance workers see to that. IBM's cleanliness does not stop at the street. Every production line inside is spotlessly clean—no paper, no grease, no metal chips, no bottle caps will ever be seen on the floor. I often wonder if E-J's exterior also reflects the working environment inside their factory. If so, making shoes must be a grim, dirty, and unhealthy task. Yet, Endicott culture praises Endicott-Johnson for providing jobs, security, good housing, and care for their workers.

There seems to be nothing but Italian restaurants downtown. The spaghetti comes piled high on oblong plates as big as the platter Mom used for a whole baked chicken. Fusco's spaghetti tastes like it was just made, and the pale red sauce is rich with garlic and oregano. Until last week, I'd never eaten spaghetti in a real Italian restaurant. Dad knew a guy named Willie Tomaine, but, as far as I knew, there were no other Italians in Orange, Virginia.

Endicott is also known as Sinus Valley. This morning, when I came out of Mrs. Lashier's house, where I'd rented a room, I looked down the hill toward Endicott, only to see Nanticoke Road fade into a fog bank thick as the fur on a weasel. The whole town had disappeared during the night. When I drove down the hill, I thought someone must have suddenly painted my windshield white. I was passing from the light into the foggy unknown.

# MRS. LASHIER

Mrs. Iona LaShier, a widowed school teacher, rented me a room in her old farmhouse on Taft Avenue extended, about a mile outside of town. There was a long chicken house out back that had been converted to a five-bay garage. The five-acre lot was the remainder of what used to be a hundred-acre farm owned by her family.

Mrs. LaShier and I became fast friends, spending most nights after dinner discussing books, her travels, and the history of the region. We have travel shows as a result of her Leica 35mm camera. I was fascinated by her tales of France, Germany and other places she visited after her husband's death. Travel was her way of recovering from grief.

Upon learning about my upcoming wedding, Mrs. LaShier had an interesting suggestion.

"How about I rent you the whole house, and let me be the renter? We can take turns using the kitchen, eat some meals together, share the living room with its music and TV, but you and your new wife can be as independent as you want," she said. "And anytime you're ready to find another apartment, that's OK."

"Wow. That's so kind of you," I answered. "That will take a lot of pressure off my search for other places. I'll talk to Joyce and see what she thinks. After all, you know I'll be going into the Army for six months starting in January."

# AFTER JENKINS

After the conversation with Jenkins, I return to the classroom to resume reading the pile of books and manuals they've asked us to read before the six-weeks class starts. I've spent the last four years plowing through technical books, and this seems like more of the same. At least I'm getting paid for doing this. It's better than paying tuition, even though I have to massage my butt every hour or so to get the blood circulating again.

At the end of the day and eating a hamburger and french fries at Tony's Dinner, I drive home and call Joyce.

"Hi. Howya doin?" I ask.

"OK. I miss you. Can't wait to see you in two weeks," she says softly.

We purr at each other for a while, hinting at what we'll do when we finally get together again.

"How's everything shaping up?" I ask, referring to the wedding.

"Got my dress today. Ordered flowers. Leonard will sing. So far, so good," she says.

"Today didn't go so well for me," I interrupt.

"What do you mean?"

"Well… Uh… Tom Jenkins, my new manager doesn't want me to miss time in the middle of class.

"What!" she says.

"I think it's going to be OK, but he wouldn't give me an answer today, asked me to see him on Wednesday."

"What!" She says again, louder. "You mean we're not even going to have two days together? You told me IBM had agreed?"

"Wait a minute. You know how important this job is," I offer.

"I used to think I was more important," she says.

"You are. You know you are. It'll work out. Just wait until Wednesday."

"I was counting on you to help with the last-minute preparations. You're not going to have time for anything."

Bong. The pay phone signals it needs another quarter.

"I've got to go. Call you again on Wednesday," I say. "Love you."

"Sure," she says.

On Wednesday, Jenkins offers me a compromise. He suggests I take Friday off and work on Thursday. That way I can still do the wedding and not miss so much of the class. He grins from ear to ear as he tells me as if he's discovered the Northwest Passage or something.

I fold. I really don't want to antagonize this guy, and Joyce is already antagonized. So, I agree.

So, with Friday off, I'll drive the 400 miles to Virginia after work on Thursday, run around like a maniac on Friday to get ready, get married on Saturday morning, stay over somewhere with Joyce on Saturday night, drive to Endicott on Sunday, then back to work at 7:30 on Monday morning. Some honeymoon. Joyce will be furious. Out-of-her-mind furious.

While I am going to the class, she is down there in Virginia doing all the work for the wedding. She probably thinks I'm up here having a wonderful time.

# MANUFACTURING PEOPLE

I suspect IBM top managers don't give a crap about manufacturing people. They talk a good game, but manufacturing people are the lowest on the totem pole. Not like sales or engineering. Even the smallest detail shows it. Take the toilet paper. Our toilets spit out small sheets of brown paper with the consistency of sandpaper. Now that is just stupid. Toilet paper can't be all that expensive. I guess it is a signal to tell us to be cost-conscious. Maybe IBM executives see us as hard-assed workers.

And we can't see outside from the third floor of the building where everyone assembles and tests computers. The windows are glass brick, letting in some natural daylight, but the primary light is from rows of fluorescent lights. Like the second-grade toilet paper, manufacturing people don't get open windows like office people have. They must think we might spend our time looking out at the trees or the constant clouds of the southern tier weather.

Apparently, they only distribute one color of paint to factories—putrid green. Everything—yes, everything—the walls, the file cabinets, the work-benches, the machine tools, even the typewriters are the same color. Boring is a color named green.

The bloody background noise is enough to drive you crazy. The air conditioner hums incessantly and makes a strange low beat frequency with the rumble transmitted throughout the building by the manufacturing machines. I wonder if we were subjects of some bizarre scientific experiment to see how much stress we can take.

\* \* \*

Jim Dawson sounds like a cross between Huey Long and Thomas Edison. "Dis mownin we're goin ta folla da path of the adda function," he says. For six weeks, 11 other guys and I have listened to him meticulously trace through each of over 600 pages of wiring diagrams.

Jim, or anyone else for that matter, doesn't seem to know what the 650 Magnetic Drum Data Processing Machine is supposed to do. To Jim, IBM's first medium-scale computer is just a jumble of vacuum tubes, wires, and relays arranged in long circuitous strings. Apparently, IBM people believe in the power of inductive reasoning—they'll give us all the details to see if we can figure out the big picture. If that's the case, I sure can't connect the dots.

When I joined the company on June 21, 1957, I didn't know what IBM made other than punched cards and typewriters. At UVA, they'd mentioned the word 'Eniac' and some other so-called computers, but I had no idea how they worked or what they're supposed to do. Calculate, I guess. Better than a slide rule (I hope) that little inaccurate piece of bamboo labeled 'log-log-duplex-deci-trig' was my constant companion for four years in engineering school. A better name would be 'estimating stick,' because it only helped me guess the right answers on exams.

IBM is famous for its small rectangular punched cards, made of thin tan cardboard into which grey machines can punch small rectangular peepholes into the cards in a code, representing numbers or other data. For instance, one of these cards might carry the data to describe my name, social security number, and address. If I inserted the card in an IBM machine designed to read the card, it would say, "Aha! This is Grant Tate." A standard IBM card is just about the right size to fit in a dress shirt pocket, although over half of its length would be visible. Maybe we engineers can figure out a way to make the cards into some sort of bizarre pocket protector.

IBM became famous after World War II, when the US government looked for a more efficient way to process mountains of data gathered by the thousands of census takers around the country. As I understand it, census takers filled out forms by hand while talking to people in their homes or fields. When the Census Department had all the forms, thousands of people, probably women, called data entry specialists sat at typewriter-like machines and typed the information from the forms. The machines translated their keystrokes into punched cards. It might take eight or ten cards to hold all the data from one family. So, after the census, there were millions of IBM cards piled up in the Census Department.

But, never fear, IBM had the solution to that problem. Other IBM machines could read the cards, sort them by county, job category, or whatever, statistically analyze data from the cards, and printout reams of reports on green and white paper—the kind with edges of pinholes, which the machines used to move the paper past the printing mechanism.

This procedure sounds cumbersome, but, hey, it's better than sorting or adding by hand. As best I can tell, the early census data was nothing but a list of people in big books. You could count them, but nobody had the time or inclination to do any statistical analysis.

Most of IBM's machines are a mass of clicking relays, cams, gears, belts, and things that make grinding noises, but the machine I'm learning, the 650 MDDPM, has replaced most of the mechanical parts with electronic tubes. The thing will add, subtract, do other calculations, and even make basic decisions, like, "if Charlie Brown's income is greater than $50,000, put his data in list A." The 650 still depends on the old-fashioned IBM card reader to enter data and a huge printer to put the data into usable form. Yet, its brain is electronic. Nobody around here seems to call the 650 a "computer," but, to me, it does some of the same things as those scientific devices.

All of my classmates here at IBM seem content to wallow around in the details of electronic circuits. They seem happy to have a job, any job. That's certainly the case with the two guys who just escaped from Communist Hungary. To them, this probably looks like heaven. And, even though their English barely goes beyond, "where's the toilet?" they follow Jim's instructions with gusto.

Unlike them, I'm bored. To overcome the boredom, during lunch, I've taken to reading *Andersonville*, the deeply depressing story of prisoners in a Confederate prison camp during the Civil War. I can't figure out why I chose such a book because the gruesome scenes have ruined many a sandwich for me. IBM is not Andersonville, but I feel vaguely like a prisoner here, wondering if I'm heading for a career of monotonous wiring diagrams, or maybe I secretly harbor hostility toward working in a factory.

# THE WEDDING

I tug at the white collar, trying to get some space so the beads of sweat can roll freely down my neck. Dad, my best man, stands close to me, both of us in front of the altar of the Lower Rapidan Baptist Church. On a scorching hot July day, the organist plays nondescript motifs, a prelude to "Here Comes the Bride." He and I look at each other with wry smiles. Mr. Floyd Binns, the minister, is on a platform just behind us.

I left Endicott, NY at 3:00 am yesterday to drive the 400 miles to Orange, VA, arriving around 2:00 pm. To pass the time, I listened to every news story: John Glenn orbiting the earth, Althea Gibson being the first Black woman to win Wimbledon, the Surgeon General finally connecting smoking to lung cancer.

Joyce greeted me like a long-lost lover even though I was half asleep and cranky from a long trip.

"I'm so glad to see you," Joyce said.

"Me, too," I replied before the kiss.

"Everything is in place for the wedding tomorrow," she said. "I still have a few things to check out, but they are just details. Leonard Norris is going to sing, and I want to make sure his nerves are not getting the best of him."

"He's always been pretty confident when he soloed in the high school chorus," I said. "How are you feeling?"

"I'm a bit frayed from all the details, and I'm a little nervous, but I'm OK," she said. "Hollie and I are going to stay at Aunt Lavie's, just up the road from the church tomorrow morning so we can get dressed there."

"Yeah, Dad, Mom, and I will drive down from home tomorrow morning. It's only seven miles."

My eyes snap to the front as "Here Comes the Bride" fills the small church. Familiar faces are out there in the congregation, but they are just a blurry mass to me now. I can see Joyce in her white wedding dress with a smile I've missed over the past months. She and her Maid of Honor, sister Hollie, walk slowly down the aisle. Sweat is creating a river down my neck.

Soon it is over, and Joyce and I are greeting people on the church's lawn. 30 minutes later, we are in my new 1957 Plymouth with big tail fins, heading to Orange for a family reception in her parent's small house.

"That was beautiful," I say. "Thanks so much for all your work in putting it together. Sorry I couldn't be here."

"I have a place for us to stay tonight in Pennsylvania, about half-way to Endicott. So, we can start driving after the reception," I say.

"I'm eager to get started," she says.

# REAL WORK

This is the last half-day of the class. We are going to start real work after lunch, and man, am I ready for it. I may not like the production line, but at least I'll get out of this damned musty classroom.

The morning has dragged by, but now, just after lunch, Tom Jenkins, looking very much the confident IBM manager, steps into the classroom. He is wearing the uniform we all wear—a white dress shirt, preferably button-down, polished shoes, and a necktie. Striped is preferred. Most guys wear dress pants, but I refuse to take a chance on messing up my good clothes. Besides, I have a big supply of khakis left over from my days at the University of Virginia.

Applying the IBM dress code to manufacturing workers is pretty stupid because safety rules require us to tuck the tie between the second and third button of our shirts when we are working on the computers, and the long sleeves are a pain in the neck. No rings or jewelry are allowed, and all of us must wear safety glasses, which look like the kind my dad wore when pink plastic frames were first introduced.

Tom came up through the ranks from technician to first-line manager and has little charity for graduates of fancy engineering schools who start at higher salaries than many of his men who'd been around for years.

He eyes me suspiciously, and I know he's thinking about our initial encounter. He's probably wondering if I'll be able to test a computer. His expression says, "Show me, Tate" and something inside tells me my first test in the corporation has begun.

"Are you guys ready to go to work?" he says with a sly smile. "12 systems are out there waiting for you."

Tom tells us he has assigned each of us to work with a more experienced test engineer until we get the hang of testing a computer.

Tom leads us out the door, through the hall, down a short flight of steps, and into the factory. We step into a room as long as a football field, holding two rows of 650 MDDPMs that stretch to infinity.

As we walk into the factory, a cacophony of sounds bombard my ears—the shrill whirr of 200 high-speed rotating cylinders, the deep hum of exhaust fans, the chi-chi chi of IBM machines punching holes in cardboard. A strong odor of ozone and cardboard dust permeates the air. The parquet wood floor is spotlessly clean. Papers and manuals lay neatly on the rows of green metal workbenches with butcher-block tops.

The scene takes me back to my first visit to the textile mill where my father worked when I was growing up. There, the noise was even more deafening as 100 looms clacked-clacked their shuttles back and forth, emitting an effluvium of oil and ozone, mixed with a whiff of Woolworth's sewing department. Maybe in a few years, I will become a manager just like Dad. I've followed his advice to stay out of the textile industry, but he never said stay out of management. I like the idea of working with people, but my challenge in IBM seems to deal with machines.

Suddenly, my stomach quivers with a pang of fear. My God, maybe I can't remember any of those 600 wiring diagrams. How will I ever be able to troubleshoot a computer when I'm not even sure what the machines are supposed to do? I've fixed amplifiers and a variety of other electronic junk, but these things are big and complicated. This is like sending a car mechanic out to fix a space rocket.

"OK, guys. I have your assignments." We gather around to hear his announcement.

Jenkins' voice fuels my fears. Maybe he's right about engineers. All that education doesn't give me a clue how to do this job. What do "Fourier Transforms" have to do with tracing signals through wires? I can see his face now, gloating about another engineer who bit the dust.

"I'll give each of you a number. That's your computer. Your teammate will be there."

Agitated, I listen as Tom reads the names. Finally, he says, "Tate, you're on 56."

When he finishes the list, each of us walks down the aisle searching for our assigned number. Over each testing stall hangs a large, printed card that lists its number plus the name of the customer who is going to rent the system. IBM never sells a machine; it rents them to customers for a monthly fee. After passing 20 or 30 workstations, I eventually come to 56. Boeing Airplane Company. My stomach begins to quiver again. Why did I have to draw one of IBM's most important customers?

I pause to look over the situation. A bluebook of wiring diagrams lays open on the table. I recognize the open page as a familiar diagram of the magnetic drum control system—and my stomach starts to feel calmer.

A dark-skinned, slightly balding fellow with questioning eyes appears from behind the computer.

"Hi, I'm Charlie Gehm. Welcome," he says, grinning through his big teeth.

"I guess we're going to be roommates," I say.

"This isn't much of a room, but I'll be glad to show you around after I finish the test module I'm running."

I stand in front of the computer, contemplating the blinking lights of the machine's central processing unit. It's about the size of two refrigerators bolted together. At desk level, on the narrow side facing me, is a "console"—an eighteen-inch, square, grey, metal panel containing lines of flashing lights, rotatable switches, and push-buttons. By rotating the switches, and pushing the "enter" button, we can transmit instructions to the machine's brain. Inside and just below the console, sits a magnetic drum, the computer's memory, whirring at about 10,000 rotations per minute and capable of storing about 16,000 snippets of information.

In addition to turning switches and pushing buttons, we can also communicate with the computer using IBM cards. Those little pieces of cardboard look simple, but it takes another mechanism as big as a five-foot kitchen cabinet to read or punch the data holes in them. This device is particularly mysterious to me because it consists of thousands of moving parts and electrical relays that never seem to operate correctly. Chads and dust from the hole-punching process tends to float all over the place, choking circuits and clogging mechanical parts.

Stepping around to the side, I see grey panels that we can lift off to expose electron tubes and circuits on large swinging gates like vertical Beautyrest mattresses, but with electron tubes replacing the springs. Black, snakelike cables connect the central processing unit to a power supply, also the size of two refrigerators. If something is wrong inside these boxes, it's my job to find out which of the 2,000 tubes or millions of wires is at fault.

All in all, this computer has five large units connected by miles of wire. It fills a space half as big as a racquetball court, emits enough energy to heat a small office building, but can make only limited decisions.

When Charlie returns from behind the computer, I know that even working together, it will take us four or five weeks to run every test, check every operation, exercise every circuit, and prove the system's reliability. Charlie has been the obstetrician; he connected the power lines that bring energy to the new computer's brain. Now I'm going to be the pediatrician who will check the health of the new child.

While facing the computer, my mind drifts to Joyce, wondering what she is doing today in Mrs. LaShier's big house where we've rented a room. In a sense, I envy Joyce's free time. God knows I could use some of it, having graduated from engineering school with a sleep deficit I calculated to be 1,681 hours. Joyce has the time to read, to hike the hills and fields overlooking the town, to explore the community, the shops, the people. But will she? I'm not sure what she will do or what she has in mind. Watch me go to work, I suppose.

I cringe to think how little we've talked about these things. I've been so involved in surviving engineering school and getting a job, there's been no space to think about life, about the future, about aesthetics, about alternatives. I just jumped on the expected path for a Southern boy. Get an education, get a job, get married, have children, go to Church. It's what one does. So far, I'm on track, blindly ahead of schedule.

At this point, I'm not sure where my job will take me. I sure don't want to spend years in this environment, testing computers. I wanted manufacturing, but, so far, it's monotonous. I want to be a manager like Dad, but is this the path? Jenkins is not the kind of person I want to be, but could I be a good manager in this department and use different methods? To really care about people? And what is the path to become a manager? A lot of unanswered questions now.

This particular term can only last six months, because I have to fulfill my six months commitment to the US Army Signal Corps base at Ft. Monmouth, NJ in January. That will be another adventure.

Mrs. LaShier's place was a fortunate find. She's provided Joyce and me a comfortable, warm place to live during this interim time. After the Army, we'll look for a new apartment, beginning the next stage. Perhaps that will give us more stability after moving around every six months. Everything is new; new location, new job, new wife, new work relationships, new food. We're only 400 miles from Virginia, but it's a long way from home.

Every weekend when the weather is good, Joyce and I explore the countryside of New York's Southern Tier, picnicking at the Finger Lakes, visiting the Corning Glass Museum, hiking at Watkins Glen, eating fresh apples at the orchards. We follow Mrs. LaShire's suggestions to find places beyond normal tourist destinations. Joyce and I are carefree, enjoying our freedom and our new relationship. We know my stint in the Army is coming up, and we will soon be entering an unknown venture.

# GETTING
## ON THE
# FAST TRACK

# LT. TATE

"Hey, does anyone know where Vietnam is?" asks Tim Johnson. Our group of 30 young army officers is in a waiting room at Ft. Monmouth, NJ, waiting to get orders for our next assignment after basic officers' training. Most of my colleagues are just starting their tour of two years, whereas a few of us are required to serve only six months of active duty followed by seven and a half years in the reserves.

We've been through six weeks of officer "basic," where we refreshed our skills in warfare and tactics and learned about the role and responsibilities of our branch, the Signal Corps. The program wasn't nearly as tough as the summer training in ROTC. That six weeks ran us through infantry basic, where instructors from the 82nd airborne gave us a hard time. At the end of that program, I realized the US Army could turn innocent college kids into killers in just six weeks.

Having grown up in a small town, a rural area, I was familiar with guns. Like other kids, I had a 22-caliber rifle at the age of 12. My parents supervised me closely, keeping the gun securely locked unless Dad and I were going out for some hunting or target practice. My grandfather Tate, Papa Tate to me, lived on a farm, survived the Depression, and brought partridges, squirrels, turkeys, or other wild game to the dinner table. That was part of his family's subsistence. I had been hunting with him—he was an excellent shot, but it seemed a necessity, not pleasure. He never seemed to delight in shooting a bird or anything else. He did delight in eating them, however.

When I enrolled in engineering at the University of Virginia after my post-graduate year in high school, the news about the war in Korea was a mixed bag. The new President Eisenhower told the Chinese that he might be willing to use atomic weapons to end the conflict. But, in July the government announced an armistice had been signed at Panmunjom. With all that, the USSR was a growing threat, having announced their development of a hydrogen bomb. All those signals told me to join the ROTC at UVA. Anticipating that I might someday be drafted, I'd rather go in as an officer. Besides, it felt like my duty to be prepared.

At ROTC six-week summer camp, over a year ago at this point, I was all of 140 pounds, at 5'10". Close to average height in the class, but still among the smallest in stature. Members of the 82nd Airborne, some tough customers, formed our training cadre at Fort Meade and A. P. Hill. The Airborne trainers were not about to let the ROTC college kids get by easily, so we had the whole boot camp experience: weapons training, grenades, patrols, tactics, heavy weapons. They had a clear mission: give these young guys the skills to potentially lead others and win battles. In other words, turn us into killers.

That may be a harsh assessment, but the moral choice was clear. If I choose to take this path, to become an officer, then I must be able to do my duty. That includes the duty to actually shoot enemy soldiers as necessary. If I am unwilling or incapable of pulling the trigger to protect my fellow soldiers and myself, then I should not be in the ROTC.

That dilemma became clear during one night-time exercise.

Our training officer selected four of us to go out on patrol across some rugged territory to capture a red flag and bring it back. This was to simulate the conditions of a real-life patrol, where a small team goes out to gather information about the terrain or the enemy.

One of the other guys was Tony, a new friend from Chicago with a long scar on his right arm that he claimed was from a gunshot during a street fight. Tony was rough and ready. The other two were unfamiliar to me. We talked briefly about our mission, looked at the map lit by Tony's flashlight, inserted blank ammunition in our rifles, and headed out toward our objective. It was an inky black, cloudy night; not a star or moon in sight. We inched our way through a field, following our phosphorescent compasses, but sticking close together, not to lose one another. As we were feeling our way around the edge of a huge hole we suspected was an old tank trap—bang, bang, bang. The flash of an opponent's rifle penetrated the dark. We dove into the tank trap.

Tony and I whispered to each other.

"All flashes from one spot. Probably one guy," said Tony.

"Yep. Looks like it. But we should make some noise to attract more fire and see if that's right," I replied.

We rustled some dry bushes. More flashes.

"You're right. Looks like one guy," Tony said. "I'll distract him from here while you go around behind."

"Good plan," I said.

Quietly, I circled around behind the shooter. I hear him fire more shots and "clang," his rifle ejected the empty cartridge.

I said, loudly, "We have you. Give up or you're dead."

Of course, we only had blanks—no one would actually be hurt. I whistled across the field and soon Tony was next to me.

"Hey, the flag is right here," he said.

We headed back across the field with our 82nd Airborne captive in tow.

"Where are those other two guys?" I asked.

"They just stayed in the tank trap when I came to you," Tony answered.

But when we got to the tank trap, no one was there.

We turned the flag into the trainer, who thanked us for doing a good job in record time. Neither one of us mentioned the other two fellows, and the trainer never asked.

I never found out what happened to the other fellows—were they afraid? Goof-offs? Or just didn't give a damn? What kind of officers would they be?

I'm not sure what the future will bring, but I've been brought up to take responsibility, do my duty, do what it takes. If this is what it takes to get those skills, I am ready for it. Many people from my hometown fought in WWII, including my uncle and family friends. So, I am ready to pull the trigger if necessary.

* * *

When my active duty assignment began, Joyce and I rented an apartment about ten miles from Ft. Monmouth from a Russian immigrant couple. The apartment is atop an unused multi-vehicle garage, located close to their farmhouse. They have about ten acres of what was once a large farm. Mrs. Savitsky is a kind, calm, 70+ woman, with homemade dresses and hair that always in a gray bun. Her husband always wears a funny, gray Russian cap, has a thick accent, and is more excitable, tending to rant on in Russian when something doesn't suit him.

Two weeks after we moved in, just as I arrived from the army base, Mr. Savitsky approached me and started yelling while pointing at the bottom of my car. I turned, staring intently at the car, trying to figure out what he was talking about. With that, he turned and retreated toward his house. A while later, Mrs. Savitsky knocked on our door and said Mr. Savitsky wants us to move out.

"Why? I don't understand," I said.

"He said your car dripped oil on the driveway and you ignored him when he tried to talk to you about it."

"Oh, I'm so sorry. I did not understand what he was saying. If there is oil on the driveway, I'll be happy to clean it up," I replied. "Please tell him

I'm sorry. We'd really like to stay."

"But wait," I continued. "Would you mind if we both went together so I could apologize to him?

"Sure," she said.

The apology went well. I talked slowly in my most articulate voice. He seemed to understand.

A week later, Mrs. Savitsky brought us a fully cooked dinner featuring calf brains with unidentifiable vegetables. I hoped that was a well-meaning gesture, not an attempt to poison us.

* * *

"Lt. Tate, the Colonel will see you now," says the private who is handling administration.

I step through the door, approaching the desk where a bird Colonel with a gray crewcut and a freshly starched shirt is sitting at his desk.

I stop in front of the desk, offer my salute, and say, "Lt. R. G. Tate, sir."

"Well Lt. Tate, I see you've had some computer experience," he says.

"Yessir," I reply. "I've been testing computers and been through IBM's training programs. Can't say I'm an expert, but at least I've had a start."

"Good. We're assigning you to the US Signal Research and Development Laboratory for the duration of your tour. You'll be reporting to Capt. Bill Luebbert over there. Luebbert is responsible for designing the Army Field Data System, the computers and networks the army will use in the future."

"Great. I look forward to it, sir. When do I report?"

"Monday morning. Here are your orders," he says. "Good luck over there. They're doing great work."

I salute again, turn, and leave the office.

"Where are they sending you?" some guy that I don't know in the class group asks.

"To the Signal Lab, designing computers," I reply loudly.

"At least it's not Vietnam," Tim Johnson chimes in.

# CAPT. LEUBBERT

Monday morning at 7:45 am, I checked in at the lobby of the complex building that houses the Signal Corps R&D organization. I'd never been inside the Pentagon in Washington, DC, but this place seemed as large. with huge multi-story angular sides. Some people called it "the octagon," but I wasn't sure there were really eight sides. Nevertheless, it is huge. How will I find Luebbert's department?

Ten minutes later, I introduced myself to a young private who must be the department's clerk.

"Good morning, Private. I'm Lt. Tate, here to see Capt. Luebbert."

"Yes, Lt. Tate. He's expecting you. Go on in."

Already I saw a difference. The private did not stand up, salute, and escort me to the office. Instead, informal greeting.

"Good morning, Capt. I'm Lt. Tate."

"Oh, so glad to see you. By the way, just call me Bill while we're in the office here. When we're in a military group, we can go back to the formality.

"Sounds good, uh, Bill. I'm Grant. I'm looking forward to working with the unit.

"Good. Let's get to work," he said.

"We already have a lot of the system designed in block diagram form, but we need to describe it in words so people can understand it. I'd like for you to take on that task," Bill said.

Wow. That is exactly what we needed back at IBM when Jim Dawson was going through all those wiring diagrams.

"That sounds good," I replied. "I'm eager to get started."

Now, almost at the end of my tour, time has flown by. Capt. Luebbert immediately threw me into the work of helping design the future data processing system for the US Army. Unlike Dawson, back at IBM, Luebbert is a system's thinker. On my first day, he described his vision for the future and how our unit fit into the big picture.

"The army of the future needs not just good communications, but good data. To win the next conflicts, our units will need the best computer system in the world. It's our job to figure out what that system looks like."

I didn't know much at the time, but Capt. Luebbert treated me like a professional. Yes, we had military uniforms, but our everyday jobs were like those in any other design firm.

Even after just four months in the department, I had learned how a design team works and experienced a professional leader as head of a department. Luebbert didn't run me through some long orientation program but gave me real problems to solve. Maybe I can become a leader like him.

For Joyce and me, my Army time was like an extended vacation. We played in the surf at the officers' club beach at Sandy Hook, NJ marveling at the view of Manhattan across the water. We became close friends with one of my fellow officers, Floyd Goodwin, and his wife, Weezie, and explored parks, local restaurants, and amusement venues. Weezie, from South Carolina and who spoke with a slow Southern drawl, was quick to point out that a good Southerner would never name their son Grant. Floyd and I were in the same military unit, experiencing many of the classes and exercises together.

I was a reserve officer, meaning that, in the long run, I would not have the same opportunities for promotion and consideration as a "regular Army" officer. Regular Army officers could retire with full benefits after 20 years, whereas reserve officers needed to serve 30.

One day, a private came to our offices at the Signal R&D Lab.

"Lt. Tate," he said, loudly.

I looked up and raised my hand.

"Colonel Mulligan would like to see you in his office. Could you come with me?"

What the heck, I thought. I've never heard of this guy. What's up?

I followed the private down the long outer hall of the octagon, while my mind raced.

Soon, he showed me Col. Mulligan's door and ushered me in. I stepped forward, offering the customary salute.

"Good morning, sir. I'm Lt. Tate."

"Glad to meet you, son. Have a seat."

I sat in one of the chairs in front of the desk. The Colonel came around and sat in the other chair, turning it to face me.

"I hear you're doing good work over there in Luebbert's operation."

"Yessir, I'm enjoying the assignment. Capt. Luebbert is terrific, and I'm learning a lot," I said.

"Well, we'd like to offer you the chance to join the regular Army. We need computer experts, and you have the potential to grow and lead in that area. That means, of course, that we would extend your assignment here indefinitely."

Wow! I'm stunned. I had never, in my wildest dreams, thought of a military career. That means leaving IBM, possible assignments overseas, and who knows what.

"I know this is sudden," the Colonel continues. "Take a week to think about it and let me know."

Arriving home that afternoon, I rushed in eager to find Joyce. She smiled, happy to see me, and I could smell a casserole cooking in the oven.

"What's up? I can see something is going on," she said.

"Sure is. Let's fix some coffee. We have a decision to make," I said.

We sat at the dining room table, sipping our coffee and talking.

"They want me to join the regular Army," I said.

"OK. What's that?" she asked

I go on to explain the offer and the implications.

"Does that mean we stay here?" Joyce asked.

"Yes, for at least two more years."

"And after that?"

"Not sure, but they want me to stay in computer development. However, that could be on some army base studying operations and finding out what computers they need," I reply.

We continue to talk, trying to visualize what an army life would be like for both of us—and for our possible children. Benefits are good, schooling is good, expenses are manageable, frequent moves are bad, opportunities for promotion are good, following military rules is good and bad.

I found it comforting to have her incisive questions and viewpoints, offering many things I'd never thought about. This also gave us a chance to revisit what we wanted in life for ourselves and our family. We talked about it off and on for the next several days, ultimately deciding army life was not for us.

Col. Mulligan was disappointed when I told him.

# COMPELO TECH

For the first time in over six months, I'm in a dark civilian suit, white shirt, and striped tie. This is my first workday after active duty with the US Army Signal Corps, and I am eager to get started. What kind of assignment does IBM have in store for me? Probably more computer testing, similar to my job before going in the Army. I'm meeting with Phil Evans, a manager in the personnel department.

"Good morning. How was your Army experience?" Phil asks, offering his hand.

"Not bad, I spent most of the time designing computer systems," I reply, thinking that I would let him know that my military experience might be useful to IBM.

He motions to the chair in front of his desk. I want to hear about my next job, but we trade small talk and Army stories for a good 15 minutes.

Finally, Phil reaches for a letter. "Have you ever taught school?"

"Yes, I was a drawing and lab instructor in college, and I did some training in the Army," I reply.

"Well, Union-Endicott High School is looking for a temporary science teacher, and we've agreed to help them out for a few weeks. Would you like to help them out?" Phil smiles.

I am stunned. I never anticipated that IBM would turn me into a teacher. Science! Do I remember enough to teach high school science?

"What subjects do they want me to teach?" I ask.

"They don't say in the letter. Why not go talk to the principal and let them explain?"

Phil was surprised to see me today; even though I sent him a letter two weeks ago. My teaching assignment could be a coincidence. Perhaps the letter from the school district and I arrived on the same day. Phil had a problem, and its solution walked in from the Army. But wait, perhaps IBM doesn't really know what to do with me.

\* \* \*

Two weeks later, I am a school teacher, drawing force diagrams and pictures of physics experiments on the blackboard for a group of defiant teenagers who are draped over their desks as if they haven't slept in a month. Soon I realize my position is perfect. I can't be fired by the school system, and my career doesn't depend on coddling students. The Army taught me discipline and how to dish it out. I'm not prone to put up with a bunch of unruly, sloppy students, so I decide to crack down.

Soon, I send one particularly disruptive fellow out of the room, telling him to return after he shapes up, then I lecture the remaining students on good manners and the importance of education.

Now, after several days of struggle, the message is beginning to take. The students begin to ask questions, allowing me to put more life into our discussions. We've turned the corner, and teaching has become fun. The students and I have achieved a good bond, and all of us are learning a little physics.

* * *

It turns out IBM does have a place for me in the computer testing department, so, after my three weeks teaching, I am poking and probing around thousands of electron tubes and wires, just the same as before the Army assignment.

"Hi. Looks as if you're really concentrating on that test."

It's my manager, Jerry, who replaced Tom Jenkins while I was in the Army.

"Got a little surprise for you. Clarence McNeil wants to talk to you," he says.

"Who's Clarence McNeil?" I ask.

"He's head of the training department," Jerry replies. "He needs your help. He wants to see you in 15 minutes."

Untucking my tie from between my third and fourth shirt button, I walk down the 100 yards of computer test stalls, down the stairs, through the machine shop, and down two flights of stairs to the administrative offices, eventually reaching a sign reading "Manufacturing Education."

A woman with drawn-back black hair greets me from her desk. "Good morning, you must be Grant. Mr. McNeil is waiting for you."

"Thanks," I say, wondering why she used "Mr. McNeil" when the company's tradition is first names only.

When I step into "Mr. McNeil's" office, I understand why. This guy is dressed like a Brooks Brothers model. His blue suit with subtle black strips is tailored perfectly to fit his trim but solid physique. His hair looks as if it was trimmed yesterday. Each hand sports a polished gold ring and his nails were probably professionally manicured. A blue and yellow rep tie graces his wrinkle-free, button-down shirt, with a silk handkerchief neatly tucked into the jacket's pocket.

His desk reflects his attire—neatly lined papers, an expensive desk set with a real ink pen, a few mementos of awards are placed in strategic spots.

A feeling of complete dowdiness creeps over me. I never thought of going to the locker to put on my suit jacket, and my clothes smell like ozone from the computer floor. My shoes are unpolished and who knows what my hair looks like. You dummy, this is an INTERVIEW!

"Have a seat. And call me Mac," he says.

"Thanks. I didn't come to work this morning expecting something like this," I fumble.

"Well, this is a bit unusual. We have a big training job to do, and we need some help. I understand that you have some teaching experience."

Laughing, I say, "Well, if you consider three weeks in the blackboard jungle, you're right. But I worked my way through school as a lab assistant teaching other students."

In IBM's typical fashion, they probably figured out they need to train some people, then asked themselves, "Who do we have that has teaching experience?" Then someone said, "What about that guy that went down to the high school? Sure, he'll do."

Mac goes on. "You know that we don't lay off people. We're introducing a new computer system that uses transistors and we'll need lots of people to test the units—many more than are now on the computer floor. We need to convert our machinists and mechanical assemblers into computer test technicians."

"That's a big job," I say, thinking that it is actually impossible, not just difficult.

I remember how the Signal Corps had given all of its officers a six-week training course in electronics and how one of my fellow officers, who had majored in liberal arts, asked how someone like me could have spent four years studying electronics when the Army could teach it in just a few weeks.

"I've looked at your background, talked to your manager and the principal at the high school, and I believe you're the best person to develop this course," Mac says confidently.

Develop the course! That's a lot different from teaching with someone else's lesson plans for three weeks. Besides, maybe mechanical people simply cannot become test technicians.

Mac continues. "We plan to give everyone in the plant a chance to take some aptitude tests. We'll use those scores to choose people for interviews. Then we'll select people who have the highest chance for success. We're looking for highly motivated people who have the ability to learn."

Incredulous, I ask, "When is this supposed to start?"

Mac goes on to explain that the testing is to start in a few weeks and that the first class kicks off in three months. He anticipates that the course will be 12 weeks long, eight hours a day, followed by four weeks of intense training on the new 1401 computer. We will call the program Computer Electronic Technician Training Program—Compelo Tech for short. In addition to me, he will hire at least one other instructor. That means that each of us will be teaching at least four hours per day. We can give homework and tests just as in regular schools, but student evaluations will be given in individual face-to-face meetings, similar to the company's employee appraisal program. Mac explains that the employees' jobs are to be good students while they are in the program.

In spite of my trepidation, I am intrigued by the idea. The computer testing job is getting dull. Every day seems like a repetition of the day before. My main entertainment has been trying to find new ways to analyze the machines and find problems more quickly. Every day makes me feel more like a robot.

"OK," I say. "I'll do my best. When do you want me to start?"

\* \* \*

For the last three months, my companion teacher, Ray Slater, and I laid out the curriculum, course outlines, handouts, overheads, tests, and exercises that will take the adult learners from basic electricity and algebra to solid-state electronics in 12 weeks. We located other instructors to teach the four additional weeks of specific computer training, but it was up to Ray and me to have students prepared for learning the new computer. In parallel, Mac and his team tested hundreds of employees. Ray and I interviewed about 50 of the top scorers and chose 24 for the first class.

At 8:00 am on the first day of the program, Mac introduces Ray and me to the learners and tells them that they are in for 16 weeks of hard work. The 24 people stare back in anticipation. Most of them have not been students for 20 years and are over twice my age. This is going to be quite different from teaching high school students. Ray and I say a few words, after which Mac and I return to our offices, while Ray begins the first four hours of class—Introduction to Algebra.

I grab some coffee and settle in my chair, longing for four or five hours of quiet. My class, Introduction to Electronics, is to start just after lunch. At 9:45, the phone rings.

"Grant, you've got to help me," Ray says, sounding desperate. "I'm already out of material, and I don't know what to do."

"Can you give them some in-class exercises?" I ask.

"We've already been through the ones I planned. Can you come and take over? We're on break now." His voice is shaky.

"See ya in five minutes," I say, already picking up my materials.

Ray meets me outside the classroom door. He's sweating and his tie is loose.

"What happened?" I ask.

"Well, we started right in," he says, "and I moved through the materials, but there was not one question from the guys in the room. I don't know if I was moving too fast or not."

"It's their first day of class. They're just getting the feel of what they are in for," I reply.

"If you don't mind, Grant, I'm going to get a cup of coffee back at the office and try to relax."

"OK," I say. "Just take it easy and we'll talk about this at the end of the day."

Whee! I'm wondering what we instructors are going to experience. The students are nervous, and so are we.

I take a breath and step into the classroom. I can feel 48 eyes staring at me. These guys feel quite different from the group of students at the high school.

"Good morning, everyone," I say, walking to the front of the room.

We are in one of the new rooms in IBM's Training and Education Building. The whole wall behind me is filled with chalkboards. An instructor's desk sits in front of the chalkboards facing the students, each of whom has a modern chair with a large writing surface in front. Glancing around the room, I see that most of the student's yellow pads contain notes, so some of Ray's topics must have gotten through. I put my jacket on a chair and sit on top of the desk facing the class group.

"How're you guys doing?"

I wait.

"Well, I'm feeling pretty nervous right now, to tell you the truth."

I recognize the speaker as John Tolson, one of the guys I interviewed.

"Yeah, me too," I reply. "You have to face me every day, but I have to face 24 of you."

Everyone laughs.

"I was feeling nervous last night, thinking not just about this first day, but about 12 whole weeks together," I say. "This is a whole new thing that none of us have ever experienced. This is an experiment for IBM, and I'm impressed that they will invest this much money and time in us."

"And, last night, I thought, 'I'm nervous,' but what about you guys? Most of you have been out of school for 15 years. How must that feel?"

"15 years! How about 20?" Says a fellow in the second row.

What I thought might be a few ice-breaking comments, now looks to be a long discussion. They talk about their anxieties about the program, the challenge of changing from a job they knew well to one entirely new, their worry about their abilities to succeed in the program, their questions about what a computer test technician really does. They also want to know about my background.

I tell them the funny story of teaching in high school just after returning from the Army, how I was selected to design and teach this program, and how I worked my way through college. I also say how I am willing to work with each person to help each succeed.

After over an hour of free discussion, I say, "We're all in this together, we'll all help each other. Now, let's take a ten-minute break, and then we'll start to learn some basic electronics."

\* \* \*

At the end of the day, I return to the office and see Ray busily working on some papers.

"How'd it go?" he asks.

I tell him about the long discussion with the class group, and how the class members were probably more nervous than we were.

"We should probably move slowly through the subjects at first, to give us the time to get to know each other. To some of these guys, these are brand new topics—and some have not been in this kind of training for a long time. Yes, they've been in apprenticeships and in skills training, but this approach is mostly brand new. We'll need to check often to see if they are getting it and if they are feeling comfortable," I explain. "Let's include a lot of little quizzes and reviews every hour to make sure they're understanding. These guys want to learn, and we need to help them."

"Yeah. I've thought about that," Ray says. "While you were over there in class, I modified my plan and realize I moved too fast."

"That's great, Ray. Let's get a good night's sleep and get a fresh start tomorrow."

\* \* \*

On the second day, things have smoothed out. Ray and I are over our nervousness and have settled into a routine that will take us through the 12 weeks. Compelo Tech has launched and we are all on board for the ride.

* * *

We trained over 200 computer technicians in the Compelo Tech program. As soon as one group finished, we started another. It was an unusual educational venture because we could immediately see the result of our work. Occasionally, I visited the manufacturing department where technicians and assemblers were building the new 1401 computer. At any point in time, there were at least 100 computers in the process of completing their test. I could see our ex-students hard at work, testing the machines, and doing it professionally. I was doing something important, not only for the company, but also for the people who moved into a new career path at the middle of their working life.

* * *

Our son, David, was born at the local hospital in Endicott during this time when Joyce and I were just under 24 years old. It was a frightening event for several reasons. Joyce had a long and painful labor, much of the time without me in the room because of the hospital's rules. I walked the floor, read half of the book, *Dr. Zhivago*, but could do little for Joyce but pray. She and David came through it all right, but I was scared out of my wits. We were 400 miles from her family and mine. It felt as if Orange, Virginia was on another planet.

In spite of the troubles, the next morning, Joyce lay smiling in the bed with our cute, little, red-headed kid in her arms. Even then, he wiggled a lot, a precursor to the energy he would display in the years to come. All three of us set out on a new adventure. I might know computers, but they aren't nearly as complicated as a child.

# A STEP UP

Frank Delaney, head of the plant's quality control operation, plucked me out of the training department to put another challenge on the table. He asked me to become a Project Manager of Quality Control for electronic products. This meant I would be responsible for making sure every computer leaving the plant met IBM's high standards and customer expectations. In addition, I would oversee the quality of printed circuit manufacturing, the tiny components that made up the brains of the computers. As project manager, four full departments of technicians and inspectors each with about 25 people and headed by a manager would report to me. I was a manager of managers at age 25. Most of my colleagues joined the company before I was born.

Frank said technology was raising the standards for manufacturing and testing. He needed someone with a strong technical background and a fresh point of view. I could attest to the fresh point of view, but what did I know about IBM manufacturing? Yet, I always wanted to be a manufacturing manager like Dad. Dad fought hard for his people's rights, and I wanted to do the same.

I was hardly a B student in engineering, but I knew I was a reasonably good problem solver and could handle complexity. What scares me most was the personality cult of the manufacturing managers. These guys are tough and proud of it. Sure, they're fair, but they yell and scream, they're obsessive about deadlines, and they go to work at 7:00 am or 7:30 pm, for God's sake. Just look at Ivan Fredin, Jud Schoonover, Tim Reeser. These guys are tough. They don't curse, don't demean people, but they're strong, loud, and assertive—intimidating without violent language.

Jud Schoonover, one of my colleagues, was responsible for quality control of the machine shop. I'd seen Jud end an argument with another manager by throwing the questionable manufacturing parts one by one into a trash can. "Do you think they're any good now?" he shouted to his opponent who stared pop-eyed at the twisted metal pieces hitting the trash can. "Don't ever dispute my men's judgment again," Jud continued. "These parts are scrap!"

I'm just a timid little mouse by comparison. Sure, I've been a 2nd Lieutenant, I'm tough on the inside, I have some courage of my convictions, and I can make difficult decisions, but verbal? Hell no, that's not me.

* * *

Ivan Fredin was one of the tough guys who had worked his way up to Assistant Plant Manager step by step with grit and hard work. Ivan's white hair stood out like a light when he took a daily walk around the manufacturing floor to see how the thousands of people who reported to him were doing their jobs. He'd stop to talk to machinists, assemblers, and occasionally a manager. He didn't depend on people telling how things were going, he wanted to see for himself. Executives at IBM didn't need a fancy consultant to tell them that hands-on supervision worked best.

One afternoon, Ivan's secretary asked Frank and me to brief Ivan about some quality control issues. How did customers feel about our new products? We went into the office at our designated time, but no Ivan. It was unusual for him to be late. We sat talking, reviewing some of the charts and statistics we had accumulated.

In 10 or 15 minutes, Ivan walked briskly into the room, face drawn, eyes narrow. We must be in trouble, I thought. He really looks upset.

Ivan sat down behind the desk, leaned back slowly, eyes down, hands on the desk.

We waited.

What in the world is going on? What's happened?

A tear swelled from under Ivan's left eyelid, sat there glistening in the light of the walnut-paneled office. Ivan slowly brought a hand to his dark suit's breast pocket, pulled out a starched white handkerchief, and patted the tear's track. Eventually, he looked up.

"Sorry. Been out in the machine shop. Tom Herndon caught his hand in a press. They took him to the hospital. Looks like he'll lose the whole hand. I talked to his wife. She's on the way to the hospital."

I sat there wondering what to say, trying to visualize how such an accident could have happened with all the safety devices and procedures the company used. I guessed that the man probably used the machine without employing the safety devices. But Ivan had no interest in assigning blame, concentrating instead on taking care of Tom and his family and comforting other members of the man's department, acting more like an affectionate father than a disciplinarian. My fear of the tough guy's loud boisterous style rolled away like the tear on Ivan's cheek, but the tear would always be a visual reminder of IBM's care for individual employees.

A few years later, when IBM was getting ready to introduce its new 360 computer system, Frank asked me to head the Quality Engineering Department.

"We're facing some big challenges in the near future," Frank said. "We need a strong Quality Engineering function to lead our technical direction."

Quality Engineering was the organization that designed the quality assurance testing, statistical approaches to quality control, analyzed failures or other deviations in manufacturing processes, and advised other departments on technically related issues.

Frank was right about challenges. IBM was introducing the 360 computer systems, a common architecture that would revolutionize computing. Often described as IBM's "you bet your company" system, the new line required extraordinary efforts of all departments, functions, and locations. Our job in Endicott was to build the 360 Model 30 computer and the complex printed circuit boards and cards from which all 360 computers and systems were to be built. We were taking all our technologies to new levels.

Executives asked my department to design programs and procedures to make sure that the new System/360 computers shipped from Endicott met the customers' highest quality and reliability standards; defining those standards as "every system should be more reliable than the system that it replaced in a customer's office," meaning that every customer should see improved productivity and reliability when a new 360 system replaced a current machine.

My team of quality and reliability engineers had attracted attention when they had designed an innovative test to root out defective "black epoxy modules" in the 1401 computer, a member of the pre-360 generation of computers.

To develop the new tests, we labored for long hours over a period of three to four weeks under the intense scrutiny of local plant executives as well as executives at division headquarters in White Plains, New York. The division president, Clarence Frizzel, a tall, lanky West Virginian, like Ivan Fredin, known for his no-nonsense, tough management style, called me every week to find out how we were doing. The first time "Friz" called, I was almost too nervous to talk. I wasn't used to having executives skip over six or eight levels of management to call a 28-year-old, relatively green project manager.

As we neared completion of the design, Friz invited me to his office in White Plains. "Come on down and show me the plan," he'd drawled. "My assistant will tell you how to get here." Every division level executive had an administrative assistant, usually a young person on the way up who had attracted the attention of management. This gave executives a chance to get to know him, and it gave him a chance to observe executives in action. Almost every high-level executive in the company had been an "AA" at one time or another. To young managers, becoming an AA to a key executive was the quick way to get attention and rise to the top.

Soon, Tom Wrangle called me.

"We've allocated 30 minutes for this meeting, so talk net," he said.

Sure, I thought. 30 minutes for one of the most complicated projects I've ever worked on.

"OK. I'll do what I can," I said. "See ya on Tuesday."

On Tuesday, I arrived at the division headquarters building in White Plains, 200 miles from home, with a fever and a nasty prostate and bladder infection that my old fashioned doctor in Vestal was treating with sulfa drugs—big yellow pills like the ones that vets use on horses. My stomach was pitching and rolling like a tugboat on a stormy sea. This was my first solo meeting with such a high official, and I wanted to get it right. By all rights, I should have been home in bed, but, no, the show had to go on.

At the designated time, I entered Friz's living room sized office carrying two rolled-up easel charts on which I had squeezed my report. He stood up behind his rectangular, sharp-edged walnut desk to greet me.

"Good mawnin, Grant. Welcome to White Plains. I'm eager to hear what you have to say," he said, sticking out his long arm, staring into my eyes. He had the stature and demeanor of Abe Lincoln, but with sandy hair, a smooth, angular face. His white shirt sleeves were slightly rolled up as if ready to go to work. On the desktop lay a few letters and memos, walnut inbox and outbox trays, and an IBM "Think" sign. The kind that Tom Watson, the founder, had distributed to every manager and salesman.

"We've made good progress," I started, putting my two charts over the pins of the easel stand in the corner of the office. It wasn't easy to find the pins, because my hands were damp and shaking and my knees felt weak. "The test program is defined, and we've designed a reliability stress test to run on selected systems. I've made a diagram of the whole program on these charts."

Friz asked a few questions about the program that I was able to answer without hesitation, but my stomach continued to revolt. Suddenly the room began to whirl. I grabbed the easel stand, trying to stay upright. Friz and his assistant must have bounded out of their seats, because I soon felt strong hands on my arms, keeping me from melting into the office carpet.

"Here. Sit here," Friz's voice sounded through the fog. "Tom, get some water and call first aid."

"I'll be alright," I mumbled, mortified that they would think I passed out from stage fright, wondering with panic what was happening to me, devastated about screwing up in front of the division president.

"You just sit right here," Friz said softly, pulling up a chair to sit next to me. "We'll have some water in a minute."

"I'm sorry."

"It's OK."

Soon, Tom, the AA arrived with a nurse in tow. By then, my head had cleared enough to see them. I sipped the water with my audience of three staring at every move.

"First Aid is just downstairs," the nurse said. "I brought a chair. Do you feel like standing up?"

"Yeah, I can make it to the chair." I stood up, wobbling a bit, but held firmly by Friz and Tom.

"Thanks so much. I'm so embarrassed."

"Don't worry," said Friz. "We'll get someone to drive you home."

"But it's 200 miles."

"I'm sure someone from Endicott is down here today. We'll find them and have someone drive you and your car back. Tom, get on it! Find out who's here today."

The nurse wheeled me to first aid where a doctor checked me over for about 20 minutes, concluding that I was having a reaction to the heavy medicine I'd been taking. I still wasn't sure whether it was the medicine or a panic attack. When I stepped out of the doctor's office into the reception area, Friz stuck his head into the door.

"How're ya doin?" he said with a smile. "We've found a ride for ya. You get on back home and we'll talk when ya're feelin better."

He sounded more like a concerned brother than a distant executive. He really cared about me. I relaxed. So this is what IBM means by "respect for the individual?" Maybe not, but it sure feels good to me.

\* \* \*

During my time with Quality Control, our daughter, Lynn, with wispy blond hair and big blue eyes, arrived after a relatively short labor process. It was as if she was born with a smile on her face. Having a daughter was an exciting experience for a guy who grew up with no sister or young girls in the family. Joyce and I now had two children two years apart in age, and an active, engaging home life. But, we quickly settled into the changes, and I was already beginning to learn that even in the same environment, people can be quite different. Male, female. Active, quiet. Wake up early, sleep late. We are all different, but trend toward common values.

# JFK

IBM worked hard to develop relationships with many colleges and universities, for at least two reasons. The first was to have good sources of engineers and other employees. Also, IBM wanted to sell computers to the university computer departments, many of which were becoming quite sophisticated. The recruiting department asked me to be a liaison with the University of Virginia because I knew the institution and some of the people. That meant an occasional visit to Charlottesville and a nice opportunity to visit Orange.

I flew to Charlottesville on November 21, 1963, dropped by to visit my parents and in-laws, then returned to Charlottesville to do the rounds. The director of the computing center and I had a good chat on the morning of November 22nd, where he told me about the university's applications and gave me a few hints about future plans. Feeling good about that, I dropped by the White Spot Diner on the locally famous "Corner" for a traditional hamburger.

After lunch I took a short walk across the grounds, weaving past the Rotunda and the Alderman Library, soon reaching Thornton Hall, the School of Engineering. As I was walking down the hall toward the dean's office, a student said, "The president has been shot. Oh my God!" Another student said a bit softer, "Good riddance."

How could someone be so crass as to express such a thing about a president I admired? A president so eloquent. A president challenging us to higher goals. A president who wanted to conquer space.

I was stunned. Stunned by the sudden shock of the attack on our president, but further stunned by a comment I felt incapable of processing. My ears started ringing. People around me seemed like mere sprites. People looked at each other though not seeing.

President Kennedy inspired us to do more for our country. "Ask not what your country can do for you, but what you can do for your country." Within the next 10 years, send people to the moon and bring them back safely. There was work to be done. Join the peace corps, build our economy. Camelot had arrived. We had new energy. We had hope for a new day.

How could this happen in the United States? Sure, Lincoln had been assassinated, but those were different times. How could this happen now? We were numb with shock, wondering how the nation would cope. Wondering how we would cope.

I found a chair and sat down, trying to think what this meant. What will happen to the country? Who did this? What will happen now?

I proceeded to the dean's office and spoke to his secretary, suggesting we cancel the meeting.

She said, "It's just as well. He's gone to join other faculty members in an emergency meeting, and we're all shocked. Take care of yourself, young man."

I went to the motel where I was staying and turned on the TV, watching the news and commentaries roll in. What will tomorrow bring? What will this do to our country? To our lives? I eventually heard Walter Cronkite tell us the president was dead. A new president, a consummate politician, grimly picked up the thread of government. An investigation, a whitewashing, an unbelievable explanation of a single assassin made me wonder even more deeply how one person could so disrupt my life—our country. We fear the bomb. We fear the USSR. But Lee Harvey Oswald would have looked harmless at the supermarket.

# FIVE-YEAR REFLECTION

Now, after just five years in IBM, in 1962, I'm a manager with over 100 people working in my organization. I've met my five-year goal. My classmates in engineering school thought I was crazy to go into manufacturing. "It's menial work," they said. "You'll be bored out of your mind. You should go into design." But I persisted. Managing a bunch of nerdy engineers didn't seem like a good target. Besides, I wanted to think we were building something. I wanted to see real stuff, not paper.

So far, I've had three management jobs and still haven't followed any incumbent. After being an instructor for Compelo Tech, Clarence McNeal asked me to become manager of Engineering Training, a new department, that reported to him. My second management job, Project Manager of Quality Control, was heading an existing organization, but the job had been vacant for a good while before I arrived. The next assignment also took me to a new job, one that had not existed before, Project Manager of Quality Engineering.

So, here I am. Yes, we are producing stuff, but the technical challenges are growing every day. Each problem is more complex than the one before it. Going into a career in engineering design couldn't have been more complicated than this. And, because there are just a few of us with engineering backgrounds in Quality Assurance, our guidance and knowledge are essential to produce our products.

A few months ago, IBM introduced a new graduate program in cooperation with Syracuse University, where I can get a master's degree in electrical engineering while the company pays all tuition. Instructors come to Endicott, about 100 miles from Syracuse. I never pictured myself moving up in the academic ranks, but I need to know more about the technologies we're dealing with and have a deeper understanding of the theory. So, I signed up.

I'm struggling. There is just one three-hour class a week, but the homework is taking me 10 to 15 hours outside of class, revealing some of the shortcomings of my studies in undergraduate engineering. The homework requires intense effort, and I need quiet. I've tried working until the wee hours of the morning, going to the local college library, staying late at work—stealing time where I can. Of course, that leaves Joyce to take care of the house, three-year-old David, and one-year-old Lynn. She is not happy to say the least. "You're giving your life to IBM, what else can you give them?" But, at the same time, in spite of my growing salary, we are barely getting by financially. We started the marriage with no savings, and we now have a mortgage and other living expenses. My salary is covering everything, but we are saving little.

My boss, Frank Delaney, has become my mentor and my model. At every opportunity, he's encouraged my efforts and expressed thanks for my good performance. My Syracuse class is once a week and starts at 3:00 pm. Several times, in the middle of a meeting in his office, he asked me, "Isn't it time for you to leave for class?" and insisted I leave the meeting and catch up later.

Because of all the pressures, I've been tempted to drop out of the master's program, but that would be letting Frank and all of my colleagues down. IBM is investing a lot in me. Since my time in Manufacturing Training, they've sent me to Basic Manager Training, Advanced Management Training, Principles of Quality Management, Advanced Quality and Reliability Techniques, and now the Syracuse program. They are betting on a return on their investment. It's my moral responsibility to deliver results.

Grandma Tate's words ring in my ears: "If you have a talent and don't use it, it's a sin."

# BIG CHANGES

Leading Quality Engineering seems like a blur: fast-paced, brutal change, crunching technical challenges, growth. The organization, which consisted of only two departments of about 15 people each two years ago, now has five departments.

New technology has driven growth. IBM introduced a new computer system, the System/360 with radical new mechanical, electrical, and software systems. Computers in the previous generations could not "talk" to one another. A software program or application written for one computer type could not be used on another without massive rewriting of the basic code and instructions. Software written for the 1401 computer, made here in Endicott, would not run on a 701 made in Poughkeepsie. The System/360 fixes all that through a massive rethinking of computer architecture and technology, and a company-wide engineering design effort.

Since mid-range computers have traditionally been designed and manufactured in Endicott, we were assigned the System/360/30, and the plant was gearing up for the effort over the last two years. We've been redesigning processes and test methods, retraining people, and designing new ways of assuring the quality of the systems.

The new systems require a whole different technology inside. The company redesigned the electronic devices, wiring system, and connectivity to achieve significantly new density of circuits. In other words, a box of a certain size could contain more computing power and speed than in the previous generation. IBM is calling its technology Solid Logic Technology (SLT).

Some of the components, the silver modules holding thousands of micro-transistors, are produced by the Components Division in East Fishkill, New York. Those modules are sent to us in Endicott, where they are mounted on SLT cards of multiple sizes. Those cards are then inserted into larger boards to make up a given computer configuration. The foundational cards and larger boards are also produced in Endicott. In previous generations, called Standard Modular System (SMS), one could observe the metal circuits that formed the connectors on the card. The new SLT cards and boards have much finer circuit "wires," and there are also multiple layers of wires on a single card or board.

Our group, Quality Engineering, is responsible for designing statistical quality control techniques to make sure the production processes are producing at acceptable quality. We also test proposed process changes to make sure they work before being added to the production line. And, we devise our own test approaches and software to independently test products while they are in process and before they are shipped to be included in a computer system. It is intense, schedule-driven work.

Tim Reeser, who was previously Manufacturing Manager and responsible for overseeing all production in the plant, was put in charge of scaling up all SLT processes and production. Reeser is a skilled manufacturing leader who is more prone to use pressure and intimidation than thoughtful logic to get his way. He's been running huge daily status meetings to check the progress on every aspect of the project, checking every milestone and pushing, pushing, pushing for faster results. One of my managers regularly attends the meetings, but Reeser will often call me if he is not satisfied with the response.

Watching Reeser work has made me realize that these old-time manufacturing people are not my tribe. Yes, my dad was a manager in manufacturing, but I'm more prone to use cool-headed logic than brute force to solve problems and get results. So far, my approach is working pretty well. People probably see me as overly quiet, but they seem to respect my approach and knowledge. I'm not sure that's true with Reeser, though. He eyes me warily, tries to ask tough questions, and works hard to find flaws in my arguments.

We have engineering departments in the factory. Industrial Engineering plans the factory layout and space, Manufacturing Engineering receives design from Product Engineering then devises ways to manufacture them. But those functions are located in a building separate from manufacturing. There are few people with engineering degrees within the manufacturing departments, although we've staffed Quality Engineering by hiring engineers.

Manufacturing runs on three shifts a day. First shift starts at 7:30 am sharp. If Reeser and his cronies need a staff meeting, it always starts at 7:30 am. And there are harsh words for latecomers. Macho mornings are part of the culture.

In spite of being "the quiet one," we had some notable accomplishments over the last two years. We developed a special reliability test for the System/360/30 computers that helps predict the system's reliability and stability over a period of time. I presented the technique at an IEEE conference in San Francisco to an enthusiastic audience.

* * *

One day, I received a call from Bob Doffelmeyer, a colleague at the product development lab.

"I just want to give you a warning," he said. "We're going to be buying 100,000 small motors and you'll have to test them."

Big deal, I thought. We can test complicated circuits and computers, so what's so complicated about testing motors?

"It has to be done really fast," Bob continued. "You see, IBM is going to put a measurement device on every computer—a device based on these motors—that will measure how many hours customers are really using their computers."

Again, I was skeptical. A mechanical motor to measure computer usage? Seems as though we could design a simple electronic device to do the same thing.

Nevertheless, soon we were testing thousands of small clock motors. In the middle of our challenges with the SLT technology, we were testing motors.

Not only that, but the motors were failing at a high rate. Jack Klein, head of our failure analysis lab was trying to figure out why.

"That little rotor inside stops turning and goes into oscillations every once in a while. I'm trying to figure out what makes that happen," Jack said. "And I have a guy over in the mechanical analysis lab also doing some testing and mathematical analysis to help me figure it out."

One night in the lab, Jack, George Allen, one of our assistant plant managers, and I watched some motors fail as Jack duplicated the conditions causing the failures. We looked at data charts, stop-action pictures, and other information.

George Allen said, "You're wrapping up your master's degree. How about writing your final paper about this phenomenon?"

Six months later, I presented my paper, "A Non-linear Analysis of the Start/Stop Characteristics of a Small Permanent Magnet Synchronous Motor," to my faculty committee at Syracuse University.

\* \* \*

Jack Klein was our failure analysis expert, a creative genius, extremely productive, intense, and difficult to manage. Jack refused to adhere to IBM's working hours, choosing to show up whenever he felt like it and go home long into the night hours. Jack's flagrant rule violations drove his managers crazy, and several of them tried to fire him for tardiness. But, Jack's ability to solve problems far exceeded the capabilities of anyone I had ever met. In my mind, he was worth his weight in gold, whether he showed up at 8:00

am or not. I pulled Jack out of his regular department and had him report directly to me. In addition, I gave him his own space to set up his lab and its equipment. He soon had all the analysis equipment he needed and, in addition, a new 1401 computer system, which he used for his calculation. Of course, Jack was also a master programmer. Whenever I had a difficult technical problem, I knew where to turn: Jack Klein.

On one occasion, we saw a remarkable increase in the number of failures on the 360/30 final testing line. With additional testing, we found that increased testing time would eventually remove the failing components, but doing so added significant time and cost to each computer system we were shipping. "We need a stress test," Jack said. "We should heat cycle the systems to cause the weak components to fail."

"How do we do that? I asked.

"Give me the weekend and I can show you," Jack replied.

When I arrived on Monday morning, Jack was waiting in my office.

"C'mon, let's go to the computer line," he said.

Jack had rigged a tent-like structure fitted with air conditioners and heaters, which he could control to sequentially raise and lower the temperature of the entire computer box (about the size of two home refrigerators bolted together). He loaded a test routine in the computer while he worked with his rigged-up tent. Soon, the test started revealing failures, and in a far shorter time than the more lengthy tests did at room temperature.

"I figure we can test all the assembled systems on the line in a few days while we're in the process of fixing the source problems," he said.

Jack went on to work night and day with the manager of the testing department to get all the computers tested.

* * *

I'd built the organization, led some important technical projects, tested 100,000 motors, and completed my MSEE degree.

Because of the growth of the new computer system sales, IBM decided to build two new manufacturing plants, one in Raleigh, NC, the other in Boulder, CO. Frank Delaney told me that I was a leading candidate to start the Quality Assurance operation in one of the two plants. I wasn't too keen on Raleigh because I had no desire to go back to the South and the rising racial conflicts there.

One day, I received a call from Jim Sullivan, the Assistant General Manager at Boulder.

"We need someone to build the Quality Assurance organization in

Boulder, and I hear you're good," he said. "Would you like to join us?"

I quickly agreed to the new opportunity, an assignment to build a new organization and to head up a whole function—to be a "functional manager," a prestigious job in a manufacturing plant.

Our third child, Laura, had just been born a few weeks before Jim's phone call. He wanted me in Colorado as soon as possible, but that would present problems for Joyce and the children. Joyce and I talked about the new job and the changes it brought, and we decided we should make the move.

# IN THE
# *SHADOW*
# OF THE
# *ROCKIES*

# BOULDER

"I thought they were still herding cattle out there," was my mother's comment when I told her I was being transferred to Boulder, Colorado. Mom grew up in Virginia and had never been west of the Virginia border. It wasn't quite the wild west, but the start-up of the new manufacturing facility in Boulder promised to give us a wild ride.

As Quality Manager, I was to be responsible for seeing that all the products and components shipped from the plant met the company's high standards and also met customer expectations. To meet that end, we monitored the various assembly and manufacturing processes and conducted tests at various stages.

One other fellow from IBM Poughkeepsie, Henry Feigenheimer, was already in Boulder and would report to me. Luckily, Henry was a knowledgeable and experienced manager with strong capabilities. It was up to Henry and me to form the Quality Assurance organization.

When I first arrived, IBM had rented an office near a downtown hotel. I walked into the building, found an empty office, took my name plate out of my briefcase, placed it on the door, and went to work. Soon, a guy from Facilities Management came by.

"Whose office is this?" he asked.

"Mine," I said.

Boulder was to manufacture products being transferred from Poughkeepsie (tape drives) and Kingston (core memories), so most of the people in the building had come from those two locations. Being the only transferee from Endicott, I knew only a few of them, and I wondered how their culture and management style might differ from my own. At the beginning, at least, our plant was the "sister" plant to the two older locations, which has been given the task to guide us along the way to competence and independence. Hence, we were able to obtain most of our procedures and processes from more experienced organizations. Yet, except for the management team and a few technical experts, most of our people would be hired from the local area. Many of us wondered how we could train these cowboys and cowgirls to be manufacturing people.

# EUTAW DRIVE

Joyce and I rented a house from two Colorado University psychology professors who were on sabbatical for the summer. Their place was previously
featured in *Beautiful Homes Magazine* and consisted of four intersecting
two-story high cylinders at the crest of a hill overlooking the city. It was
within a half mile of the Flatiron Mountains, which seem to consist of
quarter mile slabs of granite that some force of nature had caused to tilt up
far enough to stand on their ends, with opposite jagged ends reaching far
into Colorado's royal blue sky, saying, "look here, look here." The house
came fully furnished, including two Siamese cats. The lease was only for
the summer period while the owners were away and while our permanent
house was being built in Frazier Meadows, a relatively new development at
the southern edge of town.

Joyce seemed thrilled with the rental house, although she was reluctant
to move to Colorado. There was no crib in the rental house, so we prepared
a bed for baby Laura, just two months old, in a large drawer from a chest of
drawers. Laura, already comfortable with her new life, slept as if the drawer
was a natural place to sleep.

The house we're building is not so spectacular in its outside appear-
ance, but it is built to survive the hazardous winds called chinooks that
sweep down from the mountains with speeds often exceeding 100 miles an
hour. These are caused by temperature differentials between the flatlands
of the city and the mountains to the West. As a result, builders construct
houses in our new neighborhood, Frasier Meadows, using post and beam
construction, thick cedar siding, and one-and-a-half-inch cedar shingles.
Our new house is a dark green split level with double reinforced windows
that grace us with a view of the Flatirons glowing in the morning light.
The builder finished the front yard with Kentucky Blue Grass sod, but the
backyard is a typical dry desert plot with prickly pear cactus, plains yucca,
and a few sprigs of rice grass.

The team of managers who moved here to start the new manufacturing
plant banded together to make ourselves and our families rapidly become
part of the community. Joyce and I have met more people in a shorter time

than at any other place in our life. We enrolled David in the school located in our neighborhood and Lynn in preschool, and we started attending the local Methodist Church. Those, too, added to our new contacts and friends. Boulder is a vibrant, open community.

Everyone here lives outdoors, hiking the mountains, fishing the streams, skiing, running, canoeing on Boulder Lake. In addition, Denver is just over 30 minutes away and offers many accouterments of city life.

Joyce is more active than at any time in our relationship. She and Julie Kilcoyne have become good friends, and we are sharing much family time with the Kilcoynes and their four children. Our church's social group resulted in many activities with six other couples in our age group.

# CRISIS

I look down at the glistening aqua icebergs floating in an emerald sea. They are 30,000 feet below me, silent beneath the drone of four Pratt and Whitney fanjets pushing us toward Stockholm. We pass a landmass, white colors stretching far to the north. I stare at the tip of the icy land as a mass the size of Manhattan shivers, lurches, then slides into the North Atlantic, sending ice water and foam in all directions—a Niagara in reverse. I wonder about the whales, the walruses, the seals who might have inhabited or still inhabit the arctic mass. Do they simply ride it down until the thing settles into equilibrium on its path toward the equator? What about the whales circling with their pod, searching the edge of the landmass for food only to have the mass fall on them. Does the force push them away? Can they survive such a force of nature? Or does nature somehow signal its actions to creatures with more acute senses than ours? Might they hear a groan, or perhaps feel a vibration?

In another hour, the Scandinavian Air jet banks sharply right into the morning sun. I'm still groggy from a restless sleep, trying to fit myself into two coach seats on the nine-hour trip over from New York. The lucky guy by the aisle conked out just five minutes after we left Idlewild Airport and never woke up, as far as I know.

I look out the window at the sea and the city of Stockholm divided into sections by waterways. Like a tourist, I try to absorb the view below me—my first sight of a European city, so different from New York. Red roofed buildings—which seem strange for this part of the world—palaces, modern commercial structures, narrow curvy streets. And no skyscrapers.

It all seems like a dream coming to Europe like this. Imagine me, a country boy from Orange, Virginia flying to an exotic Swedish city to give a speech to an international audience! Just five years ago, I could never have imagined such an experience. No one in my family has ever even been to Canada or Mexico, much less Europe. This trip would be beyond their wildest dreams.

"Ladies and gentlemen, we are beginning our descent. Please fasten your seatbelts."

Curt Johnson, IBM Vice President for Quality Assurance invited me to make this speech while I was still in IBM's plant in Endicott, NY, before they asked me to become Quality Assurance Manager at Boulder.

It seems as if IBM has something new in store for me; it's in direct conflict with something going on at home. They asked me to go to the new plant at Boulder, Colorado at just the time when our youngest child was due. Six weeks after she was born, I was on my way to Colorado, renting a temporary house, buying a house, starting a new job, and working with strangers. All the while, Joyce coped with a new baby, a four-year-old, and a six-year-old, and she was preparing to sell the old house. The company didn't provide any childcare help, but they did take over the house-selling process. Yes, we talked about the stress the move was putting on both of us, but we decided Boulder represented an opportunity we shouldn't miss.

It's mid-morning, and in a couple of hours I'll take a plane to the Volvo factory in Gothenburg to pick up a brand new 1966 122S station wagon. This European trip seemed like a good opportunity to save about $800 from the US price, although I'll have to drive the thing for over 100 miles to get a reduction in the US duty. That'll also give me a chance to see Gothenburg and the surrounding countryside first hand. Driving 100 miles in a couple of days shouldn't be so hard to accomplish.

Three hours later, I'm stepping off a DC3 onto the tarmac at Gothenburg facing a single small terminal building. Will anyone in this godforsaken place speak English? Two Volvo taxis sit in front of the building, and I head for one of them.

"Good morning, sir," says the driver.

Well no problem with English here, I think, feeling slightly irritated he recognized me as American or English speaking.

"Morning," I say, surrendering my bags to him.

"Where would you like to go this morning?"

"The Volvo factory. I... I don't know their address," I say, shuffling for the address in my briefcase.

"Don't worry, I know where it is."

I settle back into the seat, watching the Swedish countryside whiz by. I'm here to present a new computing testing technique my group of Quality Engineers invented. A year ago, the speech had caused quite a flurry at the reliability conference in San Francisco.

The people at Boulder knew I was scheduled for this European trip and supported the idea, even though they didn't like the idea of me being away for a couple of weeks while the new plant was starting up.

Now, turning into the circular drive of the Volvo plant, I think of little but the excitement of picking up my new car. I step out of the taxi, shuffling for Swedish Krona in my pocket, and hand the driver the tab plus

20%. He stares at the money, then hands me back the tip, saying, "Thank you, sir, but that is not necessary in our country." Not like the guidebooks told me, but I thank him, grab my bags, and head into the Volvo office.

In less than 15 minutes, they checked my passport and drove up a shiny midnight blue 1966 station wagon. Its grill looks like a comedian's toothy grin. There is a chrome mirror mounted on each fender—more like a truck than a car. The Volvo representative opens the door, inviting me to sit. I admire the blue leatherette seats, the smartly, but simply designed instrument panel, and the long gearshift protruding from the floor.

"Have a good visit to Sweden," he says. "Here is your map to the hotel."

I take a few minutes to peruse his directions. There are no street names shorter than ten letters—and none bear any resemblance to English words. How will I ever remember these directions while driving on the left side of the road in traffic? But I throw the car into gear and take off into the unknown. Then I come to a traffic circle. Oh my gosh, what do I do now? I make my way to the left, circle around the thing twice, then recognize the name of the street the guy had given me. The odometer tells me I've been driving 10.6 miles—almost 90 to go before I can take the car back to Volvo so they can put it on a boat to the USA.

That was part of the intricate plan Joyce and I developed for a trip to the East coast. It sounded feasible at the time. She, the three children, and I would fly to New York. There, they'd go to see our friends, the Dillinghams, while I got on another plane for Europe. Two weeks later, I'd return from Europe, pick them up, and go to New Jersey to get the new Volvo from the docks. We'd then take a few days' vacation to drive from New York to Colorado in the new car. Great plan—we'd get to visit friends, get a new car at a bargain rate, and see the country.

\* \* \*

My speech in Stockholm goes well, and I head off to the IBM plant in Southern France to compare notes on tape drive manufacturing.

When checking into the hotel, I get a call from Jim Sullivan, my boss, saying my inspectors are rejecting 90 percent of the core storage units because of bad solder joints. He suggests I consider cutting my visit short to come home.

Crisis! Most of IBM's 360 computer systems use our core storage units. If we can't make them and ship them, we'll stall shipments of the company's main product line. I call Don Kehr, a manager who reports to me and is responsible for quality assurance of the memory units.

"Almost all the units have defective solder joints. They're all failing our pull test, and I've stopped shipments until we can figure this out. We've analyzed the process, the materials, and the tools the assemblers are using, and they seem OK," he says.

The memory units are part of the central random access memory (RAM) of a computer, the device that stores programs and data while the computer is operating.

These random access memory devices are miserable monsters to produce. They contain thousands of fragile components and thousands more of electrical connections—the primary source of failure in electronic devices.

The device stores data in units called "bits" in tiny doughnut-shaped pieces of ferric oxide called cores. In essence, the toroid-shaped core is a tiny magnet whose polarity can be set by running electrical impulses through wires strung through the doughnut's hole—a simple and basic principle. But for this principle to be useful to the computer, you need a lot of doughnuts to make a random access memory. You'll need eight of these doughnuts to store one "byte" of data. To make a RAM unit large enough to store 16,000 "bytes" of memory, you need 16,000 sets of eight doughnuts or 128,000 doughnuts. Now that's a lot of doughnuts.

But, unlike the glazed kind we eat with our coffee, these doughnuts are tiny—just a bit larger than the diameter of the lead in a number 2 pencil. And the material is similar to a pencil's graphite—easy to crack and break. The cores are stamped out like aspirin tablets, but unlike aspirin, they have to be perfect—in shape, density, and magnetic characteristics.

Luckily, another IBM plant supplies the doughnuts, but we at Boulder have to put them together to make a memory unit. We assemble the toroids into flat planes of about 16,000 cores, then string four wires—each about the diameter of a human hair—through each of the doughnuts. We have machines to help us string the wire through the tiny holes. When finished, the plane looks like an intricate screen wire mounted to a square plastic frame that's slightly smaller than a colonial windowpane. When the planes are complete, a technician tests the plane on a complicated piece of equipment to make sure each of the cores does its job. To make a random access memory, we stack eight of the planes on top of each other, solder the edge connectors, and test the whole unit.

The solder joints along the edges are critical to the unit's reliability. We test them by subjecting the wires to a "pull test," applying a certain amount of pressure on the wire. If it releases, the joint is obviously not strong enough. To get a good joint, one needs to apply the right amount of heat, soldering material, and hold it for the correct amount of time. It takes training and practice. When I left Boulder for Europe, the inspectors who worked for me were finding increasing numbers of defective solder joints on memory units—a signal something was wrong. However, I had confidence in my team of managers and technicians—thinking they could help the manufacturing people find ways to help workers do higher quality work.

"What changed?" I ask Don. "Why did the reject rate skyrocket?"

"I don't know. They've added a couple of new operators in the last week or so, but that wouldn't explain it."

"Let's get some of those bad units into the lab and have someone analyze the joints. Have them check the materials—see if they can figure out the strength of the joints. Keep me informed. Can you transfer me over to Kilcoyne, the manufacturing manager?"

I hear a few clicks and beeps.

"This is Kilcoyne," the voice says.

"Leo… This is Grant. Just been talking to Don Kehr about the…"

"Yeah, you'd better get back here. We're not shipping anything, and we need you to straighten it out."

"What can I do that our teams aren't doing?"

"Look… have you added a lot of new operators to the line? You know training and experience is critical here."

"Sure, we've added new people, but they've all been trained."

"I really think you should get back here. We've got the whole company watching us. Dunlop, the VP of Manufacturing, is coming in tomorrow or the next day. It doesn't look good to have the Quality Manager on a trek to Europe. In fact, over the phone, he suggested we get a new quality manager if you're not going to be here."

\* \* \*

The next day, arriving in Denver airport after dinner time, I rent a car and go directly to the Morgan Street building where we're manufacturing the core memories. Even though it's almost 8:00 pm and the second shift has been at work for three hours, Don Kehr is there to meet me. He's short and stocky with tousled flaxen hair and deep blue eyes. Even at this late night, his shirt and tie look neat and clean, although I know he spent most of the day on the manufacturing line—he smells like electronic manufacturing—the distinctive odor of ozone and plastic that's characteristic of high technology manufacturing.

"Hi. How's it going?" I ask, extending my hand.

"I feel beaten and bloody after the last few days, but we're holding up OK," he says.

Don takes me into his office where five memory units, each the size of a short loaf of bread, lay on top of the desk. Even from six feet away, I can see uneven and discolored nibs where solder joints have been poorly repaired.

I say, "OK. Here's my suggestion: let's tighten the qualification test. Get the best operator from the line, go through everything he does in detail. Make sure the training includes all his best techniques. Second, tighten the certification test, and let's re-certify everyone on the line. Third, let's get the engineers involved in that, and also get them to accelerate the new spot welding technique. Does that make sense?"

"Sounds good to me, but I'll need your help to convince the manufacturing guys, Graham and Kilcoyne—and also the engineering guys. They've been pretty obstinate. They think our tests are too tough."

"Yeah. Don't they always? If we start having massive memory failures in the field, it could kill the reputation of the 360 Computer system. It's our job to protect IBM's customers and the company's reputation for high quality. Don, thanks for all your good work. Why don't you go home and get some rest? You look more jet-lagged than I do, and I've been on planes for 11 hours."

* * *

After a fitful night's sleep, I'm back at the plant in a conference room with Kilcoyne, who thinks our test standards are too high and is pushing hard to keep shipments on schedule. I'm the one keeping him from reaching that goal. Tel Graham has seen the same data I have, but I'm not sure he'll take my side in the meeting. We know something changed two weeks ago on the manufacturing line, but we're not sure what, and it's going to take more time to find out what's causing the problem.

Driving from the Memory Plant in Denver to Boulder provides a welcome distraction for my problem-wracked brain. The radio blares out local traffic news, an accident on I-70 blocking traffic for miles, which, thank God, I can avoid, and news that Major Edward White and James McDivitt orbited the earth 62 times in Gemini IV. The space race goes on, as does the conflict in Vietnam. The world and local conflicts fade momentarily as I crest the hill overlooking Boulder, the majestic Flatiron Mountains lit by the morning sun and framing the city on my left, the vast plains leading to Nebraska on my right, and the tightly clustered buildings of the University of Colorado standing out in the center of the city. But knowing I'll be at the newly built IBM administration building in ten more minutes, shakes me back to reality.

The meeting with Kilcoyne is going better than expected. He and the three other manufacturing executives started out attacking me and my organization for setting standards too high—our testing is too harsh, but after showing the data collected from Don Kehr last night, they conceded that we have a more fundamental technical problem.

"Something changed," I said, showing how the defect rate tripled starting two weeks ago. "And it wasn't because we added new workers, although I'll have to say the whole department needs more training. It's some other factor: a change in the equipment, faulty soldering materials, some other contaminations. Right now, we don't know, but we're systematically testing all these variables over the next few days. In addition, we'll ask for a team of engineers from Kingston to come out to help us."

"Well, what do we do about shipments? They've got computers sitting idle in Poughkeepsie waiting for memories."

"Today, we're going to stress test ten of the units that pass our tests. If they come through all right, you can start to ship those that pass our screen."

"Hang around a few minutes," Kilcoyne said to me at the end of the meeting.

Closing the door, he returns to his desk. I sit across from him, thinking, *oh crap, here it comes*. Maybe I'll get sent back to Endicott.

"Dunlop wants me to take you out," he says.

"Why? Because I was on a business trip that you guys agreed to? The problem hadn't started when I left."

"I know, but he thinks you should have been here, or returned sooner."

"Geez, I got a plane as soon as I heard about it, and my family is still stuck back on the East coast."

We trade a few more comments back and forth, then sit in what seems like an endless silence. I suddenly realize I'm wringing my hands that are wet with sweat. My face feels red, and my throat feels tight.

Finally, Kilcoyne speaks. "Look… I believe no one is better qualified to get this thing fixed. You're the smartest QA manager in the business, but we've got to get this problem under control. I'll take the heat with Dunlop, but you'd better get this fixed fast."

"OK," I say. "Thanks." I get up slowly, open the door and walk faster and faster down the aisle.

* * *

Now, after two weeks of training and certifying operators on the memory line, the failure rate has returned to acceptable levels. The engineering department committed to a date for introducing a new spot-welding technique that yields more consistent joints and requires fewer detailed skills on the part of operators.

Don Kejr, Tel Graham, and I spent two hours discussing the sequence of events leading up to all the trouble, all the elements that threw things out of balance and exploding the failure rate. Graham was responding to the demand for memory units while taking the risk that newly trained operators could do the job. Don Kejr's team rightly detected the failures, stopped production, and subsequently, increased the training and certification. They did not need me on the scene to find the solution. They did it. But I had an image problem, the responsible manager should be on the scene.

The problem I don't know how to solve is on the east coast. My new Volvo is due to arrive at a port in New Jersey in the next five days. My plan was to be there to pick it up and take four days to drive to Colorado with Joyce and the children. It sounded like a good plan, a nice vacation before I took this promotion to the new manufacturing plant in Boulder, Colorado. My job in Endicott was going smoothly at the time, and taking a few weeks off looked like a good reward for developing a good quality engineering team there. But now, this mess....

Our friends in New York welcomed a visit from us—but for a month? Or however long it might take for me to get back there to pick up the family? It will take at least a week for me to fly back there, pick up the car, pick up Joyce and kids, then drive back here. If I asked for a week off now, IBM would probably fire me. Even if this problem is solved in the next week or so, Kilcoyne and the other top executives will still think I'm a shirker if I ask for time off. I could ask Joyce to fly back to Colorado, even ask her to pick up the car. But would she? Even then, I'd have to find a way to pick up the Volvo on the docks in Newark. What a damn mess.

A week later, the Volvo I bought in Sweden arrived at the docks in New Jersey. Kilcoyne and others agreed I could take a week off, pick up the car and my family, and drive 500 miles a day or more to cover the 1,800 miles to Colorado. It won't be a pleasant trip. Joyce will be upset and angry after feeling abandoned for three weeks, but the children are excited about getting to Colorado. I'll smile and make the best of it... not a good respite from the stress of the memory fiasco.

# MOUNTAIN AIR

The sun has been up for about an hour as I back out the white Sunbeam Alpine and take down the cloth top, putting my spinning rod, fish eggs and creel behind the seats. Tuesday traffic is light across the southern part of Boulder, no impediment to my path to Boulder Canyon Road. After passing through the Flatirons, the light dims, rays struggling to find their way through the jagged rocks lining the canyon. It's hard to forget the many pictures a Boulder native showed me of this road pummeled by huge boulders.

"It happens quite often," he said.

I hope it's not today, I thought. Top up or top down in this little car, I'd be smashed flat.

But my mind is on a mountain stream or lake, the ones plentiful in the mountains around Nederland, the tiny town 16 miles up ahead. I'll park somewhere, strap on my canteen and backpack, grab the fishing gear and hike back in for a mile or two, toss in a spinner or a fish egg, and hope for the best. Whether I catch anything or not isn't important, this is just a journey away from the day-to-day toil of starting our manufacturing plant. A day of quiet contemplation.

I shift down to second while encountering a steep, sharp turn, accelerating to third and fourth on the other side. This little Sunbeam is a joy to drive, especially on a superbly winding road. So far, only two other cars come by heading for Boulder. I breathe in the cool air and drink in the images of ages past carved in the rocks.

Arriving in Nederland, I stop at the only cafe and order a donut and a cup of coffee. The donuts look homemade, and the woman pours the coffee out of a big enamel percolator, like the ones you'd see in the cowboy movies. I tried to dress like the natives this morning, ratty baseball cap, jeans, canvas coat, and muddy hiking boots, but she knows an Easterner when she sees one.

"Where're you headed, honey?" she asks.

"Think I'll trek over to the Arapahoe Peak area and look for a fishing hole. Not expecting to catch much, though." I answer. "You know any good places?"

"Can't say I do. Haven't seen any fish coming by here. But watch out for the bears, they've been seeing one over there."

"Thanks for the hint. I'll be careful," I say.

I head for one of the two empty cafe tables. Pulling out the chair stops the conversation of the four old men sitting at the only large table. Three of them nod at me, the fourth only scowls. Funny, the scowler is the only one wearing sneakers, not cowboy boots. They return to their conversation as I sit down with my donut.

The four men remind me that someone once said all small towns are exactly alike. This scene could be here in Nederland, or Orange, VA, or my grandfather's farm village of Fredericks Hall.

I wonder what these guys are talking about. Perhaps some small controversy in whatever local government, or whether there's going to be a big snow year, or what's happening in Vietnam. One or more of these men might have a son drafted to go fight in that bloody war, still raging on in 1966.

I've been lucky to avoid the war. My seven-and-a-half-year Army Reserve obligation expired a few months ago. The Army could have called me back to active duty anytime, but my obscure military occupational specialty of Electronic Engineer, R & D probably shielded me.

But here at this moment, the war is far away, as is IBM, technology problems, or day to day conflicts. In a few minutes I'll be alone on a mountain trail with only one care—an errant bear.

# AN EXECUTIVE
# ARRIVES

Over a year after our initial start-up in Boulder, we are still under the gun to meet growing demand for our tape drives. We've moved into new buildings in Niwot, just outside Boulder. Our four buildings are blocks of 100,000 square feet and from the sky look like a giant checkerboard on the prairie.

We are way behind schedule on shipments of tape drives and core memory units, both of which are needed to complete installations of System/360 in customers' locations. We are the choke point, the one obstacle to IBM's ambitious sales goals. We are approaching 4,000 employees in the plant, and my unit, Quality Assurance, is almost 300. Most of the managers are experienced, having been recruited from other IBM locations, but, except for some lead technicians and specialists in the various departments, most employees have been hired from the western states in the region. As one manager put it, "We're trying to turn cowboys into computer makers."

And that conversion process is too slow. My quality inspectors are finding defects in all levels of production, from incoming parts to final testing. The typical IBM plant works with around 20,000 different parts, from screws to complicated mechanical and electrical components. Some of our parts are produced here or in other plants, but most come from suppliers around the world. Our fast-growing production schedule is pushing our suppliers to the limit. As a result, we are rejecting many shipments because of quality defects. With critical components, we've resorted to inspecting every part, saving the good ones, and returning defects to the vendor. Similarly, we've increased inspection and monitoring throughout the production and testing processes to ensure we don't ship defects to our customers.

We have the manufacturing blocks in place, but our warehouse, though externally complete, lacks the internal structure to store and retrieve the thousands of parts for production. Warehouses employ sophisticated systems where a given part can be automatically stored, retrieved and forwarded to the production line just when needed. Our partially completed warehouse is restraining production. Storage racks are being installed, but parts are sitting in boxes all around the floor. The warehouse team has arranged the boxes so they can find the parts they need, but chaos reigns. Assembly managers, desperate to prepare their tape drives for shipment, are slipping into the warehouse at night to retrieve parts for their department.

We were desperate for the machinery to move pallets of parts around the warehouse, so we assigned a purchasing agent, Trey Johnson, to search the whole USA for forklift trucks, which are in short supply.

\* \* \*

We are in the general manager's conference room for our daily status meeting.

"I know we're all tired," says Dick Whelan, our general manager. "But we have a big job to do here. The whole company is depending on us. Make sure you put some rest into your schedule."

Dick is a confident, mild-mannered executive with years of experience in manufacturing, having advanced through positions in IBM's Kingston and Poughkeepsie, NY locations to give him the required experience. His black hair, now interspersed with grey, speaks to that experience. Dick's chiseled features, sharp nose, and piercing eyes makes one feel confident. He knows how to listen to his people.

He continues, "You know I've been fielding calls from all the execs in both division and corporate. I've been explaining that we're moving as fast as we can. Frank Cary, our group vice president, will arrive at Jefferson County Airport sometime on Wednesday."

We all groan. "How does that help us?" I wonder. We'll have to spend all our time updating some executive when we should be working with our people to solve our problems. Yet, none of us on the management team speaks up to object. We have to do this.

"OK, Don, let's look at the numbers," Dick says, looking at Don Cross, who is responsible for tape drive manufacturing. Don goes to the front of the room and turns on the projector. Don's full head of hair is grayer now than when I met him 18 months ago after both our families moved into the same neighborhood, Frazier Meadows. Don calms those around him, here and in social gatherings. I relax seeing Don at work.

His first transparency shows a sharply upwardly sloped red line with a dark blue line underneath.

"This shows how far behind we are," he says. "We are working overtime when necessary, but lack of parts is hindering assembly. We've even had people standing around waiting to get parts to put into machines."

Tel Graham, manager of core memory assembly, presents his charts. Same story.

Next, we hear from Marty Lombardi, production control manager, detailing the lag in receipt of parts.

"Often, we're getting enough parts, but Quality Control is rejecting them," Marty says.

All eyes turn to me.

"What's going on, Grant," asks Dick Whelan.

I walk to the front of the room and show our data on failure rates in each part of our production system.

"I think you guys are way too critical," Don Cross says.

"I agree," chimes in Marty. "We can't get stuff through the warehouse because it's being rejected.

"Look, we can't put defective parts in our machines. And we can't ship machines that won't work in customer's offices," I reply. "I'll be happy to take you to each department to show you what we are finding. We have to get better at producing quality stuff. Then the rejection rate will go down."

Several people grumble.

I continue with my presentation, showing all the data.

At the end of the meeting, Dick Whelan says, "Grant, I want you to take over management of the warehouse in addition to your other duties. We know it's chaos over there. People are taking parts without recording the records. And, nobody can find anything. Go out there and fix it."

"But..." I mutter, but the meeting is breaking up.

I walk back to my office, head swirling. What the hell do I know about warehousing?

How do I make sense of the chaos out there? First, I have to look at the situation.

* * *

Stepping into the new 100,000 square foot warehouse, I see rows upon rows of boxes, tops open, containing parts and supplies. Construction people are assembling the new rack system at the back end, progressing from the back to the front. A forklift brings new boxes from the dock, placing them in rows by the direction of a guy holding a clipboard. As a box is placed, the guy notes its location on the clipboard.

"At least they've got some semblance of order," I think.

Soon, a fellow in a white shirt and loosened tie approaches me. His gray hair is tossed as if he'd just gotten out of bed. His khaki pants have a spot of grease just above his right knee. And he's wearing scuffed cowboy boots.

"Hi, can I help you?" he asks. "I'm Tom Mitchel, manager of the warehouse."

"Yeah, I'm Grant Tate. They've asked me to work with you to see how

I might help."

"Oh. Glad to meet you. They told me you were now my big boss."

"Well, I don't know about big boss, but I hope we can work together to solve some problems.

"You know my biggest problem?" he asks. "It's the people from the manufacturing line coming over here taking parts without telling anyone."

"How are they finding things?" I respond.

"As you can see, we've sorted the boxes by sections. They've figured out the system and how to find the parts. And, of course, you know, they are taking the parts before Quality Control checks them."

"OK. Let's figure out a way to fix that," I reply.

On the way back to my office, I'm asking myself, who knows about warehousing? Industrial engineers.

I go to the office of Bill Bowman, Manager of Industrial Engineering. We soon agreed I could borrow Bob Beckett, one of his industrial engineers, to help me in the warehouse.

"Bob knows his stuff, but I have to tell you he's hard to manage. He's aggressive, impatient, and wants things his way," Bill says.

"That's exactly what I'm looking for," I reply.

Now, two hours after meeting with Bowman. Bob Beckett and I are walking the warehouse together. Bob seems about a foot taller than my height, with trimly combed black hair. He looks to be mid-twenties and moves with the confidence and agility of an athlete. He has a strong, commanding voice. And, I hope, a commanding presence.

"Look, we have a lot to figure out here, but as the first thing, let's lock down the warehouse. Don't let anyone in unless they're authorized."

"OK, I'm on it," Bob replies.

\* \* \*

The next day, Frank Cary, one of IBM's senior vice presidents, arrives at the Jefferson County Airport, a few miles out of Boulder, in one of the company's private jets. An hour later, he's at our plant having been picked up by Dick Whelan. I don't envy Dick's having to endure Cary's probing questions during the 30 minute drive from the airport.

\* \* \*

Whelan, Cary, my colleagues, and I are gathered in Whelan's conference room. This is the first time I've seen Cary in person, having heard of him in his previous role heading the sales and marketing division.

Cary is taller than expected. His cherubic face, punctuated by wire rimmed glasses, belies his reputation as a hard-nosed executive. He stands in contrast to the other executives I've met, reminding me of Lavrenity Beria, Stalin's sidekick in the USSR. I am immediately suspicious and uneasy.

Dick introduces each one of us, describing our role in the organization. Cary starts to fire away without waiting for the presentations we've prepared for these sessions.

"What are you doing to catch up with the schedule for tape drives?" he asks Jim Sullivan, our Assistant General Manager.

"We… uh… uh, we're doing everything we can to get the parts, train the people, test the products," Jim replies.

"I mean specifically," Cary says.

"Let us show you the data. We prepared an update," Sullivan replies, regaining his footing.

Sullivan's face has been showing the strain for several weeks, red-faced, deep frown lines, occasional splotches of skin irritation.

Don Cross steps forward to the projector to show the production data. Don looks more confident than that projected by Sullivan. "What about quality?" Cary asks.

That's my cue, and I step forward to show that reject rates of parts and finished products are reducing but are still above desired levels.

"What are you doing to make that curve go down?" Cary asks.

"We provide detailed information to the manufacturing people to help them see how to improve, and also work with them to improve processes, training and test procedures," I answer.

Cary's mouth twists and I wonder if he is coiling for an attack. Does this guy understand my job? Does he know anything about manufacturing?

"Well. Keep pushing. Protect our customers," Cary replies.

Finally, at the end of the meeting, he offers to help.

"Look, if you need the jet to retrieve parts from the vendors, feel free to use it," Frank says.

Of course we have no idea how we could use a relatively small passenger jet to help get big shipments from vendors and through the warehouse. Yet, who could say no to a vice president for such a generous offer. Cary offered no encouragement, did not acknowledge our progress, only push, push, push for more production. This guy is different from what I'd come to expect from IBM executives. The ones I've met before focused on taking care of the people. Cary is about numbers. A beady-eyed Berea who is likely to become CEO.

Later, Dick Whelan calls Trey, the guy in Purchasing responsible for finding fork lift trucks, saying, "The IBM jet is down at Jeff Co Airport, so I'd like for you to be in charge of scheduling it to pick up parts from vendors."

Trey, being a relatively new employee who had been hired in Colorado, replies, "What kind of company is this, anyhow? I want forklifts and what the hell do I get? A fucking airplane!"

Cary and his jet left a few days later, leaving us to fix the problems. Bob Becket and our new security procedures helped put order back into the warehouse while workers constructed the new racks and control systems. Within three weeks, the warehouse was under control, and we turned our attention to other production problems.

# HAPPY IN BOULDER

The family was happy in Colorado. David attended an elementary school in the neighborhood, Joyce found a pre-school for Lynn. Laura had a safe place to play, and we immediately adapted to the Boulder outdoor culture. The children found readily available playmates in the neighborhood, including Leo Kilcoynes's children. Work brought a lot of stresses, but seldom ruined weekends, and required relatively little overtime.

Boulder Lake, about ten miles north of our house, provided an opportune place to go fishing. One windy Saturday, David and I rented a small motor boat to try our luck in the west. We attached some artificial lures to our rods, started the motor, and began trolling. Just as we were feeling a bit discouraged, a fish took David's lure, and the pole made a big whack on the side of the boat because of the fish's strength. After swirling around a bit, a fighting trout flew out of the water in front of us while trying to escape the line. David's eyes popped with excitement.

With smiles of accomplishment, David brought his prize home to show his mother and sisters.

We took off for the mountains most weekends, Joyce, David, Lynn, and I hiking, with Laura in a Gerry backpack on my back. I figured if I carried her every day, she could still be in the pack in her elementary school years. We acquired a pop-up tent trailer which became our abode on a two-week trip to Yellowstone, northern Wyoming, and South Dakota.

Through the Methodist Church, Joyce and I joined a couple's group, participated in their discussions, picnics, and parties and explored the many restaurants of Boulder and Denver. The other couples came from varying geographical areas and professions, so our conversations became rich with variety. We also became friends with several of my colleagues from IBM who also lived in our neighborhood. With some of them, we spent Saturdays in the nearby stadium cheering for the University of Colorado Buffaloes football team, for which Eddie Crowder was coach, the father of one of David's friends.

Soon, we had a new member of the family.

One Saturday, seven-year-old daughter Lynn and I, after doing some shopping, decided to stop by the SPCA animal shelter, where we found a litter of black puppies, each with silky fur, blunt noses, and squirming bodies.

"Oh, Dad, they are so cute. Just look at them," Lynn said. "That one there is really special."

"Yes. Really cute. I wonder how big they get," I said.

The SPCA attendant told us the puppies had become eligible for adoption the week before and that they were cockapoos, a mix of cocker spaniel and standard poodle.

"They probably will be about 20 pounds when fully adult," she said.

"Please, Dad, can we take one home? Lynn said. "Please, please."

I hemmed and hawed, trying to make excuses, then finally said, "Which one?"

"Oh, that one we were just watching."

"OK," I said.

Soon, Lynn and I returned home with a seven-week-old puppy in a box.

When we showed Joyce the puppy, she said, "Whose dog is that?"

I said, "It's your dog."

"That's not my dog," she said.

"Please, Mom. She's so cute," Lynn said.

"It's our dog," I said.

Joyce's initial reaction soon turned to love, as puppy Shelly worked her way into the hearts of the family. We built a six-foot cedar fence around the back yard to give Shelly running room, and also to contain a piece of the dry desert for some creative landscaping.

# A NEW ADVENTURE

Last week, Leo Kilcoyne called me to his office.

"You have been selected to go to a special management development program at Stanford University," he said.

"What's that?" I asked.

"It's a year-long graduate business program called the Sloan Program. IBM selects only two people a year to attend. You'll be in a group of people from businesses all over the world. IBM will pay for your moving expenses and other fees. And you'll get your full salary. For the year, your job will be a student."

"Wow. When does it start?"

"September, so we have three months to decide who will run Quality Assurance after you're gone?"

"What will happen when I come back?"

"Don't know what things will look like in a year, but you'll get an assignment appropriate to your current level or better."

"Well... that sounds great."

In my head, I quickly estimated the amount IBM was going to spend on me.

"That's a lot of money to spend on my development. What will the company expect in return?" I asked.

"Come back more of a manager and less of an engineer," Kilcoyne answered.

Leo Kilcoyne is the Assistant General Manager of the Boulder plant, having replaced Jim Sullivan after the production crises we faced over a year ago. The production problems caused several others to lose their positions, Marty Lombardi, Manager of Production Control, for example. I knew, at the time, that those two were feeling extreme stress. Sullivan's decisions seemed arbitrary and erratic, his forty-year-old face was taut and flushed, and he often seemed preoccupied or out of touch.

Kilcoyne, on the other hand, is calm and collected. Leo, his wife Julie, and their four young children live in our neighborhood, Frazier Meadows. We became close family friends, but that has never hindered our business relationship. Leo is a steady, sure, smart leader with strong puritan values and treats everyone with fairness and respect. Steady is right. Leo seems to have one pace for doing everything... slow. The first shift in manufacturing traditionally starts at 7:30 am, with the office people starting at 8:00 am. Leo typically walks into his office between 9:00 and 9:30 am. In many ways, he reminds me of my dad. Leo had built his own house near Kingston, NY, and has the hand skills to build anything. He knows how to get things done.

My work style is more erratic. I tend to make faster decisions, am impatient, and like to try new things, experiment. Yet, like Leo, people tell me they like working with me, that I am a good manager and am always looking out for my people.

Being selected for the Sloan program indicates upper management's confidence in me, in spite of all the troubles we went through last year, when I thought, after the core memory difficulties, that some people, such as Bob Dunlop, VP of Manufacturing at division headquarters, thought I was screwing up. He could have vetoed the Sloan opportunity, but apparently did not. Strange, even in the midst of almost getting fired, I never worried about getting fired, or what I would do if it happened. Several people, including my old boss, Sullivan, lost their jobs because of the plant problems, but I was part of the group that came through with my job intact.

Joyce is still smarting after being stuck in the east while I was in the midst of the core memory problems. I tried explaining the stress and the challenges I was facing, but she never seemed to understand. "It's obvious the company is more important than we are," was her response. She never seemed to connect my troubles with the possible threat to the family's security. What would happen if I really got fired? We had no savings, and she had no job. It was up to me.

Now, I'm wondering how Joyce will react to pulling up stakes to move to California, after just three years in Colorado. It will certainly stoke her fears of being left behind again, of moving to a new place, of leaving her friends, of changing the children's school, and of leaving the house we've come to love. We will need to work these things out together, but, in spite of all my training in management and human relations, I find it hard to work with my own wife.

She is interested in our social events, particularly if they promote our status. She likes being the wife of a rising IBM manager but doesn't have the foggiest notion of what I, or our friends from IBM, actually do. Consequently, I stopped discussing my day's work at home, even when facing a crisis. Part of my hesitation rests in my desire to forget the sources of my stress, the pressure for more production, and the on-the-job conflicts. Living them once is enough. Talking about them makes me relive the pain. So, I just bottle it up. *Soldier on, Grant, that's what you're supposed to do.* But

Joyce is a good mother, intensely interested in David, Lynn, and Laura; their schooling, their care, their development. We are living out the 1950s model: me working and Joyce managing the home.

I am self-assured at work, but a wimp at home. Nevertheless, this Sloan program is an offer only open to three or four people from the entire IBM company. It's an exceptional opportunity. I must find a way.

And it is not clear what will happen after Stanford. Kilcoyne's answer was vague. I will presumably be returning to Boulder, but jobs at Division HQ, back in the East, may be calling. I completed my master's degree in engineering while still in Endicott. I'm on IBM's "Hi-Po" list, a list of people having been identified with good potential. There will undoubtedly be another test to see if I can cut the mustard.

Since coming to Colorado, we built a new manufacturing facility, hired over 6,000 people, produced thousands of tape drives, core memory units, and computer systems—an amazing feat by most standards. My own organization, Quality Assurance, is now 300 people. We started with a few experienced people and built the organization from the bottom-up to a fully-staffed organization with highly respected managers, professionals, and skilled craftspeople. These people are fully equipped to carry out our mission whether I'm here or not. I helped build Quality Engineering in Endicott, and now the entire Quality Assurance organization in a new manufacturing plant.

My job is complete. It's time to move on. Stanford, here I come.

# SURPRISE PARTY

That night we were stuck on the elevator while 200 people drank champagne. When Joyce and finally I stepped into the room, expecting a small dinner with a few other couples, we were met with a roar of "Congratulations! Stanford will never be the same."

I quickly explained the elevator malfunction, apologizing for being late, while Leo Kilcoyne led me to a microphone and a small stage.

He stepped to the mic and said, "We all know why we are here. Grant Tate has been chosen to attend the prestigious Stanford Sloan program in California for the next school year. This is a special program for up-and-coming executives to study management and strategy. Grant helped us start this plant and grew the Quality Assurance organization to be a highly competent and respected function in our plant."

I was stunned, never expecting something like this. I scrambled to think of what to say, because Leo was certainly going to hand the mic to me when he finished.

"C'mon over here, Grant," Leo said.

"Wow," I said, looking out over the people sitting at tables in the largest ballroom in Boulder. "Thank you all for coming tonight. I'd like for this to be a celebration for all the great work you've done here. Just three years ago, IBM Boulder was a clutter of rental buildings with a big plot of open land out yonder in the plains. Now, there are almost 6,000 of us building intricate, high-quality products for customers all over the world."

"I'll never forget how Henry Feigenheimer and I sat at the table trying to figure out how to build our Quality Assurance team and how to find the right people. Now that team is over 300. Amazing! Thank you, Henry."

"Yes, we had some bumps along the way, struggling to meet production demands, learning how to build complicated units, and entertaining executives flying in on jet airplanes. But, through hard work and diligence, we got over those obstacles and made something we can all be proud of. So enjoy the night and I'll be around after dinner to say hello."

Leo showed Joyce and me to our table where his wife Julie and some of my other colleagues were sitting.

"Oh my gosh, what a surprise," I said. "We never expected anything like this."

"It's nice to take a few minutes out to smell the roses," he said.

I looked at Joyce who was grinning from ear to ear.

# STANFORD

The refreshing, mint-like scent of eucalyptus envelops me, taking me to a world quite different from the day-to-day conflict in IBM's manufacturing operation. A 15-minute bike ride, half through the forest, is now my daily commute from our rental house in Palo Alto to the Stanford campus.

Stanford Business School sent me a box of six books, economics, organizational behavior, finance, suggesting they be read before beginning the program. Do they think I'm a speed reader?

But wait, maybe I should become a speed reader. I called the training manager at Boulder asking if there was a class in speed reading. He said, "No, but I can send our instructor up to talk to you." Soon a fellow, looking more like a high school student than an IBM employee, with tousled hair, a plaid shirt, jeans, and cowboy boots showed up at my office.

"I'm Joe Carson," he said. "I understand you want to learn to speed read."

"Yes, and I want to learn fast as well. When can we start?" I asked.

Joe and I met for 30 minutes each day for instruction and drill, me the reader, Joe the drill sergeant. He showed me new techniques, ran me through reading exercises, and measured my comprehension after each exercise.

Thanks to Joe's training, I got through the six books and was ready to go in the Stanford Sloan Program.

* * *

On the evening of our welcoming reception, Joyce and I met 32 other people and their spouses from various industries including several from other countries such as Japan, Sweden, and the UK. Each person had at least ten years of management experience.

Although we came from different backgrounds, our class group quickly became cohesive. At the end of each week, one of our members sponsored a party that included spouses. Spouses, in this case, meant wives because no women were in the class. There were a few singles in the class, but most members were married. Stanford sponsored orientation and social events for the wives, helping them connect. Pool parties, boat trips, Hawaiian luaus, musical performances formed the scene of our weekends

Joyce and I rented a fully furnished house with an artfully designed Northern California garden about a mile from the Stanford campus. David and Lynn's elementary school was only a block away, and I rode my bike every day to my classes. Laura, a toddler, had a yard to play in and a safe sidewalk to ride her tricycle.

Laura, then just over two-years-old, quickly found she could use her tricycle for exploration, an early clue to her later life. Joyce and I were chatting about the day's happenings in the front yard one afternoon, so focused we failed to notice Laura was out of sight.

"Where's Laura?" I asked.

"She was right here on her trike," Joyce said. "Oh, my gosh. Where is she?"

We searched the sidewalks, up and down, until we finally found Laura on the opposite side of our block, which bordered a busy street in Palo Alto.

As I approached Laura on her bike, I said, "Where were you going?"

"Just looking around," she said, proudly.

* * *

Academically, we followed much of the standard MBA curriculum of finance, management, marketing and sales, operations, economics, strategic thinking, ethics. Still other elements gave us a broad understanding of leadership and corporate management. We dipped our toes into world affairs. Claude Buss, an advisor to the state department regarding the Vietnam war negotiations, kept us up to date. "The average Vietnamese just wants the soldiers to get out of their fields and stop the killing," he told us.

We visited a business or industry every week, Kaiser Steel, to talk to plant management and watch steel girders glowing red with heat flowing back and forth over rollers to form their final cross-section, C & H Sugar to stand high on a platform overlooking a 50-foot-deep bin gradually being filled with fresh sugar cane from Hawaii, Wells Fargo, to hear how bankers run a vast financial operation. We visited docks to see ships unloaded and talked to working level operators. I discussed life with a tugboat captain on the waters around San Francisco. Other classes seemed outside the classical curriculum. Comparative Religion and Foreign Affairs expanded our horizons.

A guest speaker every week described the challenges of running their company or organization. Frank Cary, a Stanford MBA graduate, was one of those. Frank described the antitrust case just brought against IBM by the federal government and acknowledged the challenge during the System/360 buildup.

Interesting comments, I thought, but no one, including Frank Cary, ever thanked us for our sweat and blood during our crisis at Boulder, a situation that had cost several of our people, such as Jim Sullivan and Marty Lombardi, their jobs, if not their health. As one of my colleagues said, "Keeping our jobs must have been our reward." IBM has many award programs, especially for salespeople. Their Hundred Percent Club every year fetes people for meeting their sales targets. Like the gritty toilet paper indicated back in Endicott, manufacturing people rank low on IBM executives' totem pole.

Cary's approach sounded like a typical financial analysis, once again, reminding me of how different he seemed from Thomas Watson, Jr. and other IBM leaders who always started a conversation by talking about the people.

After the talk, I, along with some of my classmates, approached Frank.

"Hi, I'm Grant Tate," I said, offering my hand.

Behind his wire-rimmed glasses, Frank's eyes showed no recognition.

"I'm one of the two IBMers in the class."

"Oh," he replied. "Nice to meet you." Then proceeded to speak to the next person.

No warmth, no recognition, no asking how it's going. I wonder if IBM is my kind of company. Now that I've seen a lot of others, maybe this is not the proper organization. Cary is a big turnoff.

The week before Cary's visit, the Sloan Program Director asked two of my classmates and me to attend a question-and-answer session with the program's advisory group, which consisted of past graduates and other important sponsors. We sat at a table in front of the room, gave a brief introduction, after which the executives fired questions at us. "In your eyes, what is the most important feature of the program? How does it fit into your overall goals? Have you gained new insights and perspectives?" We responded with confidence and emotions, drawing many smiles from the audience. Afterward, two of the executives approached me to ask more. One said, "If you ever want to reach out, call me," handing me his business card.

Although Joyce hated pulling up roots to move to California, she seemed happy with our life there. She was outgoing, developed good relationships with others, and looked comfortable for the experiences. Joyce and other spouses formed a committee to plan our group's weekly social events. My classmates and their spouses obviously liked her, and we developed strong relationships with other couples. Joyce found a commercial swimming club in our neighborhood and enrolled David, Lynn, and herself in lessons. All became good swimmers by the time the year was over. Joyce and I were thriving in this new experience, working and playing together, meeting new people, exploring new vistas.

David and Lynn were engaged in good schools and seemed happy. Every day, as I rode my bike to the Stanford campus, I waved at David and Lynn as I passed their school where I could sometimes see their class through substantial windows. Laura and I spent almost every morning together in the parks, where I read materials preparing for afternoon classes, while she played in sandboxes and swings.

Lynn, born with athletic coordination, spent every recess doing tricks on the playground's "monkey bars." One day found us transporting her to the Stanford University Hospital from which Lynn emerged with an ankle to hip cast to repair a spiral fracture. This after, of course, falling off the high hand bars on the jungle gym.

The next week, we received a phone call from her teacher saying, "Just wanted you to know I found Lynn in the jungle gym, cast and all." Lynn was not about to let a broken leg get here down.

David joined an active local Cub Scouts pack with children from a wide cross section of California culture. On one of their outings, a group of Chinese Americans asked me to join their discussions, which evolved into the Chinese equivalent of "yo momma" jokes where they compared notes on growing up in their particular culture.

Every weekend, we explored California, the missions up and down the coast, the sights of San Francisco, the restaurants of Palo Alto. Joyce was intensely interested in the history of the area, so much that we couldn't pass a historic marker on our trips without stopping to read the placards. West coast history was never taught in Virginia schools, so we were entering an entirely new realm.

The regular Stanford classes, which were in the afternoon five days a week, gave me flexibility and time to explore fascinating new topics in depth. This was the only time in my adult life where my full-time job was learning—unlike late high school, University of Virginia, or Syracuse University where I had to work to earn my living while studying for my diplomas. I also found my aptitudes were more closely aligned with business rather than engineering topics.

Seeing her passion for history or anthropology, coupled with her prolific reading, I thought Joyce might want to dig more deeply.

"We've lived in the backyard of a university in Endicott, Boulder, and now Stanford. Do you want to take some classes?" I asked.

She looked back at me, smiling, but said not a word.

\* \* \*

Toward the end of our program, I dropped in to see Dean Bud Pedersen to express my thanks for his leadership. I also wanted his advice.

"I'd like to someday teach at a university, should I go for a PhD?" I asked.

"In your case, your industrial experience is what counts, but you should also get a doctorate degree. It doesn't make much difference where you get it. Just get it," he answered.

# BOULDER AFTER STANFORD

On my return, Leo Kilcoyne appointed me to head Industrial Engineering, a position I welcomed because of its broad responsibilities for planning, plant layout, process design, and innovation. There are about 100 professionals in the organization, most with Industrial Engineering degrees, quite different from my electrical engineering background.

But I feel comfortable in this environment because my study of computer systems and various manufacturing systems has given me a well-rounded perspective on the systems and skills required to produce high-tech products. Our unit includes experts in optimization and data analytics who can analyze and solve complex problems. They, for instance, studied our warehouse, then planned and implemented a system that can rapidly store and later find parts needed by production.

My year at Stanford opened my eyes to domestic, global, social, and economic issues. My colleagues at Boulder were quick to notice my "California Attitude." One said, "Stanford turned you into a liberal."

"No, it just opened my eyes to what was going on around me," I replied.

IBM, like many large companies, needed to adjust its policies with respect to equal rights, after the passage of the Civil Rights Acts of 1964 and 1968. The company made explicit its policies of nondiscrimination in hiring, promotion, and working conditions, and set out to assure every person in the management chain implemented the policies. To do that, IBM had to retrain every manager in the company. Probably, because of my California Attitude, I was chosen to join Les Franklin, one of the few Black people in the plant, to train our over 500 managers to implement the new policies and to help them understand the nuances of working equitably with people of all racial and ethnic backgrounds.

Les and I found that most managers, many of whom had been hired in Colorado, had some knowledge of Latin American culture, but had never met a Black person. Our class on racial and ethnic slurs to avoid drew extensive discussion with the participants. At the end of the class, each manager signed a pledge to implement the company policies. The company promised to find a job outside of management for any person who was unwilling to sign. To my knowledge, every manager signed the pledge.

# THE BOARD
# OF DIRECTORS

"Who the hell are you?"

My instinctual response is to say, "I'm Grant Tate. Who the hell are you?" But I am not sure T. Vincent (Vin) Learson, Senior Vice President of IBM, has a sense of humor, so I introduce myself as one of the managers hosting members of the IBM board of directors for lunch and a plant tour, then ask him to join Mr. Amory Houghton, Dr. Grayson Kirk, and me at our table.

Scowling, Learson sits down, hardly acknowledging the other two men. He is well over six feet tall with a booming voice and greying, swept-back hair. His shadow is almost as long as his reputation for being a tough SOB. IBM managers speak of Vin Learson with fearful respect. He is the legendary management force behind the System/360, our attempt to revolutionize the world of computers. I know very well that Learson has been critical of our performance at the Boulder, Colorado plant. So, his demeanor is no surprise.

As Learson grumbles and toys with his food, I continue my conversation with the other gentlemen: "Dr. Kirk, you have certainly faced some huge challenges at Colombia," I say, struggling to ignore Learson's stare.

"Yes, but I'm happy to say that it has settled down quite a bit. We haven't had a sit-in for several months now."

It was a big day for the management of the IBM Boulder plant. Hosting an IBM Board meeting was an unusual occasion for any plant. We have practiced for weeks to get it right—going through the agenda, assigning hosts to the individual board members, driving the 30 miles from the airport to the plant over and over to make sure we know the route, painting and cleaning the plant, and preparing the plant tour route to make sure that the appropriate employees are available along the way to demonstrate their work.

The visit is taking place just over two years after we opened the new manufacturing facility in 1965. These were heady days for IBM. IBM announced the System/360 computer system in what Fortune magazine called a "you bet your company strategy." Customer orders had far outpaced even the most optimistic projections—and the company built two new manufacturing plants to meet the demand: one in North Carolina, the other in Colorado.

"When are we going to start the plant tour?" says Learson.

"As soon as Mr. Houghton and Dr. Kirk finish lunch," I reply nervously.

"Well, let's get going soon. I don't have much time."

"Where the hell is Max Femmer?" I think. According to our well-planned agenda, Max, the Director of the Development Laboratory and a senior manager at Boulder, was to have the "opportunity" to escort Learson on the plant tour. But, so far, Femmer is over 30 minutes late for lunch.

Amory Houghton looks at me and smiles.

"I guess we're ready," he says, sensing the tension.

Houghton, Chairman of the Board of Corning Glass Corporation, a seasoned executive, grins at me to signal understanding as I stand up to lead the way from the cafeteria to the manufacturing plant.

It is a relief to be walking—the exercise loosens my tight leg and stomach muscles, but how I wish Max Femmer would arrive and take Learson off my hands. I like the other two men. They could make the plant tour a pleasant experience.

As we enter the plant, I begin my well-rehearsed spiel: "The plant was started in 1965 by a management team from several other IBM plants. Except for about 200 people with critical skills, we recruited the balance of the employees from the local area. As you can imagine, all new employees have completed an extensive training program in which they learn the principles and policies of the IBM company as well as the technical knowledge and skills necessary to build the high-quality products that we produce here."

Mr. Houghton says, looking down the production line, "My, the plant is neat and clean. Is it always this way?"

"Hell, no. You can tell that they swept it up this morning," says Learson.

I feel my face redden with embarrassment. How could Learson be so discourteous to an outside director?

Dr. Kirk, President of Colombia University, looks slightly miffed. Still, Mr. Houghton smiles at Learson and starts a story: "When I was taking a group of Corning directors through one of our plants last year, a director leaned on a bench to get a better look at an operation and put both hands on a newly painted tabletop. He held up both hands for me to see and said, 'They're still ahead of us, but we're gaining fast.' So, I understand the problem."

Even Vin Learson laughs, but then he suddenly bolts to a telephone on a production manager's desk. Soon, he is giving orders to some hapless IBM manager at a distant facility. He is trying to run the whole damned IBM corporation while walking down the aisle in our plant.

I continue my pitch to the remaining two men: "We're shipping over 1,000 drives a month, but the company needs 1,500..."

A short man in a crew cut rounds the distant corner and heads toward us as I talk. Finally… Max Femmer.

"Where the hell have you been?" I whisper, meeting him halfway. "Take this tiger off my hands."

"You mean Learson? Where is he?"

"Over there on that phone. He can't seem to pass one—probably worried about this month's shipments from all the plants."

"Yeah, he's carrying a heavy load."

"Is he always like this?"

"So I've heard. But he's supposed to be smart and fair. We'll see."

"Good luck," I say, returning to my other two guests.

The plant tour continues with only Mr. Houghton and Dr. Kirk. They listen to my every word, asked good questions, and shower me with thanks.

I've never met an IBM executive like Vin Learson, and I wonder if that is what it takes to get to the top. Perhaps a no-nonsense, abrupt style is required. Yet, it seems inconsistent with everything I've learned about respect for the individual and good leadership. He reminds me of Mr. Rubin at American Silk Mill, who drove his management team to the point where most departed. If this is what it takes to get to the top, I will never be in the top ranks.

By bringing the Board of Directors to Boulder, IBM's top brass must have felt our plant had stabilized after all the start-up problems, but, to my knowledge, none of them ever thanked us for the extraordinary effort to establish this place. Some of my colleagues paid big prices in health and position, while those of us who survived with our jobs felt extreme stress. A simple thank you would have helped.

# REFLECTIONS ON COLORADO

The move had been inevitable for over a year. My job as Industrial Engineering Manager in Boulder took me to division headquarters in White Plains multiple times to present and defend our strategic and operating plans. Division executives and staff members looked to me as the person who knew what was going on in our plant. Several directors saw me as a potential member of their team.

Colorado has been good for the family. We engaged fully in the outdoors lifestyle of Coloradans, camping and hiking in the Rockies, watching bears and other wildlife in national parks, catching native trout in the Yellowstone River, and cooking them over our campfire. We put many miles on our Volvo station wagon towing our pop-up tent trailer.

We developed a host of friends, in the neighborhood, the church, the schools, and IBM. We enjoyed cookouts, good restaurants, parties, and University of Colorado football games together. Our relationships have been wide-ranging and free of drama.

While all of us in the family were surprised by the offer to spend a year in California, we came to see it as a new adventure. We could camp on the way, seeing some new parts of the West and California, we'd never explored.

Changing schools for David and Lynn created a bit of anxiety at first, but they navigated the change quite well. Laura, at three, was accustomed to long drives and camping, and seemed to see it as just another occasion. Yet, we all will always remember the bear at Yosemite that invaded our campsite, waking us up in the middle of the night, and destroying our cooler, drinking the milk inside.

Starting a new hi-tech manufacturing plant, growing it to 6,000 people within two years was truly an adventure, although some of my colleagues might have a less positive word for it. Our relatively small management team, drawn from existing IBM plants, hired the people, built the facility, established the manufacturing processes, and produced new IBM products and units. Previously established IBM manufacturing facilities grew more slowly over longer periods of time. No one had written a manual for us— and we never had time to write one.

We did this work as the wider world raged. In 1967, when we were preparing for Stanford, the Vietnam War continued, drawing ever increasing protests across the country, one almost destroying Detroit. Virgil Grissom, Ed White, and Roger Chaffee perished in a fire on the Apollo spacecraft, and the Middle East continued to boil with another Israeli war. We were uncertain what we might encounter at Stanford.

I am now 43 and have had five different management jobs, three of which required me to build new organizations. Three of those jobs, in quality control, put me in natural conflict with production managers. Although I never looked at myself as engaging in conflict, I've managed the role quite well while finding that being prepared and using good data has brought respect and good outcomes. We encountered a great deal of pressure and stress as we built the plant, but I was able to maintain a good balance between work and home life.

Many of my colleagues at Stanford were vice presidents and other senior managers. Yet, I felt confident and comfortable with them as we debated case studies and other issues both in class and in field trips to various companies around the country. I learned to ask challenging questions and have productive exchanges with the many CEOs we visited.

Leo Kilcoyne offered me a chance to stay in Boulder, but, after Stanford, I wanted to have a platform with a wider view of the company. Going to a headquarters position provides that possibility and also offers the chance to exercise my new skills and knowledge from Stanford. In addition, it is likely that Leo, himself, will be given other opportunities at other locations.

Going to headquarters will be another adventure.

# ENTERING THE CORPORATE JUNGLE

# HEADQUARTERS

I transferred to White Plains a year after finishing the Sloan Program at Stanford and serving a year as the Manager of Industrial Engineering in Boulder. Joyce, the children, and I sat around a television in a Connecticut hotel watching Neil Armstrong step on the moon, two years short of President Kennedy's ten-year promise to send people to the moon and return them safely.

Leo Kilcoyne had suggested I stay in Boulder to become Manufacturing Manager, a promotion. Instead, I opted for Manager of New Technology Planning in the division's staff in White Plains, a newly created job to oversee new technology development in manufacturing. The Stanford Sloan Program intensified my interests in corporate management and strategy. Going to division headquarters promised the chance to stand on a higher platform.

Joyce and I discussed the career possibilities for several hours one night. That part was relatively easy to process, but both of us valued the lifestyle living in Boulder had provided. We had good friends, a nice house in an excellent neighborhood, excellent schools, a local university, and wonderful weather. Yet, we agreed the opportunity to continue my upward career progression favored moving back to the East Coast.

We bought a new two-story colonial house on a five-acre wooded lot in Ridgefield, CT, a small suburban town about an hour's drive from my office in White Plains. We had quickly discovered that house prices were inversely proportional to the distance from the primary places of employment, such as White Plains and New York City. Although IBM gave me a big salary increase to sweeten their new position offer, the higher cost of living was going to be a challenge.

The commute also offered a challenge. Whereas, it was a 15-minute drive to the Boulder plant, the new commute of an hour each way, meant ten hours a week, 40 hours a month, would be spent on the road. I didn't know how much overtime my job would require, but I could remember getting a lot of calls from people in White Plains after their normal working hours. And some of those people told me of their long hours, especially the hours when one of the many "crises" boiled up.

New technologies were helping IBM pack more functions into smaller spaces, thus significantly improving the capabilities of new computers and associated equipment. But new technologies required significant changes to manufacturing methods, which forced us to reconsider how the manufacturing plants did their work and the profile of what products and technologies each plant would produce. This change in the mission of each plant often generated emotional responses from plant managers who were inclined to protect the range of products they wanted to build. I was in the middle of those conflicts.

One situation involved Tim Reeser, then the General Manager of Endicott's technology plant, where I once worked. Advancing technology was at the root of this debate.

In the early days, a manufacturing plant could manufacture a whole computer. That meant ordering the vacuum tubes, putting them into units, assembling the machine, testing, and shipping it. Such a plant was "vertically integrated." It was responsible from top to bottom.

At the next stage of technology, making transistors required a specialized process requiring specific capital equipment, special clean rooms, and highly trained technicians. Similarly, fabricating the circuit boards, adding the "printed circuits," and inserting the transistors required another set of skills and workers. Much of the work that the computer factory previously manufactured was now being completed at specialized component factories. The computer factory management said, "What? A large component of our work and value-added has been siphoned away." The next stage of technology put even more economic content in the component factors.

As Manager of New Technology, I was responsible for recommending how we balance these technology equations among the division's manufacturing plants. After much study, my team recommended that component plants continue making transistors, microchips, and standard printed circuits. Whereas each computer plant should be responsible for producing the printed circuits customized to its assigned computer systems. This required setting up printed circuit manufacturing at the computer plants at Poughkeepsie, Endicott, San Jose, and others. We called it "the customization and dispersal program."

We occasionally got pushback on the strategy. For instance, Tim Reeser said, "No way!" After many discussions and negotiations, we presented the data backing up the recommendation and prevailed after convincing Reeser's boss, Ray Boedecker, a division vice president, to support our position.

Success in the new job required strategic thinking, knowledge of computer technology, corporate politics, and conceptual thinking. I loved the intellectual and relational challenges. The knowledge gained at Stanford helped me understand and integrate the complexities needed in the job. And, my hands-on experience at Endicott and Boulder gave me the required confidence and credibility. In addition, my background in technology and management was more substantial than most of my colleagues.

While I was in Boulder, I worried that Bob Dunlop had a negative view of my performance during the memory fiasco at Boulder. He was now the president of my current division, two levels above me in the hierarchy. He certainly had a hand in choosing me for the job, so I must have been OK in his mind.

* * *

After a year in the new job, IBM sent me to the "Interdivisional Rotation Program," a six-month term, where the corporate executive development team developed an individual program for each participant to spend time with executives in the different divisions across the corporation. I was to be a shadow in each exec's office, observing, asking questions as appropriate, but supposedly learning how things get done. This was a clear signal I was on the corporate "Hi-Po List," a list of up-and-coming young executives with strong upward potential.

I accepted this designation without a flinch, no fear, no hesitation. Stanford gave me the big-picture capability, and I could finally sit with people exercising that viewpoint. I spent a week or two each with eight or ten executives, including Spike Beitzel, Group Vice President, Dave Kearns, Division President of Sales and Marketing, and Bob Evans, Division President of Product Development. I was particularly impressed by Kearns and Evans, both brilliant in their knowledge of the business, creativity, and leadership.

Bob "Bo" Evans was the creative brain behind IBM's computer development team. He was brilliant, edgy. His moderately rotund body brimmed with energy while popping out new ideas left and right. I saw him sketch out a complex technical issue on an easel chart in Beitzel's office late one afternoon while Beitzel and four other executives watched with blank faces, not having enough base knowledge to be on Bo's wavelength. When I had a chance to meet with Bo one-to-one, he described the strengths and weaknesses of each of the executives who reported to him. I was dumbfounded that he would trust me, a junior exec from Nowheresville, with that kind of information. But he profoundly won my respect and loyalty in that one meeting. I had found at least one champion.

Other executives, however, caused me to wonder how they got to their high position. Beitzel, for instance, used the same pattern of questioning in every meeting I attended with him. It felt like he had observed the technique used by Tom Watson or another high executive, then uncritically adopted it. The rotation program solidified my observation that sales and marketing were the paths to top leadership in IBM. Execs in other functions were more brilliant, but you had to be on the sales train to get to the top station.

By the time the rotation was over, IBM's product development teams were conceiving another breakthrough computer system. Called FS or Future Systems, it took the System/360 concepts to an even higher level of performance and sophistication. Outside observers had called System/360 the "You Bet your Company System" because of the enormous commitment of resources and risks of introducing that radical new concept to the market. But, of course, the bet paid off in market share and, subsequently, a spurt of growth for the company.

FS was supposed to be the next wave. The designers were already at work, but someone had to manufacture and produce FS, whatever it turned out to be. How should we adapt the company's manufacturing systems and capabilities? Division executives gave me the responsibility to answer that question. So, as Manager of Advanced Manufacturing Systems, I assembled a small team of experts and found us a location right in the middle of the systems design activity in Poughkeepsie.

Over the next year, we studied the design directions for hardware, software, components, and other support activities and prepared tentative strategies to adopt in manufacturing. To inform manufacturing leaders, I gave dozens of speeches and presentations explaining the FS concept and its impact on the company and our way of doing things. IBM eventually decided to abandon the FS concept because it would require a revolution even later than the System/360 introduction, instead moving to a next generation called System/370.

We recognized our present divisional structure probably needed significant changes, and the company formed several special organizational "task forces" to recommend changes. My serving on those task forces with senior executives led Ted Papes to select me as his Director of Organization after he became president of the Systems Products Division, one of the units our task force had recommended.

Organization Theory became one of my primary fascinations at Stanford. Hal Leavitt, our professor, captivated my interest with his insight and depth of knowledge. I committed myself to learn more of the theory. By the beginning of the task force, I had started a new engineering training unit, a new quality engineering unit, built a whole quality assurance function in a new manufacturing plant, and started two newly created positions at division headquarters. Working with large units like divisions offered a considerable uptick in challenges, but I was thrilled by the new opportunities to learn and try new things.

\* \* \*

After four years, I should be accustomed to this commute from Ridgefield, CT to White Plains, NY, the Systems Product Division's headquarters, but it wears me down, especially the hour-long drive home after a long day's work. Interstate 684 is like a race track while the last leg, State Route 35, feels like a deathtrap with its curvy two-lane road. If all the drivers are as tired as I am, it's a wonder there isn't a crash every night. The god of corporations must be protecting us.

It's not just the commute that's wearing me down. Since moving to the area, my hours have been getting longer, meaning dinner at home no earlier than seven or eight. By that time, Joyce and the children have eaten, leaving me to dine alone. Even with the overtime, my briefcase is usually full of work to do at home. On weekends, there is work to do. Every month there is a plane trip somewhere.

David, in particular, had trouble with the move. He developed a major conflict with his sixth-grade teacher, requiring Joyce's intervention on his behalf. The teacher was subsequently fired by the principal, but David's morale had already been damaged. We eventually moved him to St. Luke's School, a private school in the area. He seemed relieved when we decided on the action.

Joyce is deeply involved with the children's school activities. She is quick to sense difficulty and is an excellent tutor and troubleshooter. I admire her diligence.

We are certainly paying a price for this move to Ridgefield. We gave up a wonderful lifestyle in Boulder to come to a new place where I'm overwhelmed with work. And I know the stress is getting to me. I've lost some weight, am consuming antacids like candy, and having to check in with Dr. Safford, our local physician often, to check out various aches and pains.

Joyce and I developed some friends from the neighbors and in the church. We are also playing tennis. But most of the conversations she and I have are about the children, the family budget, or the excessive time I spend at work.

As I feared, we are close to the edge with monthly finances, covering our expenses, but saving little. Our larger mortgage and more commuting expenses have taken their toll. As a result, I feel under pressure to earn more money, while also under pressure to spend more time with the family. Quite a paradox. I often think of the roads not taken, going to a new company after Stanford, or staying in Boulder to take a promotion there. Here, in the Connecticut-New York area, I have no visibility of my alternatives. There must be some, but right now, I cannot see them. I am on a slowly deteriorating treadmill.

# GO OUT THERE
# AND FIX IT!

This morning, WCBS is reporting the story of a break-in at the Watergate Hotel in Washington, DC. It seems four guys tried to steal some secrets from the Democratic National Committee office. I can't imagine it would be worth getting arrested just to get some useless papers from a political office. Oh, well, everyone has their thing. In 1973, anything can happen.

The phone is ringing as I enter the office.

"Hello," I say, trying not to reveal my early morning crankiness.

"Can you come down?" It's the husky voice of Sharon Grogan, my boss's secretary. "Mr. Papes wants to talk to you."

"Be right there."

I hang my raincoat, straighten my tie, pat my errant hair into place, grab a yellow pad, and head down the hall, wondering what Ted would want at this time of the morning.

For nine months, I've been helping Ted untangle and organize a high technology division that designs and manufactures everything from silicon microchips to computers large enough to fill a tennis court. I tell my family that "we pour in the sand at one end and get computers out the other." It takes 30,000 people in Poughkeepsie, Endicott, East Fishkill, and several other locations to get the job done. As Director of Organization, reporting to the division president, I identify organizational issues and fix them.

Ted brought me to his staff after observing my work on a couple of reorganization task forces. It seems that IBM restructured itself so often that it needs "directors of organization" to help plan and manage the changes. We are constantly centralizing or decentralizing. One of my friends said IBM used the same explanation for every organization change—better service to the customers, more effective focus of resources, preparation for the future, blah blah blah. Whatever the reason, we are constantly reorganizing. Much of it, however, is the result of our fast growth. I developed a couple of words to describe IBM's approach: structural intervention. We design a new organization chart, select people to fill the most important jobs, then make sure that everyone can find their office and boss after the change. Because this process occurs every 18 months, everyone is constantly learning.

Ted Papes, proud of his family's Greek heritage, at about 5'10", is shorter than most IBM executives, but he makes up for his lack of stature with strong, no-nonsense decision making. He doesn't need charts and graphs to support his position; he gets his way with short, concise, definitive arguments.

I love working with Ted. To start my job, he pulled out a yellow pad and wrote down three goals for me: reorganize the headquarters staff, identify organizational issues across the division, fix them, and make sure our interfaces with other divisions are working.

A day or so after starting my job, Ted asked me to double as his administrative assistant, a position usually reserved for a junior executive. Unfortunately, the person selected was not due to arrive for a couple of weeks. The assistant's job was to arrange visits to our various plant and lab locations, field inquiries that came into the office, and accompany Ted on visits.

One day, we visited East Fishkill, a 6,000-person location in New York state that designed and manufactured semiconductor devices used in all our computers. Before joining our new division a month before, the site was in the "Components Division."

When Ted and I arrived, the General Manager and his top lieutenants were gathered in the conference room waiting to tell their new division president about their work. After introductions all around, the first speaker rose to give his talk.

"Wait," Ted said. "What division are you in?"

"Well… uh… Systems Products Division… yours," the fellow answered.

"Tell me, then, young man. Why do you still have a Components Division badge?" Ted asked. "It's been over a month."

Every person in the room began staring at another person's badge.

"Look," Ted continued. "I want every badge in this location to be changed within two days. Do you understand?"

Every person nodded their head up and down. One person, whose department printed badges, I presumed, got up, leaving the room. He knew what he had to do.

Six thousand people knew that story within 24 hours. And I learned an important leadership lesson.

* * *

Walking down the hall, I mull over the projects we are implementing: reducing the headquarters staff, re-orienting the Poughkeepsie lab, deciding how to make East Fishkill more efficient, and solving the personnel problems at Sterling Forest. I wonder which one Ted will want to discuss.

"Good morning," I say, approaching Sharon, Ted's assistant. "How's it going?" I know she's probably been working two hours by 9:00 am. I'm not sure whether Sharon combs her wiry, gray-streaked hair with an eggbeater or never bothers. Her coif only adds to her frantic demeanor. For some strange reason, Sharon has taken me under her wing, rewarding me with her rare smiles and sometimes tidbits of helpful hints.

"He's got a meeting with Cary at 11, so he's being pushed," she says. "But he wants to see you. Go on in."

Ted is sitting behind the walnut executive desk scribbling on an easel chart pad. I know that the presentation will be short and to the point. Ted does not waste words. He's going to Cary with a scribbled chart, I think.

"Sit down," he says, pushing the chart aside. I am ready for his intense gaze—a well-practiced technique to examine my soul—to find out if I have the courage and determination he feels every executive needs. Over the past nine months, I have struggled to relax rather than crack under the stare.

I smile, "Thanks." Then chose the chair closest to his desk.

"I think it's time that you go back to line management," he says without a blink.

This is the company's highest compliment—to be asked to head an operating unit, with direct management responsibility for hundreds of people. I've been in staff jobs for about two years, close to the limit for someone who has higher ambitions. I've agonized over the question of whether to aim for an executive suite. People like Ted don't seem to have much of a life—working long hours under heavy pressure, always at the beck and call of the CEO, flying around the country in the company jet, making appointments to take his children to little league, dealing with disgruntled employees. Yet, despite all this, and the division pulling in almost two billion dollars in revenue, Ted had little management autonomy, no profit, and loss responsibility. I admire Ted, but is this the life I want?

"I'm ready," I reply, burying my misgivings.

"Have you ever fired anyone?" he asks, watching my eyes.

"Yes," I say, remembering an incompetent secretary in White Plains and a thief in Endicott and knowing that this was the ultimate test question.

"Well, I'd like for you to take on Sterling Forest…"

Oh crap, my stomach tightens, my mind races. My eyes widen even as I struggle not to reveal my panic.

He continues. "After all the studies, you know the problems. There are two directors out there who are always fighting, morale is terrible, and I don't think much is getting done."

"I know that they have problems," I reply.

"I'd like to announce you as General Manager. Go out there and spend a month, then come back and tell me the problems and what you're going to do to fix them. OK?"

"OK. When do we do this?" I ask.

"I want to announce this thing next week. Go talk to Jim Hewitt and get everything ready. You'll report to him. And, by the way, build a new office so everyone will know that you're the top dog. Let me know when you're ready to announce," Ted concludes, rising from his chair. "I know you'll do a good job." He extends his hand.

"Thanks," I say, returning his firm grip. "I'll let you know when we're ready."

Sterling Forest is a software development laboratory near Thornwood, NY, across the Hudson River from White Plains, New York, housing over 600 programmers, other technical people, and a huge room of computers that form the brains of IBM's US production control and distribution system. Seven other software development groups with another 300 people dispersed in other IBM locations from San Jose, California to Poughkeepsie, New York complete the organization.

Ted was right. We've been studying Sterling Forest for months. Division executives think the unit's productivity is low and suspect a hostile culture in Sterling Forest managers and workers. The company's "Speak Up" program has received a continuing flow of complaint letters from employees who work there, conflict among managers, and subordinates is rife. Sterling Forest develops software that runs the company's entire production control and distribution system, so the organization is a vital link in IBM's success. Computers at Sterling link manufacturing plants all over the United States and in several other countries.

My team sketched out reorganization plans, but we've not decided what to do. That is, until this day when Ted decided that I should go "fix" Sterling Forest.

I knew for a long time that it had been coming because I was a Hi-Po—a high potential manager—one of the people singled out as a future executive. I was the IBM equivalent of a West Point grad in the Army, with Ranger, Parachute, and Expert Weapons training. I'd had the program: Middle management training, Divisional Rotation Program, Sloan MBA at Stanford, and had scored in the 95th percentile on their custom-designed aptitude tests. They were watching me. They knew I had the potential, but could I deliver in a real situation? This was the real situation. Take a miserably performing unit and turn it into a productive force.

Sterling Forest. The den of iniquity. Damn! Is this an impossible job?

Will they accept me? Who do I know out there? Where does this lead? Can I take the pressure? Will we have to move to another house? Can I deal with an hour and a half commute? What do I know about information systems?

# MARY LOU

Walking down the aisle toward my office, my stomach flips with excitement. Wow! Wasn't this what I'd been waiting for? A chance to run my own organization? Yet, Sterling is a troubled location. I'm being sent to fix it, and thank goodness for that. I like the idea of changing situations—exploring new things, even groping around in the dark.

Inside, I'm a bit nervous about my promise to Papes to fix it fast. I'd better get a lot more information on the problems out there.

I glance at my watch. Eight-twenty. Still ten minutes before the official starting time. Rounding the corner to my office, Mary Lou, my assistant, greets me with a cup of coffee.

"Here. I saw your coat and figured you'd gone to…"

"Hey. Thanks. Yep, you're right. Called to the boss's office even before I'm awake."

"What'd he want?"

"To talk to me about Sterling."

"Sterling. That hell hole. Are you guys ever going to fix it?"

"We'll see about that. Is Winston in yet? I need to see his presentation of the task force report about Sterling."

"Naw. You know him. He'll drag in around 9:00."

"Could you tell him to come in as soon as he gets—"

"Wait a minute. Is Papes sending you to Sterling?" Mary Lou asks. Her dark eyes focused on mine.

"Maybe," I answer slowly.

"What do you mean, maybe?" Papes doesn't even know the meaning of maybe. He's always yes or no."

"Well, yes, then."

"Oh, crap. Just when I was getting comfortable in—"

"Don't tell Winston… or anyone for that matter. It won't be announced for a few days."

By this time, I'm behind my desk, glancing at a list of unanswered telephone calls.

Mary Lou follows me around the desk. I can smell her perfume, feel her warmth.

"What?" I say.

"Can I go?"

"I don't know. You know that's not the way it's done. And you'll have to commute over the bridge."

"I don't care. I like working with you. You're the best boss I ever had, and I know how you work."

I smile. "Thanks. I'd love to have you go. I'll need someone who knows how to get things done—someone I can trust."

"Good. I want to go."

"Good morning." Winston says, leaning around the door. "Did I interrupt something?"

"No. We're just talking. Come on in," I say.

"Did I miss coffee? Looks like you're through with yours."

"Well, get your coffee and bring in the Sterling charts. I want to see them again."

"OK. Be right back," he says, leaving for the coffee machine.

"Mum's the word. OK?" I say to Mary Lou.

"Sure. But I want to go," she says.

She turns to return to her desk just outside my door. In a few steps, she stops, makes a half turn and says in a loud whisper. "Did you hear me?"

"Yes. I'll see what I can do." I smile watching her lithe body in a perfectly groomed blue suit move out the door.

Mary Lou is of Italian descent, with dark skin and intense brown eyes. I try to think how long we've worked together—five, maybe six years. I met her even before transferring to headquarters. She's smart, efficient, and assertive. She is a no-nonsense professional who doesn't put up with incompetence on the part of her bosses or colleagues. She's loyal, trustworthy, and doesn't hesitate to tell me what she thinks. I trust her judgement. And she knows the ropes—how to get things done in the screwy, conflict ladened bureaucracy of headquarters. She jumped at the chance to join me when Papes appointed me Director of Organization a year ago. I'd love to take her to Sterling with me, but that's not normal practice in the company. But—maybe there's a way.

"OK. I'm back," says Winston, walking in with a roll of charts under his arm and carrying a cup of black coffee in the other.

Winston is a professional organizational man. He's been doing organization and procedures work for 20 years. He knows how to run organization studies, write procedures to make organizations work, and figures every political angle to get reorganizations done.

"So, what's the big interest in Sterling?" he asks. "Is the Old Man finally going to do something?"

Old Man is the Army term for the company commander. Winston never got over his experience in the 82nd Airborne.

"Papes is getting impatient. I think he's ready to move." I answer. "Let's see the charts."

Winston goes to the easel, mounts the charts, and begins talking.

"Do you want to see them all or some particular part?" he asks.

"Let's start from the beginning. I want to make sure I understand this." I answer.

"Sure," he says.

The words, "Sterling Forest, Situation Analysis" emblazons the first chart. He turns the page.

> *Mission: Development and production of logistics and operational software for internal company use.*
> *1972 Headcount: 923*
> *Locations: Sterling Forest, Poughkeepsie, Rochester, San Jose, Endicott, Kingston.*

Winston steps through the charts one by one as I try to absorb and understand Sterling's problems. The organization chart was one we call "tall" with 11 layers of management between the top manager and the working level employee. There were multiple departments with names no normal human being could understand and job titles a paragraph long. Sterling's hierarchy gave everyone a fancy title.

Yet, even with fancy titles and pay rates above the company's average, morale is low. Sterling employees submit "Speak-Ups" at twice the rate of the average company location—and the rate seems to be rising. The last yearly opinion survey showed a significant deterioration from last year's outcome. Employees showed little trust in location or corporate management.

Several groups are behind schedule in delivering their software products, and the location was almost ten percent over budget for the year.

My God, this group is going to hell in a handbasket. This is a real mess. Can I fix it?

The causes of organizational issues, like other classes of problems, can be classified into the most important few. I can't determine the root causes of the problems from Winston's charts. We know the indicators, but not what's behind them. I'll have to dig deeper to find that out. That will mean lots of interviews with managers, employees, customers, suppliers, and others that associate with Sterling. All that will take time and I'll have to do it myself unless I can recruit someone I trust to help with the task. But, I'll be looking for subtleties, not just data. I want to see the facial expressions, the body language, hear the tone of voice, see who fidgets. I have to understand how the organization works, but, most of all, I have to feel the organization, taste it, smell it, sense its inner workings.

"Well, that's it," Winston says, rolling over the last chart. "What do we do now?"

"Nothing. I just want to understand. Watch this spot," I say, letting him know something is about to be announced. "Thanks for the update. Could you leave the charts?"

"Sure. Well, I hope something happens soon. I'm tired of hearing about Sterling Forest."

"I know. I know," I answer, reminding myself that Sterling Forest is all I'll be thinking about for the next two years.

As Winston leaves the office, I step in the door, asking Mary Lou to come in. She enters, immediately sits in the easy chair while I close the door.

"Mary Lou, I'd love to take you with me, but we've just signed you up for programming school that will set you on a whole new professional path, one you certainly deserve. Going to Sterling with me will set you back another couple of years."

Silence.

"I know you're right, but working together is something special," she says after the long pause.

"I know. And I owe a lot of whatever has been accomplished to you. You have way more potential than being somebody's assistant. Go follow your dream and we can still keep in touch."

"I know you're right, but this feels so bad. How can I ever replace this?"

"Your classes start in a week. Go give it a try and see how it works out," I reply. "You'll be a great programmer or whatever you want to be."

We reach for each other's hands for the longest handshake I ever experienced. A tear is smudging makeup on her eye.

Something tells me I will come to regret this conversation.

# THE
# ANNOUNCEMENT

Three days after my conversation with Ted Papes, I drive up the winding, maple-lined road leading to a five-story glass cube designed by IBM's architects to reflect the adjoining forest lake. On this sunlit New York state afternoon, it looks like a giant iridescent Monet nestled among the mature oaks, pines, and maples. Lots designed to hold several hundred commuter cars are sculpted into the hillside so as not to disturb the aura of the building.

The trees undulated by a light wind reflected green and blue fractals dancing over the cube's mirrored walls—nature's chaotic art captured on a vast glass canvas bounded by sharp architectural edges.

Approaching the building's entrance, I hope the programmers inside, though bound by the walls and limitations of a giant corporation, reflect similar creative energy. They've been working for years on massive software programs with millions of lines of code. But IBM executives take little notice of the organization's accomplishments, they are more focused on indicators of dissension and conflict at the site. Sterling Forest employees are writing more than their share of Speak-Ups and using the Open Door to access their concerns. The Speak-Up program is a way for IBMers to let off steam. There are containers of Speak-Up forms posted in convenient spots throughout the company. The company encourages people to sign their names, but the submitter is not obliged to sign.

\* \* \*

IBM's Open Door Policy lets employees air their grievances to the Personnel Department, their manager's superior, or even the Chairman of the Board. IBM believes a person's manager should be the first stop, but, if the manager doesn't give a satisfactory answer, the employee can appeal to a higher authority. The company never had a union and doesn't believe unions are necessary for a company where the employee comes first. So, the Open Door Policy is IBM's answer to grievance procedures in unionized companies. The "man-manager" relationship is the first responsibility of every manager in the company.

Everyone knows managers are sometimes removed from their job after investigations highlight their mistakes in dealing with employees. Employees also know bypassing their manager to appeal to higher authorities involves some risk. Direct retributions seldom happen, but managers are human. How is one supposed to feel after learning your employee appealed to higher management?

Top management encourages employees to use the programs. No risk, totally confidential, they say. But executives measure location managers by the number of Speak-Ups employees submit. Furthermore, they measure the ratio of signed to unsigned submissions—unsigned submissions suggesting a more severe problem. So, the company in its zeal to make unions unnecessary has given managers a paradox: Encourage employees to participate in the Open Door and Speak-Up programs, but if they do, your performance rating may suffer.

Sterling Forest's Open Door and Speak-Up rate per capita far exceeds most IBM locations, leading executives want a solution. Most employees at Sterling have worked at no other site. And the managers, although graduates of the company's mandatory training programs for supervisors lack the traditional IBM culture. "Respect for the individual," is IBM's first principle, but the managers at Sterling seem to have missed that lesson.

There are two high-level executives at Sterling, Joe Rogers, a plain-talking, gray-haired pragmatist with no college degree, who runs site services, and Marty Ziac, a Lehigh Industrial Engineer who grew up in Information Systems, who manages the programming organization. Both men report to Jim Hewitt, the Vice President of Information Systems. Jim is sick and tired of settling disputes between Joe and Marty.

So, Jim and Ted Papes decided they needed an executive on the site to fix the place. I am the guy.

Entering the glass double doors, I see Jim Hewitt's orange Porsche 911 pull into the parking lot. He's barely on time for the announcement meeting at 2:00. Advancing to the reception desk, I see lines of people moving down the ramp toward the cafeteria, toward the all-hands meeting. I'll wait for Jim to arrive, because, if I enter the cafeteria now, I'll just fuel speculation about the purpose of the meeting. Yet, I'm sure the rumors must be flying.

"Hi. I'm Grant Tate. I'm here for the meeting."

The security guard smiles. He'd seen me several times when I was Director of Organization. "Welcome to Sterling Forest, Mr. Tate. Here's a badge for you. The meeting's in the cafeteria."

"Yeah. I can see. Thanks. How've you been?" I reply casually.

"OK. Same old stuff. With some new faces here and there."

In the time it took for me to pin on the badge, Jim is beside me.

"How're you doing there, Mr. Director?" He smiles.

"Great. Looks like a big crowd down there."

"Yeah. The room holds about 300 people and I guess it'll be full. They set up a mike for us."

I feel for the stiff IBM cards on which I'd written the notes for my remarks—a bit of a crutch in case my memory completely fails me when I look at all those faces. I don't expect to get nervous, though, because I've canvassed the country making speeches to audiences of 200 to 1000 people while working on the Future Systems project. Big crowds don't scare me anymore. Yet, this audience is different. I want to win their confidence with this first talk although I know deep down it is not possible. They will be skeptical. I'm turning forty, old enough, but still look like a kid.

I can hear the muffled roar of 100 conversations as Jim and I walk rapidly down the ramp and into a sea of people with white shirts and striped ties, on chairs, on tables, standing around the walls. Suddenly, silence. Everyone stares our way as Jim approaches the rostrum. Most of the eyes are on me. They know Jim Hewitt, he's spoken to them often, but who the hell is this new guy?

I stare back, scanning the room to see a few familiar faces, Frank Contey, Marty Ziac, and others, but mostly they are strangers wondering how this day will affect their career and lives. I am an outsider, a face they don't recognize, a threat, an unknown, too young to look wise, too unfamiliar to be in their field, information systems. I must be one of those hand-picked AA's who'd been sent in to manage the place. They are right on all counts. I find a seat next to Dave Chapman, a departing manager.

"Good afternoon," Jim begins. "I'm here to make an important announcement."

A murmur ripples through the room.

He continues. "You've undertaken some important work here at Sterling. Your programs will become the nerve center for all IBM's manufacturing operations. You've completed the move from Mahwah to Sterling, and you've brought international plants into your client base. In recognition of his accomplishments in starting CMIS, and managing its early development, I'm pleased to announce that Dave Chapman, who previously managed the CMIS project here, has been appointed Director of Strategic Planning at SPD Headquarters."

The audience applauds. I wondered if the gesture is enthusiastic or placid, because Chapman is a somewhat controversial figure. My colleagues at headquarters told me to watch all my fingers when I negotiate with him—he might just take one of them home with him. In several conversations during my visits to Sterling while Director of Organization, I thought he wasn't really being straight with me. Perhaps it was his shifting blue eyes that signaled me to be careful. It could have been his evasive answers to my questions, or maybe rumors of his favoritism toward some of his people that influenced me. I saw him as a potential snake in the grass, deciding internally to treat him carefully. I was a bit surprised he had been selected to lead the planning process for the division. It was an important job.

At Jim's invitation, Chapman steps to the podium, leaning into the microphone, stating his soliloquy. With blond hair and baby face, Dave looks more like a high school kid dressed for his senior prom than an IBM executive. His constant grin indicates the slight twist of sarcasm, certainly not sincerity.

"Over the last two years, we've worked together to design a revolutionary new manufacturing system, one that will dramatically change the way we do business...."

Listening with one ear, I scan the sea of faces in front of us, silently wishing for ESP. What did they think of Chapman? What motivates them? What do they want from their careers? How much time do they spend with their families? What are their conflicts and concerns? How do they feel about working here? Will they grow to trust me? What can I do to get to know them? Are programmers different from other people with whom I've worked? How did they choose where to sit today?

The faces are young, vibrant. I guess the average age to be in the late twenties, younger than other IBM locations. The company's equal opportunity efforts are visible by the relatively large numbers of Black American and Asian faces. The audience also reflects the influx of women IT professionals. Many of Sterling's women are managers.

"...and so I begin my new assignment with enthusiasm. Good luck to you all," Dave Chapman concludes. He gives a slight wave to the audience and returns to his chair next to me. I look over the crowd to sense the reaction. There is nothing but silence.

"Good job," I whisper, referring to the speech.

"Thanks," replied Dave. "You can have these turkeys now."

Is he serious or joking? I can't tell by the half smirk on Dave's face. Maybe he's happy just to get out of this place. Jim has regained his place at the podium and is several sentences into my introduction before I refocus on what he is saying.

"As you know we've had two different organizations here, one under Dave and another under Joe Rogers. After much consideration, we've decided to consolidate those two organizations under one Director of Sterling Forest. And I'm delighted to announce that Grant Tate, formerly SPD Director of Organization will be joining you as your new Director. Many of you know Grant from his work with organizations, and he brings a solid record of management and leadership to this position. He was part of the founding management team at our Boulder plant, having served several technical and manufacturing assignments there. So let's give Grant a big hand."

Big hand, I'm not so sure, but there was a lot of clapping.

"Would you like to say a few words, Grant?" Jim asks.

I walk quickly to the speaker's platform, scan the eyes of the audience from right to left, leaned into the mike to begin my talk.

"Thanks, Jim. First, congratulations to Dave Chapman. He's built this organization and will bring great talent to the division planning department—a key position for planning our future."

"It's a great honor to accept this challenge and an honor to work with people like you (motioning toward the audience), who're building applications on which the whole IBM manufacturing operations will be built."

My speech sounds like platitudes to me and I am sure others feel the same. They want to know how someone with my lack of direct experience in the information systems function could have been selected to head the site. Every plant and lab had an organization whose job was to design and run the intricate programs to make the business go—payroll, design automation, accounting, process engineering. I'd never worked in one of those operations—nor had I ever managed an information technology group. But they didn't know I'd had years of computer testing, had programmed the monsters, and used them in every job. If I'd been totally honest, I would have told them the division president wasn't satisfied with their performance, they were overstaffed, over budget, and had low morale. I was selected because I'd worked as Director of Organization for the Division President, and he'd sent me out to fix the place. At that moment, I didn't want to stir up resentment or make the people defensive, so I poured on the syrup.

After the talks are over, I stand by the door like a politician, shaking hands with everyone who wants to greet me. A surprising number of men and women line up to say hello. At the end of the line, Joe Rogers, Manager of Site Operations, who now reports to me and manages the people who take care of the building, run the cafeteria, take care of human relations, and all of the other support functions walks up with a big smile.

"Feel like walking around the building?"

"Sure," I reply while turning to Jim Hewitt, saying, "Do you want to go with us?"

"Naw, I've seen it enough, you guys go ahead. I've gotta head back across the river. I'll talk to you tomorrow."

"OK. See ya soon," I reply.

Every IBM building in the world must look like this inside, I think. Gray and white polished vinyl tile floors bordered by white walls and cellulose tile ceilings with fluorescent light fixtures. IBM Headquarters established standard office sizes along with guidelines of what kind of office each jobholder should have. For instance, a junior programmer was to share an 8 by 10 office with another junior programmer and was entitled to a metal desk, a standard office chair, one two drawer file, a shared telephone and perhaps a computer terminal if such a networked system was available in his/her location. An associate programmer was entitled to his/her own office. A manager was entitled to a fancier metal desk, more furniture, and an 8 by 12 office. The guidelines covered all positions up to the corporate executives. You could immediately tell someone's rank by their office arrangement and furniture. Everyone was allowed to customize their space with family pictures, mementoes, or whatever. But the "clean desk policy" urged employees to remove everything from the top of their desk at the end of each day. This was supposed to make sure unauthorized eyes didn't come in at night to read IBM confidential material. This ultramodern building with its spectacular exterior looks like any other corporate office building inside.

I can tell the rank of the people by looking at their offices, but there was no way to sense the organization of the place. Every office looks pretty much the same, lined up along pristine antiseptic halls, more like a hospital than a home for people who create amazing software programs. Except for one thing—the pictures. Apparently, Dave Chapman also thought about hospitals and wanted to avoid the image because the walls were adorned with paintings of 18th-century ships sailing on stormy seas. The stormy sea was a good analogy for the challenge that I am facing, but I hope to be better prepared than an old fighting galley.

"Who chose the art?" I ask Joe.

"Someone from the Real Estate Division came down one day to survey the place. I think she was the corporate art director. Anyhow, she and Chapman agreed on this theme," Joe replies. "How do you like it?" He asks tentatively.

"It's a strange theme for a programming center. These pictures are right out of Blackbeard's Cave. How long would it take to remove these pictures?" I ask.

"Two or three days. Would you like to get rid of them?" he replies.

"Damn right. We're going to change this place. Let's start with the pictures." Joe smiles and says, "I'll call the decorator."

"Let's get them changed by the end of next week," I reply. "Let's have some modern, abstract art we can be proud of. We want creativity, not battles."

"By the way, Joe, I want you to build me a new office on the third-floor corner, overlooking the lake," he says.

"Yeah, I know. Jim Hewitt already told me. We're starting on Monday. In the meantime, I've set you up a new office on the same floor. We'll contact you to pick some furniture for the new office."

"Really? I thought I'd get the old standard stuff."

"No," says Joe. "We're starting something new here."

\* \* \*

I continue walking down the halls, glancing into offices, and stopping to introduce myself to people working at their terminals. Each person is polite, a bit glassy eyed from staring at a screen with green text, but eager to finish writing their assigned lines of code for the day.

Some described their job to me in intricate detail, proving conclusively I really didn't know what they were doing. Geeze they must be bored. How can they spend eight or ten hours a day sitting in a small office grinding out computer code? Their 12 lines of code were a few stitches on the massive tapestry of the Common Manufacturing Information System.

We have hundreds of people like this in the building, how do we keep them all coordinated? Who are the geniuses who guide the processes? They are the first people I have to meet.

We stop by a large room filled with desks, typewriters, word processors and fax machines. About 20 women sit typing at the desks. A tall woman dressed in a green skirt, white blouse, and cardigan sweater approaches us. "Hi, I'm Marlene O'Keefe," she says with a smile. "Welcome aboard. I'm the manager of this center."

"Hi. Glad to meet you. What goes on here?"

"This is a secretarial center—a place where the "girls" type, file, and do administrative work for the departments on each floor. Office Products Division has been pushing the centralized typing pool concept, called word processing centers, because the division develops productivity tools and machines to support administrative centers. Each of these centers has 15 to 20 secretaries or administrators managed by a manager. We all report to Ben Cacia," Marlene answers.

"And Ben Cacia reports to me," put in Joe.

"So the administrative people aren't part of the department they support?" I observe. "How well does it work?"

"We get some grumbling from the programming departments sometimes, but we think this arrangement is a lot more efficient than when the secretaries reported to each department. This way they can more easily share work and the center manager makes sure the work flows freely," Marlene continues.

"So everyone who wants a letter typed walks from his or her office to this place, hands it to the manager, who then assigns it to someone to type. A day later, someone calls the person to say the letter is ready, and they walk to the center to pick it up? Does anyone use dictation? Can I call in my letter?" I ask.

"No, we're not set up for dictation," answers Marlene, defensively. "Most people write out their letters by hand."

"Good grief. I hope we don't write a lot." I grumble, thinking whoever invented word processing centers should have their head examined. This is a throwback to the early days of the industrial revolution. Someone thought secretarial work could be organized like a manufacturing process, so let's put every typist, secretary and administrator in one room so we can control the workflow. I picture myself walking down the hall bringing my letters to the center. I know the system won't last long.

"How's the morale here, Marlene?" I ask.

"Not bad, we went up on the last opinion survey, but, I admit, sometimes the girls feel like second-class citizens."

"Why is that?"

"Well... they aren't treated as part of the team—just someone to get the typing done."

Joe motions it is time to move on.

"We'll talk more about this later. Thanks a lot for the tour," I say.

"That looks like a hotbed of grumbling and gossip," I remark to Joe as we head down the hall again.

I step into the computer center occupying a space about the size of a football field, almost gasping at the sight of the sea of blue and white refrigerator-sized boxes whirring with computational power. Two operators sit staring at blinking lights on a control panel in the center of the room.

"Here are the brains of IBM," says Joe Rogers. "The company's logistics system runs from here."

"Well, I hope we're smarter than this," I say, smiling, hoping the company is more than a collection of stupid robots.

I stare at the computers, their blinking lights, their tape readers whirling this way and that and wonder what is going on inside. Will Sterling Forest be as inscrutable as these machines? There are 900 people in this organization, each working at a job someone else designed, each working for a manager, who, himself, was nothing more than a transistor in a mass of circuitry. How can I rewire the organization so it works better? How can I turn those somber faces I saw today into ones of joy and satisfaction?

With enough time, I know it's possible, but I have only two years. Two years sounds like a long time, but it's a short time to change an organization this big and complicated—not time enough for a quiet evolution. I have to create a revolution. I'll have to restructure the place, get rid of old managers, find new ones, and change how the place does its job. And right now, I don't know anyone here but this guy Joe Rogers who runs the cafeteria.

And what about my life? There won't be time for anything but work. I'll spend almost three hours each day commuting on top of ten or more hours over here working. We could move, but that's a lot to go through for a two-year assignment. Oh, hell, maybe I'll just get a Porsche like Jim Hewitt's and learn to enjoy the drive. Big office, Porsche—seems like the right image.

"Want to see your office?" Joe asks. "It should be OK while we're building the new one."

"Sure, let's do it," I say.

Walking toward the elevator, I'm rolling plans and tactics around in my head. I think about the notes I made last night—the start of a plan—a plan to take this place apart and put it back together again. I know deep down I can do this, but, right now, I'm not sure of the price I'll pay.

Completing the walk, I thank Joe for the tour, and we set a time for a more comprehensive update of his function tomorrow. He knows the building like the back of his hand. He also can identify a lot of skeletons.

# MY CONTRACT

The end of my fourth week found me again in Ted Papes' office.

"You told me to come back in about a month; after I'd had a chance to look over Sterling Forest," I say.

Staring at the charts I had placed on the easel, he says, "I'm eager to hear how it's going."

I outline my activities over the last month, listing some of the people I talked to and the reports that I'd read. Then, I flip to the first chart, entitled "FINDINGS" and begin describing the organization's mission, performance, accomplishments, failures, and challenges, using graphs and numbers. For the last several weeks, I interviewed people, scoured over personnel surveys, analyzed financial reports, and looked at chart after chart being flipped on an easel stand by an endless stream of men in blue or gray suits with striped ties and a few women in skirted dark suits.

"OK. Got it. What's the program?" Ted asks.

I flip to "The Plan" and describe a program to evaluate the role of the top managers, examine the organization's goals and mission, restructure the organization, and begin new programs aimed at improving morale.

At the end of the presentation, Ted asks, "How long will it take?"

"Two years," I reply.

"Keep those charts," he smiles.

I have a contract.

# DARLENE

Darlene McDonald, my secretary, quickly became my closest confidant—although I was never quite sure of her motives after the day she stood in front of my desk, looked deeply into my eyes, and said, "Grant, uh… I have something to tell you."

"Yeah," I say, wondering what piece of bad news she is bringing.

"You know I love you."

I stared back at Darlene, not believing what I was hearing from a devout Catholic woman who had been married for over ten years.

"Thank you, Darlene. I need that kind of support," was all I could blurt out, not wanting to touch the subject of love. Darlene watched my eyes for what seemed like ten minutes, then smiled and strolled out of the office. From then on, she reminded me every week that she loved me. It is almost as if she had written a weekly note on her calendar.

The love, or whatever it is, became a comfort to me. Darlene had neither eyes nor loyalty for anyone else and guarded my time, interests, and feelings. I did not doubt that she would defend me to the end. Occasionally, Darlene would warn about someone's motives, tell a story about hidden liaisons in the organization, or just say, "Watch out for that guy."

# TRUSTWORTHY TONY

Partly on Darlene's advice, I hired Tony Croce, a 5'3" product development manager, to be my administrative assistant and company bodyguard. After ten years of working at Sterling Forest, Tony knew the people like his own family. Tony's toughness is only exceeded by his sense of fair play. He never did anything that he would have to talk about at confession. He also is dedicated to the idea that Sterling Forest needed an overhaul—organizationally and morally. Tony had sized me up as the person to fix the place.

He watched over me like a protective father, sometimes lecturing me on executive morality, warning me to be careful of people that he didn't trust, and sometimes tactfully telling me that maybe I didn't understand how the organization worked. Tony was the one out of the almost 900 people in the organization whose loyalty, honesty, and integrity were above reproach.

Tony showed his protective instincts early in my tenure. One day at lunch I suggested that we take a walk around the property. After all, we were located in a gorgeous, natural forest within a few miles of the Hudson River—and I wanted to enjoy a summer lunch on the trail. Soon we were deep in the virgin forest; two hikers in blue business suits. But Tony insisted on walking six paces in front of me.

"What are you doing up there?" I asked. "Am I too slow for you?"

"No, I'm just checking the trail," Tony said over his shoulder, then quickly checking around the next bend.

"The trail's fine, wait for me," I shot back. But Tony persisted in leading the way. I rushed to catch up with him. "Just what are you doing?" I persisted.

"I'm checking for rattlesnakes," he grinned.

"Are you serious?" I asked. "I've probably seen more rattlesnakes than you have."

"Yeah, but a couple of our programmers saw two big ones out here last year." He looked serious.

"What would you do if you saw one?" I smiled. "Are you sure that's what you're looking for?"

After more prying, I learned that Tony had a second agenda. He was afraid that we would encounter employees on the trail.

"There were a couple of programmers making out on the trail last summer," he said shyly.

"Was that the same day that they saw the rattlesnake?" I quipped.

Tony and I completed the hike without encountering either lovers or rattlesnakes, but the incident convinced me that I had hired the fellow who might keep me sane during my lonely assignment at Sterling Forest.

Darlene and Tony help me keep in balance as I play out my role. I am never alone at work—people line up at the door to talk or to get my decision or approval, the telephone rings constantly, and the division headquarters exacts its toll in meetings and reports. My long commute gives me time to chill out or think, but often dealing with the traffic adds stress. Sometimes, during a visit to headquarters in White Plains, I find an empty office to have an hour or so of quiet, thinking time.

# ORGANIZATIONAL CHANGE

The early morning sun, filtered by the trees, lights up the lake like a shimmering peacock feather. Rays of sunshine stream across my office creating artistic silhouettes from the easel stand, Danish chairs, and pencil holder. The tranquil scene belies my typical daily routine.

During my drive this morning, NPR reported calmly about the Yom Kippur war, another of the occasional fights between Israel and her neighbors. Some reporters spoke of a possible gasoline shortage as a result of the conflict. Crap, I'm driving over an hour to get to this place. Gasoline shortages or high prices add another irritant.

Tony Croce knocks gently on the open door. "Morning, Grant. Good to see you so early in the morning."

"Thanks, Tony. You'll soon find out I'm not a morning person, but, in fact, a big grouch until 10:00 am," I reply.

"I haven't seen that yet," he says. "By ten, we've done three hours of work together."

"And here we go again. Let's get started."

We scheduled this meeting to lay out the plan to reorganize Sterling Forest. In the past two weeks, I removed one level of management, having placed Marty Ziac and Joe Rogers in positions in other IBM units. There are now 12 functional managers, not including Tony and Darlene, reporting to me.

In the past six weeks, I've interviewed every manager, whatever their level in the structure, for 45 minutes or more; exploring their experience, their training, their ambitions, their attitude toward the organization, their listing of the top challenges they face each day. I gave each the freedom to call me anytime they wanted to continue the conversation.

Whereas all managers in Endicott, Boulder, and other locations received standard management training within the first few weeks of their appointment, Sterling Forest had not used that practice. Some managers had the training, others not, leading to inconsistent approaches to departmental leadership. Most people I interviewed did not know the company's core values, for instance, "respect for the individual," we revered at Endicott.

I found many managers did not trust higher leaders and thought the organization was rife with rumors and poor communications. Also, promotions and pay increases went to the favored and powerful clique. Despite HR's pressures to conduct annual performance evaluations for all employees, many managers had not received their evaluations from their bosses.

"Tony, it's obvious we need to change the culture and the organization. Let's see if we can lay out a plan with a timeline today," I say. "I know you're called Administrative Assistant, but I want you to be the project manager of organizational change—develop the plan, lay out the schedule, organize the meetings, measure the results. Are you OK with that?"

"Sure. That's what I signed up for. I know damn right we need it," he replied.

"Here are some things I've thought about: We need a communications plan to let everyone know what we're doing and why. Let's get Fred Caplan, Manager of Communications in here to see what we can do. I'm thinking of more frequent newsletters, frequent all-hands meetings, frequent managers' meetings, maybe some posters and guides."

"Check. I'll set it up," Tony says, writing on his yellow pad.

I continue, "Next, I'd like to have each functional manager, those reporting to me, to give us a formal presentation on their function: goals and responsibilities, measurements, their customers, an overview of the people, high and low performers, results of the last all employee survey with action plan, list of major issues and obstacles."

"Already have a tentative schedule for that. I'll set the meetings up and put them on your calendar. I'm thinking it will take an hour and a half for each," Tony replies.

"Yeah, that's about right."

"Look, there's a basic principle that says, 'strategy before structure,'" meaning you have to know where you are headed before you can organize how to get there. We don't have time to do a complete strategic plan yet, but we do need to set some short-range goals and strategies. You and I can meet later this week to write those down."

"Works for me."

"We have nine remote organizations, each in one of the various plants, some over 100 people. I know they're there to support the installation of our programs and processes in their respective plant, but how do we know if they are doing a good job? Are they still needed, now that the programs have been installed in many plants and operating properly? Maybe that effort is best managed by the local plant instead of us. Let's get those managers in here to present their work, but I also need to visit to meet their people and talk to the local plant management."

"So noted," Tony says. "These are good steps. I have other items on the list and can lay all these out in a plan we can review."

"Another thing. We have all those competent women in the three secretarial support organizations cooped up in one place. I'd like to break up those departments and send each person out to support the operations across the organization. Let's get the three managers together and ask them to develop the plan."

"How right you are. We've needed to do this for a long time."

"OK, Tony. Let's see your list. Another thing, let's set a target date for announcing the reorganization. We're in a hurry here. But let's keep in mind, this is phase one of our organizational development. After this wave, we'll be well situated to do a new strategic plan and organize to implement it.

"One last thing. Let's set up an all-hands meeting in the cafeteria next week so I can talk about our goals and give them some reassurance. They need to know who I am even if it scares the crap out of them."

By the end of the meeting, Tony and I have the skeleton of our plan and have set a target date to announce the reorganization within 60 days.

# PORSCHE

The commute to Sterling Forest from my home in Ridgefield, CT seemed daunting: the curvy State Route 35, the Saw Mill Parkway, Tappan Zee Bridge, NY Thruway to the country road leading to the site took 90 minutes even on a low traffic day. IBM would probably pay for a family move closer to the site, but it's hardly worth it for just two years, the length of my agreement. So, I decided to make the most of it, buy an exciting car. My current second car, a Toyota Corolla, sure wasn't exciting. Economical, maybe, but not exciting.

On a Saturday, a couple of weeks after my appointment, son David and I visited a Porsche dealer. I could not afford the fancy models, but a white 914 mid-engine model with orange trim and fitted out in racing suspension caught my fancy. A two-seater, with a removable top, started with a purr, but roared with pent-up power with the accelerator. We spun around the Westport streets testing it out and returning to the sales office to sign the deal.

Driving the Porsche became my major stress relief. I chose a commuting route that included the most challenging curves and would push the svelte sports car to the limits. One June night I tested my mettle near Casper Lake. The sunroof was open to the cool night air heavy with musty lake mist. I glanced through the roof to see two egrets searching for a roosting place. I loved the approach to the lake—through a series of switchbacks lined with pine trees, down the hill, and across the dam. It seemed strange that the only part of the road that made me nervous was the quarter-mile straight section over the dam. I often held my breath most of the way across—thinking of how I might escape if by chance it went into the dark water. With the top off, that would be easy: swim out through the sunroof. I would probably have to wait until water filled the car because it would be hard to swim against water rushing in.

During those drives home at night, it never occurred to me that someone might want to do me in. Yes, an accident would put me out of contact on a dark, abandoned road or in a lake, but some deliberate kidnapping was not even a remote thought.

That is until Tony came into my office one day and said, "Corporate has asked me to prepare a safety plan for you."

"Huh? What's that? "I asked.

"All executives must have a plan to protect them against kidnapping and other risks," he answered.

"Really? Who would want to kidnap me?"

"You're an important person in the corporation. You know it's been happening all over in countries like Italy and Germany, even here."

"Seems crazy, but do what you have to do," I said.

That night, driving home up the four-lane followed by roads through the dark woods, I realized someone could have me in Mexico before anyone even knew I was missing. The next morning with Tony, I was enthusiastically working on the plan. Leave work at different times at night, take different routes home, call home when you are leaving, and give your wife an estimated time of arrival.

"And that damned Porsche is like a bright light saying, 'here I am, come and get me!'" Tony said.

A new world crisis, an oil shortage, helped us out.

Motorists were waiting in lines for fuel all over the country. States and communities placed new restrictions on gasoline sales to help people plan their driving. In my case, that meant those with an even-numbered license plate could buy gas only on certain days, while those with an odd-numbered plate on other days. The restrictions soon meant I would not have enough fuel to commute every day to Sterling Forest.

Fred Caplin, our manager of communications, lived in my community, so we teamed up to share the driving. That saved fuel and also allowed us to plan communications, discussing the next newsletter, and bitching about the fuel shortage together.

Fred's nondescript car gave us additional cover from kidnapping threats if there ever was going to be one. Those kidnappers would have to be desperate to aim for a low-value target like me.

# SECRETARIAL CENTERS!

A few months after talking to the manager of one of the secretarial centers, the departments of primarily women employees who provided administrative and secretarial services to all our departments, I invited the three center managers to meet with me.

Three days later, three confident-looking women gathered in my office; Marlene, tall and blond, walking with slow broad steps as if feeling the floor with her feet. Marjorie, sporting a red silk scarf tied down with a modern silver brooch, eyes actively looking for the first available chair. And Harriet Lee, pulling up the rear, looking as if she would rather be somewhere else. After introductions and hearing about the backgrounds of each manager and an overview of their people, I said, "As you probably know by now, I've had some doubts about whether having all the support centered in departments is better than dispersing everyone among the departments. I know you're working hard, and your teams are dedicated to their work, but let's see which is the best way to provide these services.

"Yes, we've had these questions, too," Marlene O'Keefe said. "Our people spend a lot of time walking back and forth to the users' departments. And, a lot of time on the telephone. Seems to me that more person-to-person proximity might work a lot better."

"OK," I said. "Could the three of you take a couple of weeks to study the situation and report back with your recommendations?"

Marjorie Cook said, "Sure. We've already thought about this, so we have a running start."

"Yeah. And we already have some feedback from managers of the departments we serve, but we can do some more formal interviews, and maybe even a questionnaire, to see what they think," Marlene said.

"Sounds good," I said. "Who do you think might not like this idea?"

"Some of the managers might not want to manage a secretary again, but that would be a rare case," Harriet said, finally speaking.

"Well, what about you three?" I asked.

"What do you mean?" Marlene asked.

"If we close down the centers, we'll have to find new jobs for all of you," I replied.

"Of course," Harriet said, "But that might be a good thing."

"You're right Harriet. Your manager, Ben Cacia, is out today, or we would have invited him. I'd like for each of you to think about your desired career path and be ready to discuss it. That's good to do whether we retain the centers or not. And, by the way, you've all developed some excellent skills while managing these departments—people management and workflow," I said.

* * *

Two weeks later, the three were back, this time with their manager, Ben, to recommend closing down the centers and dispersing the employees. Their plan included a timetable and a list of employees showing where each should go in the organization. Tony, my assistant, working with Ben, recommended the next assignment for each of the managers. Three weeks later, we announced the plan to wild cheers from the employees and all the managers in Sterling Forest.

Soon after the change was announced, Ted Papes, my division president, called to say he'd received a call from the president of the Office Products Division (OPD) complaining that my move was contrary to their division's primary sales concept—Word Processing Centers. Anticipating the call, I had briefed Ted before our announcement, saying not only was the Word Processing Center concept inefficient, but it was also a major deterrent to good communications and work satisfaction.

Ted told the OPD president I had responsibility for my site and had the freedom to do what was best for the unit.

# THE GEYSER

Sterling Forest, like most large IBM sites, had its own cafeteria. In our case, a space large enough for 300 people seated at cafe tables. Plate glass, revealing the surrounding forest, formed three of the four walls. A long sloping walkway lined by white walls formed the entrance from the main building and displayed the art and photography exhibitions we sponsored as part of our culture change campaign.

John Desmond, the cafeteria manager, also a master chef, delighted in his daily creative lunches. Excellent cuisine on a budget, he called it. But our special private lunches with small groups, retirement lunches, promotions, special guests, was where John shined. I learned early to avoid specifying a menu but be surprised by his creations.

One day in the spring, I was honoring a team for some particularly outstanding piece of software they'd designed. We enjoyed poached salmon with all the trimmings and were ready to dig into dessert, when Joe Thornton from plant services opened the door, coming to my place.

He leaned over speaking into my right ear and said, "Sorry to tell you this, but we have a water break."

I was thinking, "What? You interrupted the lunch for this. Just fix the damn break."

But he continued, "You'd better come with me."

I excused myself from the group joining Joe outside the room. "What's going on?" I asked.

Joe was nervous as a cat, pacing, talking in spurts, looking rattled.

"Joe, tell me." I continued.

"This is not just a break, it's the main water line to the building. We have a geyser out there that's 12 feet tall."

"Oh, my God," I said, knowing our computer center, which controls the whole IBM manufacturing logistic system, needs air conditioning to keep running. Otherwise, they will effectively melt. "How long will it take to get it repaired?

"We have a crew out there now working with it, and we've asked the town to shut off our main supply to stop the water flow."

I stepped to the phone, calling Frank Contey, manager of our data center. "Frank, we're losing water and the AC will be ineffective in a few minutes. You'd better start a cold shutdown of the center. You don't have much time."

Ten minutes later, we had an emergency staff meeting, where each person volunteered what his or her unit had to do. We called every IBM location we served, told them what was going on, giving them instructions to protect data and inform their users. I alerted Ted Papes and other important executives about the situation.

Ted asked, "How long will it take to get back online?"

"I don't know for sure, but my target is start of shift tomorrow. We'll be working all night.

By the start of shift the next morning, AC was working, and all our computers were back online. Our crew, with the help of a construction team, worked around the clock, creating an alternative pipeline into the building.

During our "lessons learned" discussions we discovered the main water pipe, which was buried over ten feet underground, was resting on a large rock. When the soil settled over the years, the pipe wanted to follow the settling soil, but the rock put a fulcrum in the way. No one ever imagined that a data center like ours might need a backup water supply in case there was a failure. I wondered about the risk of putting so much of the company's nerve center in one place, but that was above my pay grade.

# CARY AGAIN

The Angelic Asshole of Armonk has arrived. Like a corporate lemming, I'm standing by my rental Ford at the only helipad close to Sterling Forest. I cover my ears and squint my eyes like the classic monkeys of see no evil, hear no evil, speak no evil, as IBM's blue and white Bell Jet Ranger II helicopter explodes a dust cloud from the tarmac.

I understand why local towns hate these machines. They may be good for rescue operations and fighting wars, but they're loud and obnoxious, the perfect way for beady-eyed executives to flaunt corporate power. This is one-upmanship gone out of control. Any company can have corporate limousines and airplanes—but you have to be really big to have helicopters.

The co-pilot, part of IBM's "air force," opens the right-side door and reaches a hand to guide Frank Cary, IBM's CEO, down the steps. Frank ducks his head as if trying to keep the whirring rotors from scalping his cue ball head. Like most IBM executives, he's over six feet tall, although his cherubic face, disproportionately small teeth, and close-set eyes belie the tall frame. You'd expect someone being whipped by helicopter rotors to come dressed in a flight suit; but, no—Frank wears the standard IBM blue suit, white button down shirt, red and blue striped tie, and brogue shoes.

He hits the ground walking—the typical fast, deliberate stride designed to tell everyone "Look at me. I'm a busy executive, I have no time to stroll."

I stare through the blowing grit to read Cary's demeanor. Intense, man. Intense. No smile, no pleasantry. Just business. That's OK. I don't trust his smile anyway. Doesn't seem sincere when he reveals the undersized teeth. His fangs are deceptively hidden in a face more suitable for a grocery clerk than a corporate executive.

Now I wonder how to treat this dude? Like some general in the army? Military protocol would make this encounter easy. Just approach your superior, salute, take his bag and escort him to the waiting car. Here, the rules aren't written, but your career depends on doing the right thing. Suppressing my instinct to salute, I mirror Frank's fast pace to meet him halfway.

We got the call just three days ago.

Darlene had leaned around the doorway looking nervous. "Frank

Cary's administrative assistant is on the line and wants to talk to you."

"Oh, crap," I cringed, turning to pick up the phone. A call from his office never bore good news.

"Good morning, Charlie. How the heck are you?" I offered, faking enthusiasm.

"Great. Look. Frank wants to visit Sterling Forest on Thursday," he said. "Do you have a place for the copter to land?"

"Thursday! What's the urgency? Is something wrong?" I asked, trying not to reveal my irritation with the helicopter and the short notice. "What does Frank want to see?"

"We had a break in his calendar, and he just wanted to visit the site. Wants to tour the building, meet some people, review your programs. Let us know the agenda by Wednesday," he said.

"We don't have a place for the helicopter to land on the site. It's too dangerous," I said. "But we can find a place nearby." Why did Cary have to come in the damned helicopter? His office in Armonk is only 45 minutes away by car. "We'll check it out and let you know."

Hanging up the phone, I called, "Darlene! Get Tony and let's talk."

Soon, Darlene and Tony Croce stood in the office. I moved out to join them around the square glass coffee table. Tony sat in one of the leather and steel chairs, placed his yellow notepad on the table, while adjusting his position to keep out of the sunlight that was just beginning to wash the room with morning radiance. Tony's freshly starched white shirt glowed like radium in a bottle.

Darlene took a seat next to Tony, tugging her red miniskirt in a futile attempt to cover her bony knees. "Guess you heard, Cary's coming over on Thursday. We need that like a hole in the head, but we'll have to do a good job," I started.

We were only six months into our reorganization, still in chaos, trying to get everyone trained, selecting people for new positions and transferring others. Cary wasn't particularly sympathetic to personnel issues and I resented his disruption.

"Why's he comin?" asked Tony.

I really suspected that his real agenda was to test me—to find out if the "Hi-Po" assigned to manage Sterling Forest was up to the task.

"According to his AA, he wants to tour and review our programs. Don't think there's a hidden agenda, but could be. Never can tell with Cary." I answered. "Anyhow, make an agenda. He ought to understand our mission—what we're up against here. Second, he should meet the management team and some of the people. Then, we ought to talk about the personnel issues and the reorg. Is everyone in town?"

"Jack's at Endicott, but everyone else should be here," Darlene said.

"Well tell them to freeze Thursday. Tell Bill to clean up the place, and by the way, find a spot for the lousy copter to land."

"You serious? He's coming in the copter?" Tony cringed.

"Yeah, can ya believe it?"

"There's a pad over in Ringwood, but it's a full 20 minutes by car."

"Yeah. By that time, he could drive from Armonk. He just wants to let us know we really need a helipad. Darlene, call Jim Hewitt and Ted Papes' secretaries to let them know what's happening. I'll call Jim later to see if he knows what this is all about."

We reaped the whirlwind over the next two days. We reworked the agenda five or six times, rehearsed presentations, practiced touring the building, and polished every wall, floor and flat surface. On Wednesday morning, I arrived at the building's front door as a crew of maintenance people polished the lobby. I greeted them with a smile and stepped into the elevator, only to have my face sprayed with Lysol by a fellow who had been assigned to shine the elevator. The man was horrified to see that he had deodorized not only the elevator, but the executive manager of the place.

"I guess we're ready," I smiled, wiping the spray off my cheek. The man grinned sheepishly and stepped off the elevator as I pushed "4" and the door closed.

\* \* \*

8:00 Thursday morning finds me in the big Ford Hertz car headed for Ringwood's helipad. What should I say to IBM's CEO? Most guys on the way up would welcome an opportunity for private time with the top dog. Yet, I don't know what to do. I'd met Cary several times, and they were all unpleasant.

But today, I'm bound to meet Frank halfway. Sticking out my hand, I say, "Welcome, Frank. I'm Grant Tate." IBM executives starting with Tom Watson, the founder, wanted employees to call them by their first names.

"Good morning," sacrifices Cary with a slight smile.

On our way to Sterling Forest, the conversation is stiff and cold. Frank seems as if he'd rather be somewhere else. Why the hell did he come if he is so disinterested? I plow ahead anyway, explaining our agenda for the day, giving him statistics about the site, telling him I've interviewed every manager at Sterling Forest. But, I'm too wrapped up in my own problems to consider that the CEO might be worried about bigger problems, such as consumer prices advancing 11 percent in 1974—or what was going to happen to the country since Nixon had resigned a few days earlier on August 9th.

Arriving at Sterling, we walk to the conference room where Tony and eight of Sterling Forest's top managers are waiting. I introduce them all, feeling thankful at being able to remember their names, motion Frank to a chair at the head of the table, and step to the easel to begin the agenda for the day. My stomach is doing the rumba, but my first words sound confident.

"We're honored that you could be with us today, Frank," I lie. "We're looking forward to the day." I turn to the easel chart to describe the agenda. I'm halfway through the chart when Frank says, "I don't want to hear about your organizational and personnel problems, I want to see your projects. This is a waste of my time."

"But the success of our programs depends entirely on our ability to turn around the organization," I protest.

"Charlie made it clear that I wanted to see your projects and the numbers, didn't he?" he says, tight lipped.

"That's not what I understood," I shoot back, struggling hard to control my anger. Why hadn't this come out on the ride from the helicopter? I had told him what I wanted to accomplish today, and thought that it was clear. Why didn't he say something then? He probably hadn't listened to a word I'd said. I'm embarrassed this conversation is happening in front of people who reported to me. They watch me with questioning eyes. Tom Hays, the guy on my staff who can't stand me or my style, wears a slight smirk.

"We can revise the agenda, but it will take a few minutes," I concede. "Let's break for coffee." Luckily, we have a table of coffee and cookies.

While several people scramble to get Frank coffee, I confer with my project leaders outside. Sid can explain the logistics program, Harry the ordering program, Frank the testing program, and others can explain theirs. While they race to their offices to pick up charts and additional information. Cary sits alone at the table, watching us run around like maniacs. Is this some sort of management lesson?

15 minutes later, we stumble through unrehearsed presentations while Frank picks apart every number and every point. He is clearly gunning for us, and I'm not sure why. What the hell is he trying to do? We struggle to defend our programs, but, while not feeling defeated, we don't win many points either. We are just being hassled. Frank thinks we're a bunch of screw-ups and he's out to prove the point.

Finally, the morning is over, and we walk to the executive dining room for lunch. I had cautioned John, our facility manager, that we wanted a good lunch, but not too elegant. Entering the room, the table is formal, but tasteful. Good so far. The chef had designated our seat assignments by small name cards, with Cary assigned to the seat at my right. We struggle through small talk while eating the salads. When the main course arrives, I want to run for the hills. This "not too elegant" course includes stuffed lobster with all the trimmings laid out in a way that would do credit to Landon in Paris. Frank's face freezes as the waiter delivers his plate. Oh no, this could be the final straw.

"*Bon appetit,*" I say as we turn to our five-star meals. Frank eats without comment. He knows we had a good chef if nothing else.

After lunch, I take Cary on a tour of the building. We had stripped the 18th century sailing ship paintings that mocked the modernity of the building when I had arrived. Now, new, modern graphics and sketches, that would be a credit to the Museum of Modern Art, grace the halls. We were proud of the result. Cary glances at the art but says nothing as we walk the four floors of working space; two devoted to offices, a center floor almost completely occupied by computers, and, at the lower level, the employee cafeteria featuring picture windows on three sides overlooking the forest.

I lead Cary to the computer room, a space as large as a football field. It is neatly arranged with square edged blue and white boxes containing the brains and stored intelligence of IBM's vast manufacturing empire. The room smells like a new car laced with ozone. The monster computers emit a sound that reminds me of hundreds of Buddhist monks humming their mantra. I explain that this room controls most of the company's US parts ordering and logistics. Cary listens without comment. He's probably scared to death that the company's fate is in the hands of a bunch of guys who can't even make decent presentations. I introduce him to the two computer operators, sitting at a console, who seem even less interested in meeting him, than he is in meeting them. They just want him to get out of the way so that they can do their jobs.

Exiting the computer room, we stroll down the pristine halls, passing office after office as I explain that we organize the huge software programs into logical and manageable modules, with responsibility delegated to the different programming groups.

Frank stops at one of the offices, steps inside and says to the programmer there, "Hello, I'm Frank Cary. What are you doing?"

The programmer looks up from his terminal as if to say, "Who the hell are you?" hesitates a moment, then says, "I'm writing an optimization method for the allocation module of the monthly supply/demand balancing program."

"Tell me what it does," replies Cary.

The programmer launches into a stream of words that sound like PL1, Cobol, Chinese and Arabic rolled into one.

Sheepishly, Cary says, "Thanks, keep up the good work." And we move on. After that encounter, he merely speaks to people as we pass.

We stop at the control room of the public address system from which we can address everyone at the site. We sit at the two chairs in front of the microphone. I stare at the on-off switch, trying to remember the mini-speech I'd practiced for days. Frank shuffles in his chair and I can feel his eyes staring coldly at my face. "Aren't you going to introduce me?" he asks.

"Of course," I say, not explaining my hesitation.

I stumble through my introduction, fumbling around, barely connecting the words. I thank Frank for visiting us, and for honoring us with his perspectives on the state of IBM's business. He leans to the mic while I listen blankly. His presentation is a lot smoother than mine, but the words go straight through my head without pausing for absorption. Traditionally, CEO's offer words of encouragement and praise for good work on such an occasion, but because I doubt his sincerity, I hear not a word he says.

Finally, at the end of the day, I shuttle the big boss back to the helipad where the bird was waiting. We waste few words on the way. We shake hands, he steps into the machine, and I wait to wave as the copter lifts slowly into the air, turning toward Armonk. There, being lifted into the sky, goes our killer angel.

A few days later, I stop by my division president's office to ask if he'd received any feedback about the visit.

We had prepared "The Sterling Forest Story" to explain the issues and our action plan, which, of course, emphasized the morale issues and what we were doing about them. Frank, however, only wanted to see the numbers—what are your programs? How much do they cost? What is your budget plan for the coming year? He forced us to change our whole agenda for the day to emphasize only the business measurements. In my naivete' I missed the fact that he didn't give a rat's ass about human problems. Later Ted told me that Cary had called to tell him that, "Tate was not aggressive enough." I bit my tongue to avoid saying what I thought about the company's top executive.

In spite of Cary's criticism, the charts that Ted told me to keep were my measuring stick. Each month, I looked at the objectives to gage how far we had to go. After 18 months, I reported that the goals had been met.

# JUDGE DIXON

Frank Cary apparently didn't like the idea of landing in a site other than close to our building.

Tony came into my office to tell me he's received a call from the CEO's office. "They want us to build a helipad, so they can land a helicopter here."

"What? Why would anyone want to do that? We're only 45 minutes from Armonk, the company headquarters, by car. They could drive here by the time some pilot is warming up the damned helicopter," I said. "Tell them no. I'm not going to cut down trees, flatten some land, destroy the site design, just to have Cary or one of his lackeys play executive."

"C'mon. You know we can't tell them that," Tony said.

"Yes, we can. Just pretty up my language a bit. I'm serious."

Tony negotiated over two weeks, finally getting them to agree we could clear part of our existing parking lots whenever they needed to use it, as long as we received a 24-hour notice. But we will need the town's permission to land a helicopter here.

IBM's legal department, owing at least partly to the anti-trust suit, was top drawer, attracting some of the best corporate lawyers. We were fortunate to have a young lawyer assigned to our site to help us with everything from labor laws to intellectual property protection. Our guy was Judge Dixon, a Black ex-lineman of the Wake Forest football team, with a soft voice, and a barrel of good advice. We often laughed about the expectations a mother placed on a child by naming him, "Judge." He would smile and say, "I guess there was no choice other than law school. How could I ever be a doctor with a name like that."

Thanks to Judge Dixon's good work, we found the zoning ordinances of the Town of Warwick, where we were located, restricted helicopter landing. We needed a special zoning permit. The corporate office in Armonk insisted we apply to get it.

Two months after Judge filled out the paperwork, we got a call to testify before the Zoning Board of Appeals for the Town. Judge and I geared up to attend.

I asked Darlene to call the Town Office to find out how they dress for the meetings. The answer came back, "work clothes," whatever they were wearing during the day. Further investigation found the board's members were everything from farmers to construction workers to executives.

I said to Judge, "We can't go down there looking like slick corporate people. Let's skip the white shirt and tie routine. And by the way, you do the presentation."

We were right. Our casual attire was the right move. Judge used his best person-to-person persuasion, and we got the agreement—a 150 pound White guy and his lawyer, a 250 pound Black guy, working together on this task. We got it done. Neither one of us even thought about the racial difference. We were two professionals getting our job done. Judge's competence and counsel made my job easier.

# TURNAROUND
# COMPLETED

Sharon, Ted's assistant says when I arrive, "It looks as if you've lost weight."

"Yes," I reply. "Who has time to eat when you're in the midst of organizational change."

In fact, I lost 15 pounds over the last year and a half. Stress and the long commute were now visible for all to see.

Joe Isole, a fellow I know from Poughkeepsie steps outside Ted's door, having completed his meeting. Joe, well over six feet tall, with a prominent bent nose and pocked face, knows more about the company's logistics system than anyone else I know. He's brilliant, spins about a hundred ideas a day, and talks a mile a minute. He's been successful because he has a 5'6" sidekick who can pluck the one good idea out of the hundred and put that idea into practice. It's a wild combination, but it works. All of Joe's associates, including me, put up with his frantic demeanor because he's brilliant.

"Hey, Joe. How did the meeting go?" I ask.

"He's tough, as usual. You can have him now," Joe replies.

"OK, Grant, go on in," Sharon says.

Ted greets me warmly and I put my charts on the easel, the same charts from the meeting 18 months ago.

"How did it go with Joe?" I ask. "Did he pound your desk with his shoe?"

We both laugh, remembering the meeting where Joe, trying to emphasize his point, started pounding his shoe on Ted's desk.

"And the crazy thing was he was pounding in cadence with his own speech," Ted said.

We laugh again.

I step to the easel stand, flip to the first chart, and say, "We did it. We've completed the program."

With that, I present each chart demonstrating goals having been met. We talk about the primary leaders we'd recruited and how the team can continue the progress.

We reduced the total size of the organization from 900 to 650 people, flattened the organization chart by eliminating two levels of management, placed 22 administrative assistants into real jobs, and started new training programs for managers. I flew around the country to close five of the seven remote software development sites. Rumors say that the name of Sterling Forest would be changed to "Grant's Tomb." However, in good company tradition, we avoided layoffs and successfully placed those whose jobs were eliminated in other company groups.

Our productivity and morale indicators inched up month by month. This, along with my monthly reports, relieved some of the pressure from the company executives who wanted to just eliminate Sterling Forest. During a particularly stressful time, when union workers from a contractor were threatening to picket our front door, John Opel, a senior vice president, sought me out at a meeting to say, "We know you've got a tough job. Keep up the good work." He soothed a lot of doubts with his short sentence.

I talked to an endless stream of people discussing their problems— programmers upset because they thought that a female manager is having an affair with her superior manager; a sobbing woman who had falsified her time records but wanted her job back; a manager who is trying to get his reporting executive replaced, an executive who couldn't stand what I is doing and just wanted out. I began to feel that Solomon was a better role model than Thomas Watson.

"What now? Ted asks.

"I'd like a two-week vacation. And I suggest finding a new leader for Sterling, now that it is stable," I say.

"Good job, Grant," Ted says. "Have a good vacation."

Driving back to Sterling Forest, I think of the battles we went through, the good days, the bad days, the funny days. I met all the goals with flying colors. And six months sooner than I predicted. We reorganized the place, improved productivity, decreased expenses, and dramatically changed to a more positive culture.

But, at what price on me and the family, and on the relationship be- tween me and Joyce? Has anyone else in the company ever done anything like this? Yes, we started new plants in Boulder and Raleigh, one of those in record time, but changing the culture at Sterling Forest was far more challenging than starting up from scratch.

Once, just a few months ago, Tod Ellis, from corporate education asked me to speak to a managers' class at the corporate training center. I present- ed the "Sterling Forest Story," showing how we set goals and implemented the strategy. When the participants' evaluations of my presentation came in, most said, "This sounded like fiction. It could never happen at IBM." Yep, they were right, it was impossible, but it did happen. Unbelievable, but true.

Leadership is a lonely role. Yes, Darlene and Tony were people in whom I could confide, but neither had walked in shoes similar to mine. They never felt the internal emotions of leadership. Frank Contey, one of the managers at Sterling said it well, "Every decision you make affects the lives of someone or perhaps everyone here."

After the meeting with Ted, Joyce and I decided to take a ski vacation with all the children. While in Breckenridge, Colorado, I received a message to call Ted Lassiter, an executive from IBM's world trade group. I finally got through to him from the hallway of the ski lodge. While scores of people slammed by in ski boots, Ted interviewed me for a job in a new international division. It took me about five minutes to say yes.

# BAD MOVE

Spike Beitzel, a Senior Vice President, once told me during the Interdivisional Rotation Program, "Here's the way to get ahead in IBM: One, hire people smarter than you. Two, always be learning. Stay high on the learning curve. Three, move toward a crisis. Work on really important things. I've done those in my career so far.

At Sterling Forest, I did not want the attention, the spotlight. Just the opposite. I just wanted to see people thrive and be happier in their jobs. Even the 250 people we moved out of the organization were put in meaningful jobs, probably more satisfying because of new challenges and opportunities.

Sometimes, it was up to me to protect people in our organization from quirks of bureaucracy or bad executive management decisions. One year, the corporate personnel department released the new salary plan that dramatically reduced the traditional salary increases given to people. Yet, their materials and messaging were designed to mislead. We decided to level with the people, telling them corporate growth and profits were less than expected, therefore we needed a new salary plan.

I wanted to follow in Dad's footsteps, trying to make working people's lives better. At what price? The question haunts me. No doubt, I am driven. Almost obsessively focused on meeting the goals we set. I feel the responsibility deep within my soul. I may not be aiming for recognition, but I love the loyalty I inspire in people around me. "You're the greatest manager I ever worked for" is a constant reminder of that loyalty. Is that what I crave? Not public, but private recognition? Blind loyalty?

If those loyal people could see my inner doubts, they would be severely disappointed. They would see a small country boy from Orange, Virginia; a kid needing a hug. I don't want to disappoint them. My vulnerability will let them down and that is not helping them.

The inner drive has exacted its toll on the family.

After 19 years of marriage, how much has Joyce seen me? I have been constantly working. I get up at six, gobble a breakfast of granola and fruit, and leave for Sterling by 7:00 am. On a typical night, I walk in the door at nine, too tired to talk or even watch television. I'd say hello to David, Lynn, and Laura, ask about their day at school, then eat alone. Joyce never asked, "How was your day?" Nor did I volunteer to tell her about my work. She has no idea what I was doing or why I did it. My work friends are intensely loyal, but I cannot win the loyalty of my wife. She doesn't know me, does not understand me, and sees me as a hostile force.

It seems as if Joyce asked every week, "When are you going to stop this?"

"When we learn to live on less money," I snapped.

And that usually ends the hope of any civil conversation. Joyce returns to her book while I go to the den, open a briefcase, and go through the mail that I swept off my desk at the end of the day.

Sometimes I long for a sympathetic word—even some recognition that my efforts are appreciated. But bridging the gap that has grown between Joyce and me is like swimming the English Channel in January. Sometimes, she says, "Are you going to leave me?"

I am always surprised by the question. Why would she ask that? Where would I go? Yet, I know that she, too, is feeling insecure and lonely. It is probably up to me to break through the barriers—to find ways to talk to her. After all, isn't that my responsibility? The leader must take care of his people. Responsibility—what is that? The legacy of a boy raised in the South where responsibility and reputation were valued above all else? The burden of a lifetime, never to be shed—never to be lifted even for a day of rest?

We had a good life in Colorado. Perhaps, I should never have accepted these jobs at headquarters. What would life have been like if we had stayed in Boulder?

Yet, Joyce has a good life in Ridgefield. She has lots of friends, many of whom are tennis partners. On weekends, we go to dinners and parties with other couples. We go to church together, although I dropped out of any leadership activities several years ago. And we have some good family vacations in the summer and the winter. Joyce is an avid reader and is keenly interested in the children and their school work, though teenage years are always challenging.

Joyce and I are heavily focused on the children, the house, or other family maintenance issues. We are woefully short of substantial conversations about each other, our feelings, or what we want for the future. We have a good family, good friends in the community, and I am respected at work. Yet, I have this deep sense of loneliness that lies unaddressed. How can I feel so alone when I have so many blessings?

To the people at Sterling Forest, I was "Mr. Cool" who never seemed to get excited about anything. Darlene always watched my eyes—she said they turned from blue to steel gray when my anger rose. At such times, my words could cut like a Samurai sword—slashing at the heart of an opponent's arguments.

Yet, I never thought of myself as someone who could get power by fear. I prided myself as a skillful negotiator who could mediate tough disagreements. In my previous job, Ted Papes took advantage of that ability by sending me to settle disagreements between warring barons of the division. Yet, I never knew if my success in negotiating was because of my skill or because I was flying the flag of the division president.

Demotion was as bad as firing got in those days. Because IBM is not a company to put people on the street, division and corporate headquarters were filled with managers who had been assigned to staff jobs after failing as manager of a manufacturing or sales unit. The common phrase is "John is in the penalty box." Some of the Johns regained some influence, but that is a rare case. More likely, they faded off to some ambiguous assignment in the planning or personnel departments. They would have been better off if the company had fired them. At least then, they could have reconstructed their self-esteem instead of letting their talents rot away in the obscurity of a demeaning job.

I know that I have neither the style nor the looks to make it to the top. I am more like someone out of a Woody Allen movie than out of the slick, blue-suited, top management club at Armonk. I am only 5'10" and, as I figured it, about four inches short of top executive stature. Although I attempt to blow dry it, my sandy, curly hair is usually rumpled. The horn-rimmed glasses might remind some of John Opel, IBM's senior VP, but then, John is well known as the smartest executive ever to work for the company.

But my attitude is my primary disqualification. My growing disdain for Frank Cary and other top executives, their perks, privileges, and their yes-men is thinly veiled. I suspect my eyes often betray my feelings. Jim Hewitt, the vice -president to whom I report, once said, "Grant, you've got to show these men more respect if you want to get ahead."

I walked away from that conversation wondering what I was doing to convey my feelings. Maybe the man of steel is not so mysterious after all. I also knew that apart from Ted Papes, John Opel, Dave Kearns, Bo Evans, and Jim Gray, all the executives were a bunch of jerks. Vaguely, I knew that my alienation from other managers added to my feeling of isolation. I was distant from the people who report to me, other managers, and my family. Who else is left?

# INTERNATIONAL DIVISION

At the beginning of my assignment at GBG/I, the General Business Group, International division of IBM, I felt thrilled. It was a new division designed to produce small computers, typewriters, and other devices in 11 international countries, some European, others in Latin America, and Australia. It was another chance for me to start a new organization in a newly formed job.

Ever since Josef Spies, from Germany, and Antonina Skapars, from Latvia joined my high school class in Virginia, I've had an intense interest in learning about and visiting other countries. I was fascinated by their stories, the kind of food they liked, and their descriptions of their early life in their home countries.

I had talked to Ted Lassiter, the division's Vice President of Manufacturing on the telephone, standing in a ski lodge in Breckenridge, CO, where the family was on vacation. He wanted me to join him at the new division in White Plains becoming responsible for planning, new product manufacturing, and technology transfer—a perfect match for my skills and experience. And, it was up to me to find people to build my staff. Perfect! I had met my goals at Sterling Forest just 18 months into a two-year assignment and was ready to move on. In addition, the new position meant a thirty-minute shorter commute than the ninety-minute drive to Sterling Forest.

I first met Ted Lassiter when he was the Assistant General Manager at IBM's plant in Lexington, KY, the plant I came to know well when we tried to connect electric typewriters to computers made in Endicott. It was fundamentally a good idea to think one could enter data from a typewriter keyboard and print material from the computer on paper in the typewriter. But a computer could put a year's worth of wear on a typewriter in just one day. We were beating them to bits. I knew, of course, that typewriters could not take such a beating, but our designers thought the idea would work if Lexington could build in better quality. Even with the impossible task, I developed good working relationships with my colleagues at Lexington, including Ted Lassiter.

Ted was a Mormon, holding some important leadership positions in their hierarchy. He was square-jawed with dark laser eyes that could find flaws in any presentation. His tailor-made suits and Hermes ties created an aura that reflected his calm, even management style. Ted prided himself on truth and fairness to everyone and cared deeply about his people.

* * *

Ted took me on a short European tour to introduce me to the new division's plant managers. Paris was our first stop, checking into Hotel Meurice on Rue de Rivoli after eight hours in the air and a long taxi ride from De Gaulle Airport. No one tracked dirt into Hotel Meurice. Everything is polished, pristine—brass railings, marble floor, classic furniture unlike anything I'd ever seen in the Waugh Furniture Store, high society people hanging around in the lobby, a murmur of talking from the bar across the hall. What was I doing in a place like this? It was a long way from Orange, Virginia. And it was also a big difference from my first trip to Europe from Boulder, CO, in cheap airline seats, bargain hotels, and low-end restaurants.

The following day a car met us at the Meurice awning and whisked us to the IBM Europe Middle East Africa (EMEA) building for the day's meetings.

That evening after sole meuniere at the Meurice, I walked on Rue de Rivoli, admiring the shops, the wide streets, breathing the cool night air. A sporty Renault screeched to a stop next to me. The passenger window rolled down, revealing a young woman's face in the dim light.

She muttered something in French.

Seeing my blank face, she said, "You come with me?" in perfect English.

Naively, I asked, "Where do you go?"

"To my place. It's not far," she answered.

I could see her broad smile,

"No thank you, not tonight," I said.

"Another night, then?" she asked.

"Probably not."

Wow! I'd just encountered my first high-class French prostitute. This sure wasn't 42nd Street.

* * *

Over the next few months, we built a staff of 50 people from the 11 countries we served, becoming a truly international organization. Most people came on a rotational assignment with the agreement to return to their home country after three years. Frank Contey, an American and close colleague in my previous jobs, was one of the first hires. Frank was a genius at planning and building business processes. He set out to design the division's new strategic and operating planning processes. I need not worry; Frank was on the scene.

In 1975, electric typewriters were an essential element of IBM's business. Our new division was manufacturing Selectrics in Amsterdam, Boigny, France, Berlin, Germany, Bogotá, Colombia, Buenos Aires, Argentina, and Guadalajara, Mexico. The group that previously oversaw those plants planned to build two more facilities in undesignated locations to meet overseas demands. Typewriters were full of mechanical and electromechanical parts and required significant labor to produce. When we took over the planning, I immediately deleted plans for the two additional plants and decided to meet any increasing volumes by subcontracting some operations.

In addition, we thought strategically about the future of those plants already producing a product that technology would make obsolete in perhaps not so far future. One day, I attended the Office Products strategy session, a yearly event where each development group laid out its extended range plans. The Office Products Division designed and built Selectrics and other office products in their massive location in Lexington, KY. After listening to their pitches, I rose to say, "Sooner than you think, we can replace all that mechanical junk with a semiconductor chip." Everyone groaned, and I left the room.

My department decided which products would be produced in each of our ten manufacturing locations. These decisions determined a plant's profitability, employment level, and tax base. Each decision went to top executives for final approval. Bob Dunlop, IBM Vice President of Manufacturing, also had to approve. As a result, my staff and I became practiced and proficient in making decisions and presentations.

An incident on one of my European trips illustrated how important plant managers took these decisions. While I was visiting our plant in Vimercate, Italy, we were also considering sourcing a new office product in Amsterdam or another location. George Prinz, plant manager of Amsterdam, found out about my plane change in Paris while returning to the USA. When I arrived at Paris de Gaulle airport, airline attendants met me on the plane, escorting me to a rented conference room where George and his team waited to lobby me on the Amsterdam decision. They quickly presented their case, after which the airline attendants whisked me to my connection and put me in my seat. We decided against the Amsterdam position, anyhow.

Another day, we invited Jorge Ober, plant manager of Buenos Aires, and two of his staff members, to our office in preparation for manufacturing a printer soon to be released from product development. Jorge and I once traveled together to a plant manager's meeting in Madrid, developing a good friendship while having fun in Flamenco clubs and shops.

To manufacture in Argentina, we needed occasional support from American product development engineers. So I arranged a meeting in Atlanta with Chuck Branscomb, Vice President of Engineering for the product development division.

The Argentines and I sat on one side of Chuck's conference table, he on the other, while we laid out the case for our decision about manufacturing the printer in Argentina. Chuck said, "Absolutely not, it's too far, it's too expensive." We argued back and forth until Chuck and I came to a silent impasse. I could feel the Argentines shuffling in their seats, wondering what would happen next.

After what seemed like ten minutes of silence, I said, "Good. I'll set up a meeting with Beitzel, our mutual executive, to settle this.

"I agree," said Chuck. "See you there."

Two weeks later, we met with Beitzel, who decided in our favor.

This was an excellent example of IBM's escalation practice. If two executives cannot reach an agreement after discussion, the decision goes up the ranks to the appropriate executive. No hard feelings, no retribution. It was part of the process.

\* \* \*

One day, John Reynolds, one of the managers in my unit, came into my office and said, "I may have to fire Shirley Jackson. She's late almost every day."

"Have you talked to her about it?" I asked.

"Of course, but she only says she'll try harder. Yet, the next day it's the same thing all over."

Shirley was one of five Black people in the unit, three from other countries, she and another person from the USA. Almost six feet tall, she was hard-working, engaged in her work, and willing to express her views on things. Shirley had excellent typing and administrative skills. Having grown up in North Carolina, she and I had an immediate cultural connection, often trading inside jokes and talking about things "down-home."

"To me, that doesn't sound like Shirley. Let me talk to her," I said.

At two in the afternoon, Shirley entered my office. I walked from behind the desk to sit with her in the two office chairs.

"What's going on with this lateness, Shirley?" I asked, jumping right into it.

Shirley looked down at the floor, saying nothing.

"Shirley, what's going on? Are you alright?"

"I know John is upset with me, and I've tried to fix it, but just can't make it work."

"What do you mean? Fix what?"

She hesitated, then said, "The lateness. You know I have a three-year-old son."

"Yes."

"Well, I have to drop him off at the babysitter's place at 8:00 am, but then can't get here until 8:15 or 8:30—15 or 30 minutes late. I've asked the sitter to start earlier, but she can't budge, and I don't want to change sitters. You know how hard that is."

We kicked around a few more options to consider, but Shirley had thought about them all.

"OK, Shirley. What about changing your arrival time to eight-thirty? We might have to adjust your lunchtime, but we can do that."

"Wow, that will be great. Thank you so much."

After the meeting, I called Jim Flood, VP of HR, to tell him I'd just changed an employee's reporting time.

"You can't do that," he said. "That'll create a precedent for other people."

"I just did, Jim," I replied.

# SOUTHERN SHERIFF

Usually, our semi-annual General Manager's meetings are in one of the overseas countries, but 1977 was the year to meet in Atlanta. It was a typical three-day agenda with elements of strategy, operations, finance topics. But we did the most critical work at peripheral meetings and social gatherings. On our last night, three staff members and three plant managers met in my Omni Hotel room to review important but highly confidential decisions, going through graphs, spreadsheets, and recommended decisions prepared by my staff. During the meeting, I placed a file folder full of confidential material on the floor beside the sofa where I sat. An hour later, we completed the session, went for some drinks, and had a jolly good time.

I checked out the next morning and walked to the IBM building meeting room. A couple of hours into the meeting, I reached to retrieve the folder I used in the night meeting. The company confidential folder wasn't in my briefcase. *Oh, crap, it's still in the hotel!*

In a panic, I rushed to a phone and called the Omni, finally getting through to the desk manager.

"Has anyone turned in a folder from room 1054, where I stayed last night?" I asked.

"Hold on. I'll check," she said.

My anxiety rose with every waiting minute.

Finally, she returned to the phone, "No one turned it in, and the attendant on the floor did not see it."

"Could I come over and look for it?" I asked.

"Of course, but it's Friday, and a couple just moved into the room for the weekend. I left a message for them. But come on over, and I'll have security help you out."

I almost ran to the Omni. Arriving at the desk, the manager said, "Here is Fred Higgins, Manager of Security for the hotel. He'll help you out."

Higgins was the Southern Sheriff right out of a Faulkner novel. Over six feet, 250 pounds, belly protruding through a partially unbuttoned tan shirt, a crooked security badge, and brown striped pants. And, of course, a holstered 38 caliber Smith and Wesson and a ring of keys dangling off his belt.

Higgins and I headed to the elevator. He's on his first mission of the day. On the way to the tenth floor, I asked, "What do we do if they aren't there?"

"We'll cross that bridge when we get to it."

"Geeze, is he going to break in if no one is there?" I wondered.

Arriving at 1054, Higgins shuffled with his keys, identifying one I suspected was a master. But, instead of inserting the key, he rapped three times on the door.

We waited, looking at each other. Finally, we could hear a noise inside the room. Someone was walking.

The door slowly drifted open. Higgins leaned in, looking inside. I tried to peek around his bulk.

From behind the door, a figure leaped out, grabbing Higgins around his big chest. He's fighting to pull back.

"What the hell is going on?"

Higgins pulled back while the figure backed away.

"Oh. Oh. I'm so sorry," a woman's voice said.

In her early twenties, she was a young woman with disheveled blond hair, starting to straighten her blue and yellow flowered dress.

"I thought you were my husband," she said. "Who are you? Why are you here?"

Higgins tried to explain. I jumped in to tell her about the lost file folder.

"Oh, I found that and put it on the desk. I was going to call the front desk. We are here for the weekend, my husband went for some Cokes, and I was going to surprise him."

"Well, you sure surprised us," I said, thinking, "I'll bet she was surprised, too, to get arms full of Southern Sheriff instead of a husband."

"Thank you so much for your help," I said.

Higgins and I went down on the elevator, laughing out loud.

"How's that for the start of a weekend?" I asked.

"Better than most," he said with a smile.

# INNER SANCTUM

Thomas Watson, Sr., the founder of IBM, stared down from his life-sized portrait as if to say, "What do you know, son?" The perfectly illuminated pictures hung on finely carved walnut panels. A sofa and five or six chairs were designed to make guests comfortable, but I doubted if anyone was ever relaxed enough to sit, for this was the waiting room for those who entered pleas to IBM's top team—the Management Review Committee (MRC).

It was my day in court. I was there to ask the MRC to approve a new manufacturing plant we wanted to build in Australia. Bernie Clark, the energetic and foul-mouthed manager of our plant in Wangaratta, a city halfway between Melbourne and Canberra, had been manufacturing typewriters in broken-down rented buildings for several years. He needed better facilities to meet future sales projections. Bernie and I had planned for several months, carefully calculating the kind of building that we needed. Then we set out to win the approval of legions of IBM's vice presidents before going to top management. We knew that if any VP disagreed with our plan, we'd have an open fight in front of the CEO. But, our plan was convincing—most agreed with it.

I shuffled anxiously, almost turning my ankle in the plush maroon carpet, hoping that none of my fresh shoe polish rubbed off to mark my place. All of the 15 or so vice presidents, dressed in the stereotypical blue suits, white shirts, and striped ties, were now gathered in the gallery. Al Zettlemoyer, my boss, was busy lobbying with someone that I did not recognize.

"Are you ready, Tate?" It was the gruff voice of Bob Dunlop, the VP of Manufacturing.

"Sure, Bob." I replied.

"Well, let's hope that Cary likes it," he said, referring to Frank Cary, IBM's CEO.

Just then, the door opened revealing Tom Liptak, the secretary of the MRC.

"Next item, proposal for a manufacturing plant in Wangaratta," he announced in a loud voice.

20 corporate lemmings filed into the inner sanctum, with me taking up the rear, carrying my roll of presentation charts—my only security

before this tribunal.

The VPs dispersed to find their places in the back of the room, leaving me all alone at the podium. There I found two upright stainless steel palettes and carefully placed my charts on one of them. A muffled rumble of voices reminded me of a distant freight train destined to flatten me in my tracks.

The voices quieted as I turned to face the group. My eyes bulged as they took in the full impact of the chamber. I was at the focal point of a semicircular rosewood table with a radius of about 40 feet. The CEO, Frank Cary, sat on his throne at the table's center, about six paces in front of me. John Opel, President, sat at Frank's right and executive vice presidents filled out the 12 other chairs. They seemed miles away from me. The vice presidents that had waited outside with me sat in rows behind the circular table. Bright lights focused on the podium where I was standing, while theatre lights like stars above a sky of blue suits lit the voluminous chamber. How can I ever reach these guys? Will my voice hold? Or will it reveal my shaking knees?

Tom Liptak stood from his place at the end and said, "The next item is the proposed plant in Wangaratta presented by Grant Tate." I felt 28 eyes burning holes in my charts. They can read them, I know, but I must get closer. How can I convince them from here?

Luckily, the chart stand had wheels and I used them. Quickly, I dragged the device directly toward Frank Cary and turned to the first chart. I detected a slight smile.

In five minutes, I explained three months of planning, telling why we needed the plant and how it would generate more profits. After reaching my conclusions, I asked for questions—hoping that there were none.

"How much land do we own in Wangaratta?" It was John Opel, whose intelligence I admired.

"About a square mile," I replied.

"How large a manufacturing plant could you build on that site?" he continued?

"1,000,000 square feet," I estimated.

"Then I guess we'll give you 50,000," he said with a smile.

"Thank you," I said, smiling in return and taking my charts off the stand. I wanted to get out of there.

* * *

A couple of years into my GBG/I job, Al Zettlemoyer asked me to consider becoming the plant's General Manager in Amsterdam. "It's a promotion with better pay and good benefits. You know their problems and could do a great job."

"I appreciate the offer, Al," I said. "But what will happen when I come back?"

"You know we can't guarantee anything," he answered. "But remember, a corporation has no soul."

"Then my answer is clear. Thanks, but no thanks."

Al's words seared into my memory.

\* \* \*

In the beginning years, meeting new people and international travel presented exciting new adventures, but it became tiring in a while. My calendar showed me out of the country almost half the time. Catching up on expense accounts, writing papers for my doctoral studies, or trying to overcome jet lag characterized my time at home.

In the fourth year, son David was having trouble in school. We got him to see Dr. Ron Raymond, a well-respected psychologist, to help address the issues. But progress was slow. One day, deeply concerned about both David and Joyce, I called Dr. Raymond from my office.

"I need help," I said. "Both David and my wife are frantic and unstable. And I have no idea how to deal with it."

"See if you can get all three of you to my office and let me know when you'd like to meet," he replied.

I told Joyce about the call that night, urging her to take up Dr. Raymond on his offer.

Despite my pleading, she refused to go.

A few weeks later, David was expelled from St. Luke's school for the semester. It was his senior year, so it threatened his graduation.

The St. Luke School Headmaster and I agreed on a homeschooling plan for me to teach David's required classes over the semester, following their instructors' lesson plans. I approached IBM division executives, who granted me a moratorium on travel for six months to facilitate the project. David and I completed the studies allowing him to graduate with his class. He learned a lot, and so did I.

Last year, I began working on my doctorate dissertation, working in parallel with David's schooling and carrying on my full-time job, though without travel. No one said my job performance was attenuated, but I wondered if the approach would affect my career. Whatever the case, I need some rest. I've been in this job five years, two years longer than any other assignment in my career, and it's getting tiresome. The constant travel has worn me down, and it seems we've done a thousand operating plans. Now, they all seem the same. And the unit is operating so smoothly they don't need me anymore. I'm a change agent, not a crank-turner. I'm turning the crank every single day.

IBM continues to sputter along in 1978. The stock's growth slowed, even declined. We're still fighting the Justice Department's antitrust suit, creating a raft of internal restrictions, continuous training on acceptable behaviors, new protocols for saving documents, and all of it has cast a pall over morale and growth prospects.

Joyce and I have settled into a suburban routine, each playing tennis with our particular friends, occasionally playing doubles with other couples, attending weekend parties, going to Jesse Lee Memorial Church. For a couple of years, I led several committees in the church, but dropped out when some of the old-time members objected to the innovative programs for young people that the Minister, Craig Haight, and one of my committees started. We were trying to combat the growing drug problems among teenagers in the community. When Craig left out of frustration, I dropped out of all committees. I became a passive member of the church.

David is in Lyndon State College, a small school in northern Vermont and Lynn is in Green Mountain College in central Vermont After attending St. Luke's School in Wilton, CT, and Laura is doing well socially and academically in the public school system.

I'm feeling adrift. My graduate work at Pace University in New York, coupled with an adjunct professorship in their MBA program, has kept me engaged. Still, overall, I'm numb, going down an endless track, more alone than ever, having lots of "contacts," but no deep friendships. People like me, tell me I'm the best manager they ever had, call me empathetic, so what is wrong with me? Am I fundamentally a loner, afraid to trust anyone with my deepest, darkest feelings? Why am I so unhappy? I have what every successful man was supposed to have in my culture: a good job, a house in the suburbs, three children, a beautiful wife, and a dog. I am on the path, but it feels like a treadmill.

A professor in one of my classes asked us to take five minutes to look at the future and describe success. My classmates described my situation—professional job, good family, nice house, and whatever. My paragraph said, "I've just sold my business for $10,000,000 and am starting a trip around the country on my Harley." I described freedom. Just let me the hell out of here!

What next?

IBM introduced a program to help colleges and universities improve their services to minority students and communities. Under this program, the company would let the institution "borrow" an IBM professional for a year to help build curricula and programs. Reading the announcement, I said, "Yeah!" and almost jumped up to cheer. That evening, I wrote a letter to Jack Burton, the coordinator of the program, declaring my interest, and requesting a location in the west, because of my love for Colorado.

Unbeknownst to me, Burton already had a request for assistance from William Gross, Dean of Engineering at the University of New Mexico. Burton must have immediately seen a match, and a week later, I flew to Albuquerque for an interview.

# NEW MEXICO

The 737 took the expected steep turn to pass over the Sandia Mountains gap headed into its final descent to Albuquerque. I stared down at the lush green forest, once again amazed at the contrast with the surrounding desert. My mind drifted back 24 years to the first time I flew this gap in 1957. I was on my way to an interview with the Sandia Corporation, a defense contractor. It was one of about 25 such invitations in a year—companies were starved for engineers. I boarded the four-engine TWA Lockheed Constellation in Washington, DC and ate two delicious airline meals on the seven-and-a-half-hour trip to New Mexico. A middle-aged woman with dark, swept-back hair, wearing a fur coat, and smelling of expensive perfume sat next to me, a vivid reminder that this was a long journey for a naive young Virginian who was out of this woman's class. Now, I am returning as an experienced professional.

\* \* \*

The morning sun has cleared the Sandia range creating long shadows across the courtyard. Students dart in different directions, most probably a few minutes late for their nine o'clock class. I follow a few into the engineering building, quickly sighting the sign for William Gross, Dean.

Three women, two apparently Latina, the other Anglo, look up, smiling.

"Good morning. May I help you?" the Anglo woman asks.

"Good morning. I'm Grant Tate, here to see the dean," I answer.

"Oh, yes. Happy to meet you. Go on in. He's expecting you," she says.

Bill Gross, dressed in suit coat and bowtie, walks around the desk and greets me with a big smile and a hearty handshake.

"So glad to meet you," he says. "You have an impressive background," he says. "By the way, call me Bill."

Bill is shorter than I, about 5'6", relatively thin, and reminding me of a lot of bibliophilic engineers I've worked with. There are pictures of Ampex tape drives on the walls, not surprising, since my research showed me that he'd worked on development of storage devices.

"OK, Bill. I've been really excited about our conversation. This place is beautiful," I say.

We compare our experiences, working for hi-tech companies, designing, and manufacturing tape drives, working for IBM. Over the next hour, Bill gives me a background on the university, the engineering school, and his efforts to recruit Native American and Latino students.

"While you're here, you'll report directly to me, but I'd like for you to support Tom Cummings who heads our minority programs. I'll also appoint you as Associate Professor of Mechanical Engineering," Bill says.

"Wait!" I say. "Mechanical Engineering? I'm an electrical engineer."

"I know, but I'd like to have you join that department to help get some balance over there. Also, they are responsible for our new entrepreneurial courses, a great fit for you," Bill says.

"Sounds good," I reply.

"Also, we're looking into starting a program to help hi-tech start-up companies in New Mexico. So, I'd like for you to work with Ray Radosevich, in the business school to get that started."

"That's a full plate. But I look forward to the challenge," I say.

Bill introduces me to the staff in his office, then to Tom Cummings, Pete Salazar, Jim Shorty, and others with whom I will be working. We walk around the campus, leaving me awestruck with the Southwestern adobe architecture. I breathe the fresh, New Mexico air— stress-free air.

In the afternoon, thanks to advice from Bill's staff, I lease a small condominium in the northern part of the city, across from a desert golf course and close to a school for Laura.

A month later, Joyce, Laura, and I are in Albuquerque; David and Lynn are in their respective colleges in New England. As an introduction, we drive to the peak of the Sandia Mountains, eating fiery hot green chile stew, and looking over the city from above. We feel Sandia's cool, crisp air smelling of pine needles and fallen wood.

"This is gorgeous. Quite different from Colorado, but still the charm and beauty of the West. But I'm not sure I want more of that chili," Joyce says with a smile.

"Yes, we should be able to explore the area. There's a lot to experience here. And my schedule will give us time to do it," I say.

* * *

New Mexico is different from any other place—even Colorado, its neighbor to the north. New Mexico is the fifth-largest state, but has just over 2,000,000 people, less than half of which are White/Anglo, the rest Native American and Hispanic. Over half of the people live in the Albuquerque metro area.

To learn more about the state and local economy, I spent several days exploring documents, maps, and statistics in a university department that compiled that data. Poverty levels were high, especially in Native American and Hispanic communities. There was a complex social and political structure with 19 Native American pueblos and other tribes, such as the Navajo. The "Hispanic" community had many subcultures, some people tracing their legacy directly to Spain, others native to the area, still others having migrated from Mexico or other places. Ranchers from the Eastern plains had strong voices in the legislature, while there was a strong White business culture in Albuquerque. Santa Fe and Taos had vibrant artistic and creative communities with strong tourism economies. Many New Mexicans were bi-lingual, speaking both Spanish and English.

Jim Shorty, a Navajo man, headed the Native American Engineering program. Yes, he was indeed short. Stocky, with intense black hair and a round face, he conveyed trust and sensitivity with his warm smile. Jim and I spent many hours together with him patiently educating me on Native culture.

"Remember, we're all different," he said. "Each one of the pueblos and tribes has different beliefs and customs. Listen and learn. And be patient."

One day, he gave me this advice, "When you go to a meeting with the Navajos, they'll think they can wear you down and you'll forget what you came for. If you go to their meeting, take a backpack, and when you arrive, throw it in the corner and say, 'Let's talk.' They'll think, 'How can we ever get rid of this Anglo? He's here to stay.' That way, they'll listen to you."

Another time, five Native American engineering students came to my office to discuss the engineering math course.

"We need a different math course," one of them said.

"Tell me more," I said.

"The exercises and examples mean nothing to us on the pueblo or reservation. Some of our students don't get it."

I was fascinated to hear them describe their dilemma.

"You are all probably good students. Since the professor is Anglo, perhaps you could suggest some exercises that might be meaningful to other students. I'll chat with him to open the door for you."

How many of our educational programs across the nation are blind to cultural differences? I wondered. Is this a major deterrent to learning?

Jim Shorty and Pete Salazar, Jim's equivalent for Hispanic students, wrestled with that issue every day. They spend the majority of their time helping students adapt and learn in the university environment. We all learned our programs had to start in elementary school. If students graduate high school with insufficient math and reading skills, they could not qualify for engineering school. I spent much of my time talking to any group that would hear me, advocating for more math and science in all grades. And telling students about the joy of working for the good of society through an engineering career.

'What next?' was a big question for Native American and Hispanic graduates of engineering. Once they graduate, where do they go to work? Even though it was at the end of the seventies, many organizations still lacked programs to hire minority professionals. And, I quickly learned, women engineering graduates also faced similar challenges.

One young woman, a chemical engineering major, told about one of her first experiences as an intern at a refinery.

"These guys gave me a big ten-pound wrench and asked me to climb a 50-foot ladder to turn on a valve. They were testing me to see if a woman could do it."

And Native American students sometimes faced ridicule from their own community, for many reasons. Landing an engineering job might mean leaving your reservation, your family, your culture. As Peter Macdonald, president of the Navajo Nation said, "Go out to learn the ways of the White men and come back to help your people." But everyone knew there were few jobs in Native country.

\* \* \*

In my role in the Mechanical Engineering department, I began teaching a course on Entrepreneurship, helping students develop ideas and plans for new businesses in the state. This corresponded closely with the launch of the New Mexico Technical Innovation Center, which I helped Ray Radosevich spearhead. This was part of the National Science Foundation's program across the country.

The scientists at the government high technology laboratories at Sandia, and Los Alamos, and similar organizations, developed new technologies, ideas, and devices, many of which had commercial possibilities. We designed our center to help scientists and engineers translate those developments into commercial use. We helped them develop business plans, find funding, and launch new companies. I also helped the Four Corners Regional Commission establish other economic development programs across the four states, Arizona, Colorado, New Mexico, and Utah, and advised the City of Albuquerque about economic development programs. The president of the Albuquerque

Chamber of Commerce gave me the compliment of a lifetime when he once introduced me in a public meeting as "A great New Mexican."

The work routine gave me plenty of time to write the dissertation for the doctorate program at Pace University. Joyce and I fashioned a nook in the condo as my work and writing space. I aimed to finish the work within the coming year. The data from IBM has formed a strong foundation for the thesis. Fortunately, Dr. William Freund, Chief Economist of the New York Stock Exchange is chair of my dissertation committee. Once he approves a chapter, it is ready to go. Other members of the committee serve a lesser role.

This is my place. I am serving my purpose in life, learning every day, experiencing a wide range of cultures and working in a role where people appreciate my good work. Perhaps this is the time to stay on this career path and leave IBM. I have a reasonable possibility of joining the faculty, either in business or engineering at the university. In addition, my colleague, Ray Radosevich, invited me to partner with him as a consultant.

Leaving IBM, however, would mean giving up a large portion of my pension, increasing financial risks for the family. Yet, those were risks I was willing to take.

I presented the possibility to Joyce.

"I had a long chat with Ray Radosevich yesterday. He had an interesting proposition," I said.

"What's that? He's been a good person for you to work with," Joyce said.

"He suggested I stay at UNM and work with him in his consulting business. He thinks I could get a faculty appointment in the business school or engineering. That would mean eventually leaving IBM."

"You mean we'd move to New Mexico?" she asked.

"Of course. We've already established ourselves here, in the university, in the community," I said.

"Well, what about the children? They'd hate it here." Joyce said.

"I don't know about that, but I'll ask them," I said.

"Whatever they say, I want to go back to Connecticut," she said.

"But both of us would have lots of opportunities here. We're back in the West we love, there is a lot to learn and explore. It would be good."

"Well, you can stay if you want. I want to go back."

"Do you mean that?" I asked.

"Sure. I want to go back to Connecticut."

Every move we made was difficult for Joyce: from Endicott to Boulder, Boulder to Palo Alto, Palo Alto back to Boulder, Boulder to Ridgefield, and from Ridgefield to Albuquerque. Maybe I was asking too much but moving seemed to attack her basic sense of security. We were in our twenty-second year of marriage. She is completely dependent on me, never having a job outside of the four post-high school years back in Orange, VA. Despite my urging, and living in the shadow of great universities, she would not consider taking classes, while at the same time, making fun of my interest in learning. Does she understand or know who I am?

Soon, we moved back to Connecticut, and I returned to IBM, feeling deflated.

# *WHERE* THE HECK *AM I?*

# BACK TO IBM

Returning to IBM after my sabbatical in New Mexico has been hell. Before leaving for New Mexico, I was Director of Manufacturing and Technology Planning with a broad set of international responsibilities and a staff of over 50 professionals from 11 different countries. My job put me in daily contact with high-level executives to help decide where and how to manufacture our products across ten manufacturing plants.

My performance ratings were excellent. The title of "Director" was influential in the corporate hierarchy, somewhat like a bird colonel in the military; not as high as a general, but carrying significant responsibilities, authority, and prestige. Yet, upon my return, the division assigned me to a marketing position a field in which I had little experience. I became responsible for a dying international product line, IBM Supplies, which included typewriter ribbons, IBM punch cards, and various other small disposable components for the company's machines and systems. This, as far as I knew, was the only retail business in the company's portfolio, and it was dying—sales declining in every country. My unit reported to a divisional vice president, Paul Kaufmeil, who demanded we turn it into a growth business.

I learned of the assignment shortly after Dad died. I was disappointed but could not find the energy to fight. It was like the third strike: my deteriorating marriage, losing Dad, and now a slap in the face from IBM. I could have stayed in New Mexico launching a new path, breathing fresh air, seeing new horizons. Instead, here I am back in the old grind, the old box, working for a family completely dependent on me. There was a way out of this dilemma, but I folded. I am the lone provider, the responsible one, the one who always has to be good.

With my positive performance records, what could have derailed me? A few things came to mind.

It was my day to present our operating plan to Bob Dunlop, Vice President of Manufacturing for the whole company. As I was getting ready to leave home in Connecticut 45 minutes' drive away, Joyce and I got into a heated argument about David's schoolwork, my work overtime, my study time. Soon, she dragged David and Lynn into the accusations, seeking their reinforcements. By the time I rushed to the car, I would be at least 45 minutes late for the meeting. Returning to the noisy house to use the phone was not an option, so instead I headed to Armonk, entering Dunlop's office to face the music with my tail between my legs. I was too embarrassed to say "family problems" made me late.

Another incident upset Dunlop, also souring me on him and the company. Paul Merritt, a manager who worked for me, conceived a new strategy, the North American Strategy, to consolidate our two plants in Canada with others in the United States to distribute our products more efficiently. It was an ingenious plan that would save the company millions of dollars and shorten time to market. We engaged one of Dunlop's staff members, Mike Haight, to help us obtain Dunlop's agreement to the plan. We eventually won approval and started implementing the plan. Later, we found Mike had claimed it was his idea, even winning an outstanding contribution award for the project. My objections did not sit well with Dunlop.

Another day, while working on the annual operating plans, Dunlop called me saying we should add two more manufacturing plants to our strategic plan.

"Why?" I asked. "We don't need more capacity."

"Paul Rizzo is looking at a revised pricing strategy, which could greatly increase demand."

I replied, "Two years ago when I first joined the division, they were planning two more plants to manufacture typewriters. I cut them out. We could soon replace all that mechanical stuff inside with a semiconductor chip. So, Bob, we'll submit our plans reflecting our current forecasts. You can reject them if you want."

Dunlop grumbled and hung up the phone. A month later, he approved our plan.

Although, on the face of it, the interaction was insignificant, the call raised ominous questions. Why would IBM's top leadership be considering radically lowering prices to increase our manufacturing volumes? Was the company in trouble?

It seemed my division could have found me a job in Manufacturing upon my return. Dunlop may have squashed the idea. On the other hand, I was too depressed to ask.

A few years ago, my friend in HR, Tom Viola, noticed that a lot of high-level ex-executives were put out to pasture to rot in the graveyard of IBM obscurity. They had been removed from their jobs and were still trying to be useful but were never told the reason for their removal. Tom studied 19 cases and found that almost all ex-executives had significant psychological and marriage issues. Their most common question was, "why?" It looks as though I'll be number twenty.

* * *

Morning light lights up my empty desk top, and it's just the place to plop my briefcase. The office is a standard IBM issue for a person of my reduced level: simulated wood desk top, pressed wood credenza, an adjustable desk chair, and two hardback sitting chairs. A box labeled "Supplies" sits on the floor near the window and I place it on the desk. I pick up the phone on the credenza. Yes, it's live.

The walls are decorator brown, blank—utterly devoid of pictures. Just like me. Blank. What the hell am I doing here?

Lifting the top from the file box, I choose three folders and place them on the desk while realizing my hands are shaking.

# ADRIFT

I am officially adrift, both professionally and personally.

My upward momentum in the company apparently stopped the moment I requested the assignment in New Mexico. At the time, my performance rating as Director was at the top of the scale. My manager and others praised my good work. Yet, they assigned me to a lower-level job managing a dying business with no chance of success.

IBM had awarded me stock options during the assignment at Sterling Forest. The program provided the means for a person to purchase IBM stock for a price fixed at the moment of the award. In other words, if the stock was $200 per share on the day of the award and the stock was later $300, the person could still buy a certain number of shares at the lower price. Then, it was necessary to hold the stock for a certain period to get a tax advantage.

But buying the stock at any price required cash. So the company arranged a New York bank to offer relatively low-interest loans to stock option recipients. This seemed to be a good deal when IBM stock continually went up, as in the early days of the company, but was significantly risky when the stock declined. In other words, if the stock went below the stock option price, say $200 as in this example, a person who borrowed money and bought shares at $200 would be caught with a loan and lower valued stock.

As a result of the poor performance of IBM stock and my choices, I am left with $60,000 of debt to a bank in New York. Another set of chains binding me to this company.

I was on the high potential list, had received all the education and training anyone could get, a big investment for the company, had received stock options as a result of my performance, yet they assigned me to a bad job.

Why?

I asked around, but no one would give me a straight answer. I went to see Ted Papes, who had been promoted to a higher-level VP job, and asked him bluntly to give me answers. Ted is one of the most straightforward people I know, but he said, "I see nothing that was a problem. You did a great job with that miserable Sterling Forest; you didn't blunt your sword there."

I wonder if IBM executives became aware of my family issues. But there is no evidence of that. Yet, it is no secret that my family is estranged from me. I had requested a sabbatical from travel because I needed to homeschool my son, David. That was a clear signal of home problems. That happened before I went to New Mexico.

I am still employed, drawing a stable, but not increasing salary and have good benefits. That much is a comfort. But…

The problem is me.

And I wonder how much it is obvious to my managers and my co-workers. I am completely disillusioned with the company, with my career, my marriage. Who the hell am I? How could they not see it? But no one has addressed it.

I felt a purpose in each of my jobs over the years, helping other people learn and thrive in their respective roles. Early on, we trained hundreds of people helping them succeed in a new path. In any other company, many might have been laid off had we not developed that program.

In my management jobs, I focused on helping members of my organization develop more skills and find their place in the company. In New Mexico, I helped Native Americans and those of Latin background become engineers to help their people.

But now I am a castaway from the company I once admired. Al Zettlemoyer's words ring in my ears, "Remember, Grant, the corporation has no soul." Perhaps the change in me came when I began to realize the truth in that statement.

# JIM MORGAN

I call Jim Morgan, my primary friend in corporate human resources. Jim grew up in rural South Carolina and was one of the first Black Americans to join the IBM HR staff. Jim's calm advice and decision-making helped me talk through some problematic people issues in my previous job.

"Hi Jim, this is Grant Tate."

"Well, hey! When did you get back?"

"Got back from New Mexico over a month ago, but my dad died down in Virginia, so I've been with the family," I answer.

"Oh… I'm so sorry. It must have been sudden. Last time you mentioned him he was in good health."

I explain what happened to Dad and the impact on me.

"Jim, they've put me in an impossible job at a lower level, and I don't know why. I'm thinking about throwing in the towel and leaving this place."

"Do you have time to talk?" Jim asks.

"Sure. That's why I called."

"Well, let's slow down and see what we need to do."

We talk for 30 minutes, stepping through my concerns one by one.

"Well, Grant, you know we have an excellent Employee Assistance Program (EAP). I recommend you go to them today to get some help. Would that be OK with you?"

"Sure. I have nothing else on the schedule."

"Great. There's a person over there that would be perforce for you. Let me call, make an appointment, call you right back. OK? But another thing: You might want to stick with this job. You are probably overqualified for it, but while you're going through these personal issues, it might just be the place to be."

An hour later, I'm on my way to the EAP.

# SALLY

It began on a train.

A few months after Dad's death, I boarded Amtrak from Washington to New York, choosing the window seat to see the countryside on the way but pulling a book out of my briefcase to read just in case. Soon a woman stopped at my position, lifting her Tumi roll-on case to the luggage rack.

"Hi, I'm Sharon," she said, extending her hand. "Are you headed to New York?"

"Hi, I'm Grant. On the way to Connecticut via New York," I answered.

"Great. We'll have three hours to talk," she said with a smile.

Just what I need, I thought. A chatterbox to bend my ear for three hours.

Sharon wore a tailored blue business suit accented by a silver brooch on the lapel. Her white blouse and a blue Hermes scarf neatly tied in a square knot completed the image.

"What brings you to Connecticut?" she asks.

"I'm headed home."

"OK, then, what were you doing in Washington?"

"I was visiting my mom. My dad died a few months ago and she's taking it pretty hard. In fact, we're all taking it hard. It was a surprise; he died of a heart attack while on a treadmill stress test."

"Oh. I'm so sorry. I know that must be difficult."

It didn't take Sharon long to read my distressed face going right to the heart of the matter. I learned she does government relations work for a firm in New York, riding the train almost like a commuter.

After a while, Sharon asks, "What are you going to do about it?"

"About what?"

"About the doctors' negligence of putting your father on a treadmill when they must have known he had a heart condition."

"Well… my brother and I have thought about it, but so far, haven't done anything about it."

"I have a friend you might want to talk to. She's a medical doctor and knows a lot about these things."

Sharon pulls out a notebook, writes an address, rips off the page, and hands it to me. "Why don't you give her a call?"

I read the paper. It says, "Dr. Sally Fried." I folded the paper and put it into my shirt pocket.

Yeah, sure, I think. Am I going to call some woman out of the blue and ask for advice?

But a couple of weeks later, I made the call.

* * *

She's tall, probably 5'7", just over thirty and trim, with long blond hair that appears to be natural. She walks confidently, even athletically, to the table while I rise to greet her. Her smile is warm, accenting a classical model's face. We're at the Pace Gourmet Deli, just a block away from the University.

"Hi, I'm Sally," she says, offering her hand.

My hand, somewhat damp with perspiration, contrasts with her warm, relaxed clasp.

"I'm Grant. Thanks so much for meeting with me."

"Sharon prides herself on making connections, so I'm not surprised that's where you got my name."

We sip our coffee while I gingerly step into describing Dad's death on the treadmill. She tells me about her medical school and that she's finished journalism school and just accepted a job at a major network. She asks about my family, my background, and how I am feeling about Dad's death. Jim Morgan had asked a similar question, but suddenly my tears flow.

Sally reaches for my hand, saying, "It's OK. Just let it come out."

"I'm so sorry. So sorry," I mumble, feeling like running out the door. Where did this come from? I cried in Dad's workshop for the first time in 20 years. This is the second. Why? I should be able to control this. What's wrong with me, bawling before a complete stranger?

"It's OK to feel that way. You deserve your feelings. Let it happen," she says.

After talking for another 15 minutes, I need to catch the train back.

"I'd love to pick up the thread some other time if you like," Sally says.

"Yes, thanks so much for your help and understanding. I'll call you." I answer as we head in different directions on the street. I can still feel her hand as I'm walking the block to the number 4 uptown train.

Finally, there is someone to hear my grief.

# THE GRADUATION

I was on the program with Leonard Silk, the foremost economics columnist of the New York Times. He was receiving Pace University's award for outstanding contributions to the US economy, and I, the tiny little cog that I was, was receiving the Pace University President's award for outstanding academic achievement, an unlikely event for someone who was barely a B student in engineering.

Business studies were easy in comparison with differential equations. I worked through finance, international business, and management to achieve my doctorate from Pace University. One course, Mergers and Acquisitions, was a mystery. The professor, a specialist from Wall Street, talked in riddles. He gave me a grade of B, which spoiled my quest for a straight 4.0 average.

On the day of the big event, my Joyce and I started glaring at each other in the kitchen of our Connecticut house. "You bastard, you're going to leave me after all these years. Well, it's about time. Just get out of here!" she shouted.

"I'm sorry. It's been coming a long time, but every time I've tried to talk about it, you change the subject. Finally, I just exploded," I retorted.

She continued the yelling, the recriminations, the accusations, and the insults.

Finally, I said, "I've got to go to New York. Are you coming or not?"

"Damn right I'm going. I wouldn't miss this for the world," she said.

The atmosphere was so tense, I thought the air inside the car might explode. Why does she want to go, I wondered. To see me fall on my face? We eventually made it to Stellar Hall, Pace University's grand auditorium.

I am vaguely aware of the president's words; platitudes and praise, I supposed, for Mr. Silk and me. He introduces Silk first. The crowd stands and roars, surprisingly enthusiastic for a business school audience.

Silk goes to the podium and begins analyzing the Reagan economy and pointing out the barriers ahead. Other than the topic, I hear little of it, even though I've followed Mr. Silk's column for years. I should be thrilled to actually meet him, to share the stage. But how can I with the clouds surrounding my head?

The president calls my name and describes my four years of academic diligence and leadership in class. Meanwhile, my wife sits fuming by my side, thinking it was all a lie, hoping I would stumble and fall in front of 500 people, and knowing I'd be tongue-tied with fear, conflicted and emotion. I went to the podium and looked at the audience and Joyce's grimacing face—the hatred, the fury. My notes were a blur, my thoughts a tangled mess.

Finally, I got a sentence out.

"Thank you, Mr. President. It is a great honor to be here and share the podium with such a distinguished person as Mr. Silk, whose work has inspired me for many years. People like him are why I enrolled in the Doctor of Professional Studies Program." The crowd clapped.

My voice is clear, confident, and determined. I continued without notes, describing the high ideals of the program and thanking Dr. Zack, my mentor, and my other instructors and students in my class cohort. At the end, I held up a hand to thank the audience for their support.

Joyce was grimacing now. Her lips moved silently, and I read, "You bastard."

I responded with a smile, thinking, "you've criticized me long enough. Just listen for once."

\* \* \*

After five years of struggle, I earned a doctorate degree while working full time, but there is no celebration, except for these 500 people in the audience who knew the meaning of study, hard work, and achievement. By contrast, the new degree is a symbol of my wife's hatred. My dad cannot congratulate me from his grave, and the people at IBM seemed not to care. When I told my division president about my degree, he said, "I'm glad that's over." Little did he know that my classes in international finance were the foundation for many of our important strategic decisions.

Will it help me make important life decisions now? I need a new path.

# WHITE PLAINS Y

"That'll be $27, Mr. Tate," he says, standing behind his makeshift desk at the downtown White Plains YMCA, where I ran round and round on their indoor running track for 30 minutes each day at lunchtime.

I hand the guy three tens and take the three ones he offers me.

"Your room is 17 down that hall over there."

Picking up my over-the-shoulder travel bag containing a spare blue suit, three shirts, underwear, and other items, I walk down the long hall, reading the numbers as I go. How many other people like me are here like me, I wonder? The place is well-worn, green walls reminding me of my early IBM days, dark green metal doors now showing scratches and wear spots from years of use, two doors whose locks appear to have barely survived someone's attempt to pick them, and, finally, number 17. I fit my key and push open the door, which answers my push with a high squeak, and flick on the ceiling light of a single hanging 40-watt bulb. A metal cot, covered with a thin mattress, a dented sheet metal closet, and Formica topped tapered leg desk await me. A blue plastic shaded light sits on the desk. I toss my bag onto the cot and sit down, head cupped in my hands.

I tried to talk to her. I wanted to tell Joyce about how I was struggling, how unhappy I've been, how confused, how lost, how alone. But I didn't know how to tell her—or anyone else, for that matter. I have been too embarrassed for being out of control, too guilty for not living up to standards, and too scared of losing my job, of losing everything. When I tried to talk, she shouted, screamed, and went into the hall telling the children, "Your Dad is leaving us!" Then to me, "Get out! Get out!"

I am devastated to leave the children, who mean everything to me. Perhaps I was wrong to keep my unhappiness hidden from them. Yet, I did not want to burden them with my problems or let them know the father who was supposed to be strong, to provide for the family, was folding at the knees.

My only brother, Warren, is ten years younger than I. By the time he was seven, I was off to college, so we both grew up in a single-child family—and we never had a sister, so we never experienced being around a young girl growing up. I've been astonished by how different three children in the same family can be, each embodying similar core family character-istics, but with dramatically different styles, talents, and emotions. We've been to a lot of places all across the country as a family, but one-on-one time with me and one of the three has often been the most memorable.

David, the oldest, loves to write and was a star running back on the St. Luke's football team. He ran like the wind, faster than any of his classmates or any opposing player. David's writing teacher, Ed Scovner, encouraged good writing and stoked David's interest in writing, movies, and current events. David enrolled in Lyndon State College way up in northern Ver-mont, a place with one cafe where everyone in town gathered for breakfast. David has a lot of talents, but he often doesn't recognize them.

Lynn, next in line, has keen human relations perceptual skills, using them to get to know everyone and where each person fits into their envi-ronment. After she and I visited Green Mountain College in Vermont for the first time, she said on the way home, "I've always wanted to run a ski shop. Their program in retail management is just what I want." Two weeks later, she told me she was going to major in art. What the heck? Neverthe-less, I trust her to find her way. She's a great problem solver.

Laura, the youngest, is still in high school, and is the most industrious academic in the family. She would never classify herself that way, but her determination drives her to her goals. One day, she decided it was the day to learn skateboarding. Although she may have fallen 20 times, by the end of the day she was proficient. When Joyce and I were out of the house, it seemed that although Laura was the youngest, she was the adult decision maker.

I don't know what will happen next, to me or to my relationship with them, but I have to find a way to take care of myself.

So here I am in the Y, not knowing what to do or where to go. My family ties are precarious, my job situation is perilous, and everything I worked for is threatened. My God, I need a shower. Where do I shower? Men's locker room? At least I know where it is and where they keep the towels. Maybe I can take a deep breath and go to work tomorrow. I'm only a couple of blocks from the office. How will I work in this condition?

How did I get here?

# MOVING IN

A day after checking into the Y, I call Sally. We chat a while about the weather and our jobs, a lot of trivial warming up. She finally asks, "What's going on? I can sense you're upset."

"You're right. I finally had to escape and walked out of the house," I said.

Our many conversations since that first meeting boosted my trust in her intelligence and compassion. I was on the edge, ready to jump off, but she reached out a hand. I sensed my vulnerability, but for once in my life I took the chance on talking to someone about my feelings; feeling trapped, disillusioned with the corporate world, in conflict over my family, unsure of my future, no identifiable close friends.

"Why not move in with me? There is room for two in my New York apartment," she said.

"Really? Are you sure?"

"Sure. We know each other really well. We can make it work."

The following week, I move my suitcases into Sally's apartment in Greenwich Village. There are some visible downsides. First, I'll have to commute to White Plains by train every day, although that seems easier than the 45-minute drive I had endured. She has two cats with silky, brown, wispy fur—a definite threat to my allergies. And the cats don't seem very friendly. Sally smokes, especially when she is nervous—another threat to my breathing. And she is a nail-biter. Every single nail—on fingers that a concert pianist would dream to have—is hardly visible, seemingly embedded into the flesh. I am a bit wary about what all this means, but I take the leap.

I also had this week, my first session on the Upper East Side with Dr. Bernstein, a pipe-smoking psychotherapist wearing a tweed coat, someone straight out of the movies. I'm an out-of-control kid from a small southern town drifting around in a hostile environment.

I'm a castaway from the company, but a fugitive from the family. By leaving Joyce, I also left the family. I tried to talk to her, to get her to join me in family therapy, but it never worked. We never learned to talk sensitively, deeply, to solve problems together. I had those skills at work, but why couldn't I apply them at home?

Dr. Bernstein suggested that breaking away probably saved my life. Yet, I feel profoundly guilty. I broke every rule, every value, every thread of the way I was raised. I gave all that up, but for what purpose? Just to relieve the pain? It couldn't have been to relieve the loneliness, because I feel more alone than ever now. Except for Sally and my counselor, I have no one to talk to. I am ashamed to talk to anyone—family, friends, colleagues. I failed to reach out, to let anyone know what was going on, but neither has anyone called to check on me or to ask what the hell is going on? The church minister stopped by to comfort Joyce, but never bothered to seek me out, to consider that, I too, might be in pain.

Working with the counselor may help me get stabilized, unfrozen so I can work, I can think, I can plod. The fire, the hope, the drive is gone, but I can at least function. I'm not sure where my path might lead, but I need to take one step. Since I don't know the right direction, I need to build some stability and explore some options. Is this drifting or exploring? Perhaps it will be clear someday.

# THE PERSONAL COMPUTER

My stint in Marketing upon my return from New Mexico was a disaster. They assigned me to revive office supplies, a dying segment of the international business. We tried everything, new advertising promotions, discount programs, lower prices, but more agile competitors with lower overhead costs and cheaper prices were eating our lunch in every country.

To cap off the experience, Paul Kaufmeil, the Vice President of the division, asked me to lunch with one of my colleagues and spent the whole meal berating me, in front of my colleague, for my bad performance. My primary defense was recommending IBM get out of the supplies business. I returned to my office, called Jim Lindner, my immediate manager and requested a transfer.

"I don't need that kind of crap," I said to Jim.

The following week, I transferred to Derek Harris, a British guy responsible for preparing our division for new products, and the driver of a classic old Rolls Royce he brought over when he transferred to the US. Derek suggested I go check on a project called Acorn at Boca Raton, Florida.

Returning from Boca, I told Derek that developing the manufacturing and marketing plan for the Acorn Program, the IBM Personal Computer (PC), should be my full-time job. Preparing for new products built on my past experiences. And, strangely enough, working with supplies boosted my knowledge of retail business. IBM anticipated selling PCs through retail outlets. That meant we'd have to prepare creative business plans for the 11 major countries our division served that were quite different from other product plans.

It was 1981 and we were preparing to introduce the IBM Personal Computer into the United States and Europe. Apple had announced its early machines and also hobbyists were patching together components to make small computers, but, in general, ultra-small computers were the domain of tinkerers. Businesses were not using the current devices on the market.

The project was on a fast track. IBM president, John Opel, assigned Don Estridge, a project leader from the Federal Systems Division, to lead the project, asking him to develop a product that we could sell for less than

$1,000 and announce it to the public in less than a year. In addition, he gave Don the freedom to run the project as an independent business unit, freeing Don of many of the restraints normally faced by other product teams. For instance, other IBM products used proprietary internal components such as semiconductors and software operating systems developed by IBM's own development teams. When Don went to the company's component division to find an appropriate semiconductor chip set, the components people told him it would take over two years to design and build it, and the cost was much higher than required. So Don purchased the 8088 from the Intel Corporation to use in the PC. It was a similar story with IBM's operating system development team. Don purchased an operating system called DOS from a small company soon to be called Microsoft, headed by Bill Gates.

I hired a small team of people at White Plains, our division headquarters to help manage our division's PC program. A month after we started, I asked one of our team members, Kevin O'Brien, to bring us an operating PC when he returned from a trip to Boca Raton. A few days later, three boxes arrived at my office.

Kevin and I eagerly opened the boxes, placed the printer, display and processing unit on my desk, plugged them together and pushed the on buttons. The first PC at our division headquarters sprang into life. Kevin put a floppy disk into the slot and fired up a scheduling application. We were in business!

Most of IBM's other products required hours, if not days, to set up and get operating in a customer's office. We were in operation almost immediately. In addition, this device could provide computing services at every person's desk at every small to large organization, quite a contrast to the current situation where only big companies could afford computers and where anyone in those companies who needed computing services had to deal with the organization operating the big computing center.

We were witnessing a major breakthrough. I heard some shuffling outside my office door and looked up to see a small crowd of our colleagues gathered around to see the miracle.

* * *

Normally, IBM prepared detailed market forecasts before the release of any new product. The forecasting professionals looked at past history, similar products, different pricing models, customer surveys, and meetings with individual or group interviews.

We planned to announce the computer in August, just six months away, but we had no idea how many we would sell. IBM's forecasting techniques were honed to a fine edge, but our forecasters had little or no experience in retail or dealer sales. The PC forecast was close to guesswork, so we asked people in each of IBM's country organizations to do whatever they could to estimate the first year's sales. Now it was time to visit these people, look at the marketplace and try to develop an overall production and sales plan. That task fell to me in my role as Product Manager for Entry Systems.

In London, I was to meet Jerry Spence and Dave Conrad from the PC development group in Boca Raton. I flew from White Plains expecting a quiet, but eventful, trip with two people with whom I had worked comfortably for several months. After my arrival, we were to rendezvous in a British restaurant close to my hotel.

When I arrived at the restaurant, four people, not two, were there to greet me: Jerry, Dave, Dave's wife, Amanda, and Ron. Dave's wife was no surprise since he had told me that he might bring her on the trip. But who was Ron and what was he doing there?

To use a phrase common in the TV industry, Ron had a great face for radio. He was between 30 and 35 years old, had a bulbous face, and hair that he had combed with an eggbeater, his horned rim glasses barely hung on his nose, and his clothes looked as if he had slept in them all the way from Florida. As he was introduced to me, Ron pulled a crusty pipe from the pocket of his tweed jacket and began to stuff it with tobacco from a crumpled bag. I glanced at Dave, as if to say, "Where did you find this mess? And why is he here?" Dave grinned slyly and rolled his eyes. Explanation to follow.

Ron mumbled something about this being his first trip outside the United States and I wondered if he should have said, "outside of his cage."

We ate our salads with Ron munching lettuce between pulls on his pipe. I ignored him and turned my attention to the other three. I passed around itineraries for the trip, explained some recent changes and began to describe some of the people that we were going to meet in the next 15 days. Our trip was to cover the UK, Denmark, Netherlands, Belgium, Germany, Italy, and France. In each place, we were to meet members of the forecasting staff and marketing people, then visit stores and office supplies dealers.

My discussion was interrupted by the waiter bringing the main course. But the odor was steak mixed with burning wool.

"I smell something burning," I said to the waiter.

"And I do as well, sir," he replied, looking around noticing a wisp of smoke arising from Ron's right side.

"Sir, your clothes are on fire," observed the waiter coolly, looking at Ron.

"My God!" shouted Ron, jumping upright from his chair and banging against the table.

Glasses and silverware went everywhere. Ron grabbed a glass and tossed water in his pocket. Dave rescued a napkin and patted the wet spot on Ron's jacket, while the rest of us stood aghast. I'd heard about pipe smokers burning their clothes, but always thought them to be tall tales. Now it was happening before my very eyes.

Ron said, "damn, shit, stupid," and pulled the still hot pipe out of his pocket. He stared at it with the soft eyes of a mother examining an injured child.

"I guess it's OK," he said while the waiter reassembled our table.

After dinner, Dave explained Ron's presence.

"Ron and I reported to the same fellow in Boca Raton. Ron was responsible for mechanical design. One day, one of Ron's engineers brought some material in an enclosed can to Ron's office."

"One of my engineers wants to use this stuff on the production line. But I told him it was inflammable," he said.

"It's OK, it's not inflammable," replied Ron.

Put off by Ron's disagreement, the engineer held his ground and a strong argument ensued.

Finally, Ron said, "Here, I'll show you," pouring some of the viscous material onto his desk and pulling out a pack of matches.

He lit a match, tossed it onto the glob, which exploded into flame. That afternoon, our manager removed Ron from his management job. To get him out of the location for a while, he asked me to bring him on this trip."

"Well, I hope he doesn't burn down all of Europe while he's here," I said.

\* \* \*

Our visit to IBM's UK offices was uneventful. They were excited about the pending introduction of the personal computer but had little idea how it would affect their business. During these meetings, Ron was relatively quiet, leaving most of the discussion to Jerry, Dave, and me.

Two days later, we loaded into a traditional black London cab for a trip to Heathrow airport. Ron arrived in the hotel lobby with his battered, broken briefcase, and a box-like brown suitcase held together by straps, big enough to carry his mother.

"I forgot to tell you about this," Dave offered quietly. "He's just separated from his wife, and he brought everything he owns."

The hotel bellhop face turned red and groaned, "aarg," as he strained to pick up the monstrosity. I thought the handle would surely tear as the leatherette bowed under the weight of the bag's contents. The bellhop dropped the bag to the concrete and dragged it to the cab, lifted the front end into the door, then pushed the back with all his weight.

"Well, there's enough room for Ron in that cab, we'll get another one," I said as Ron crawled over the luggage into the back seat, while placing a small British coin into the Bellhop's hand. The man opened his hand, stared a moment, looked up at Ron in the cab, and, with typical British aplomb, said nothing.

On the way to the airport, I said to Dave, "Just remember, you're Ron's babysitter. Keep him out of trouble. And, by the way, don't ever carry his bag."

Our next stop was Copenhagen, a much-anticipated stop for me. Helga, a bright, highly experienced forecaster from our Danish office had been studying the European market and was ready with her report. Her presentation promised to be captivating, not only for its content, but also because Helga was exceptionally knowledgeable, blond, almost six feet tall, with wide, blue eyes. Her analyses had been particularly helpful to me on several past projects.

Helga greeted us warmly and led us to a small conference room where she had arranged her data and charts. We seated ourselves around a small rectangular table. Ron chose the first chair to Helga's right.

After some brief introductions, she presented detailed data on well-prepared flip charts. "I've looked at all the available references," she said in perfect English, "and pulled together data from the various countries. There's not a lot of conclusive information, but we can estimate the interest in small computers."

She moved through the charts, showing graphs by country, explaining her sources and conclusions—all the time, staring to her right—watching Ron's every move.

I was dumbfounded. Could this be some strange attraction? How could such a beautiful woman find this American, who looked like an unmade bed, attractive. The rest of us interrupted her several times to ask questions. Helga would look at the questioner long enough to answer the question, then turn her gaze back to Ron.

In about an hour, the discussion was finished, and we headed across the plaza to the cafeteria for lunch. I drifted to Helga's side and asked softly, "Thanks so much for the good analysis. This will help us a lot. By the way, what do you think of Ron? Would you like to help us escort him around Europe?" I grinned sheepishly.

Helga stopped, her blue eyes staring directly into mine. Smiling, she shot back, "If you give me a leash, I'll do it!"

She renewed my faith in women.

In LaGaude, France, we talked to a group of over 100 engineers and program-mers who gathered to hear the story of how the PC was being developed. When Dave described how IBM top management had freed the PC design team from bureaucratic procedures, we were met with cheers of enthusiasm.

After the presentation, a line formed to ask questions and to trade ex-periences. I was shocked to see the pent-up emotions caused by the long list of approvals IBM had instituted for any product announcement—proba-bly a consequence of long years in fighting the Justice Department's anti-trust suit. Don Estridge, the leader of the PC Development team carried a dog-eared roll of charts that explained the PC program. He joked that, even with all the freedom that he had been given, he still had to make 47 presentations to obtain approval to announce the PC in the marketplace.

Finally, after three weeks of touring, I was on the plane to New York and the other three, including Ron with his exploding suitcase, were on the way to Boca Raton. As we traveled from place to place, I compiled the information we were gathering about the market for PC's in Europe.

We had met with IBM marketing managers, office supplies dealers, computer clubs, and retail stores. In the end, all we had was anecdotal data. Helga's analysis of the European market was the single exception. By the time we finished the meeting in Nice, France, I knew that estimating our sales for the first year would be no better than a guess.

I remembered an occasion in my early career when my manager, Ever-ett van Heusen asked me to estimate how many units we should manufac-ture for a certain product. When I said that we didn't have enough data and probably couldn't get it, Van Heusen replied, "Who is in a better position to estimate the number that you are?" I did the estimate. Now, once again, it was up to me to guess. Probably no one knew more about the potential PC market than our small team.

Several days after arriving home, I invited Bob King and the head of the European forecasting group to lunch in downtown White Plains. Over our elegant salads, I described our trip, the people that we had met, the stories that we had gathered, and how the team saw the prospects for the first year of PC sales in Europe. Finally, I suggested a sales quota for each country. I didn't write the numbers on a napkin, but the discussion was informal. At the end, Bob said, "Call the Country Managers and give them their quotas."

* * *

A year after the PC was announced, I was riding with Don Estridge, the leader of the PC group, from one location to another in Boca Raton. Don was a thoughtful guy, more nerdy than executive-like, but built a great product and a successful team. He had achieved success in spite of IBM's bureaucracy. The Personal Computer had just surpassed a billion dollars in sales. By that time, Don and I knew each other well.

"Hey, Don. Congratulations on passing the billion-dollar mark," I said. "You know, if you were an independent company, you and your execs would all be millionaires."

Don smiled broadly and said, "Well, you know we have good security here, great support, a solid future, and many things to be thankful for."

Then he paused.

"Isn't that a crock?" he said.

But passing the billion-dollar sale may not have been good news for the PC operation. To some IBM leaders in other product lines, the PC program was getting too big for its britches, essentially diverting customer choices away from their products toward the cheaper PC. It was relatively easy to find ways to connect PCs to the big computers, creating a "smart terminal," where users had some memory and computing power at their own desk, but also the immense computer power of the large computer system if needed. And, of course, that interconnectivity opened the door for email and other communications systems. That was a good idea, but displaced a lot of "dumb terminals," that had no computing power built in.

So, instead of investing heavily in the PC organization and perhaps growing a fast-growing independent subsidiary, IBM placed more controls on the PC program and moved Don Estridge to be corporate Vice President of Manufacturing. They called it a promotion, but they, in effect, replaced an entrepreneur with another guy, a bureaucrat.

IBM could have founded a fast-growing company to compete in the small computer market, but, instead, it folded its hand.

Eventually the press and even IBM's internal documents listed the other fellow, Bill Lowe, as the person who started the personal computer project. Lowe may have been the person who convinced the executives to start the program, but Don Estridge is the person who was actually responsible for building the IBM personal computer. Bill might have been up there in the IBM clouds somewhere, but Don Estridge deserves the credit.

Not long after that meeting, our division, General Business Group, International (GBG/I) was absorbed by other divisions as part of IBM's periodic reorganization. Subsequently, I was transferred to the European Middle East Africa (EMEA) division, making it clear my job was done. The

PC business was growing fast across all countries. Our plan worked. The countries sold three times my forecast in the first year.

But a meeting in Paris sealed my fate with the PC project. I had fought hard to get the new division's leaders to assign a top international program manager for the PC, located in Paris. Lack of leadership there was starting to impede the project. In exasperation, I wrote a memo to Bob King, my VP, saying my work, as part of the division in White Plains, was going for naught without leadership in Paris; also saying I was taking a vacation until something was decided. Four days later, Bob called to say they had chosen a new program manager.

Two weeks later, I was called to Paris to provide a status update to the new program manager and Kap Cassani, a senior VP and a Swiss citizen. During the meeting, Cassani told the executives in the room that they had too many Americans on the project.

I returned to the United States and immediately filed a request for transfer from the PC project. My time was up.

# THERAPY

I still don't know if I would have pulled the trigger.

I stare out the window watching a sullied gold leaf searching for a path to the ground. It swirls, tumbles, and lifts out of sight beyond the green plaster rim of the window. A few minutes later, it enters my view again, this time from a different angle, but again, loses its battle with the rising current determining its flight path.

Like me, I think. Disconnected from my tree, tossed about, carried aloft by circumstances beyond my control. Set adrift by unknown currents. A dingy old leaf, a tired body—both pitching in the wind.

The room is plain. The bed is a standard hospital issue, mattress bound as tight as a drum with starched sheets. For guests, there's a puke green plastic and metal chair—just like the one in my college dormitory room. Another utility chair sits by the door. A metal bedside table holds a box of tissues, a water glass with a flexible plastic straw, hand lotion, a 1940s desk light, and a paperback book with a red cover. A matching locker holds my blue suit, red and blue striped tie, knee-high socks, black shoes, white button-down shirt, and balled-up dirty underwear. When I checked the pockets in the suit this morning, there were no car keys, no pocketknife, no money, no billfold—just my dirty handkerchief. At first, I thought someone had stolen everything. After all, this is New York City. But the nurses told me they'd stored everything away for me—so they would be safe. I pondered the word, "they." The nurses probably meant to say, "So you'll be safe."

The tan tiled floor shines like glass. Some guy with a big machine polished it three times since I got here yesterday afternoon. This place is clean if nothing else.

I'm in the cardiac ward of St. Luke's Hospital—not the psychiatric ward as I expected. I guess Dr. Bernstein is trying to protect me from the stigma of having "psychiatric patient" on my medical records. Nice guy. Glad he thought of that. I know someone called my manager yesterday to say I was sick, but I don't think anyone said why.

"Hello, Grant. How are you feeling today?" Dr. Bernstein enters the room.

"Better. A bit calmer than yesterday," I reply, turning to face him.

He still reeks of pipe tobacco even in this no-smoking zone. He's taller and balder than I remember from yesterday. He wears the same ratty Harris Tweed coat, rumpled khaki pants, and unpolished loafers. His ironed and starched button-down shirt is the only evidence he didn't sleep in his clothes. I smile to myself, thinking he looks like something out of *One Flew Over the Cuckoo's Nest*, although in that case, he'd be wearing a white coat. But, this is no joke. I'm wondering what's going to happen next, but, strangely, don't feel very anxious about it. They gave me some gray pills last night and this morning; that probably took the edge off my fears.

"Do you feel like talking today?" he asks softly.

"I don't know, I'm pretty groggy."

"That's understandable. You've been through a lot," he says, as if trying to be sympathetic.

How does he know what I've been through? Especially when I'm not even sure. And I'm not sure I want to talk—to open up my feelings for the world to see—to show them what an idiot I am.

"I'm not sure I feel like talking," I say, knowing he'd stick around for 50 minutes, whether I talked or not. "I was pretty confused when they brought me here yesterday."

"Yes, I know. That's why I suggested we wait until today to talk."

His eyes watch me intensely as if trying to read my mind. Psychiatrists always take note of a patient's "affect." He's probably trying to measure mine, although I'm not exactly sure what an affect is.

"What shall we talk about?" I ask, struggling to sound cooperative.

"Anything that you want to."

"I don't know where to start."

My mind races, but I can't get it all together. Everything seems so jumbled up. It's like I've been rolling down a long hill for 20 years and just tumbled into this place. How can I talk about yesterday or last week without talking about my whole life? Where can I start? How can I ever explain?

Sensing my indecision, Dr. Bernstein says, "Why don't you tell me what happened on Saturday."

"I... I'm not sure I know what happened on Saturday. I mostly remember not being able to get on the plane."

"Start there if you want."

He sits in the visitor's chair and shuffles to get comfortable. He digs in his coat pocket, apparently looking for his pipe, then abruptly jerks the hand away as if remembering where he is. From my perch on the high bed, I can see the overhead light reflecting off his head. His brown eyes are intense, but his expression shows no emotion. I expect to see judgement, want to see compassion, but see only a blank face. Can I trust the person behind such a face? Yet, I sure to God need to talk to someone—anyone—who can help me untangle the contorted web of my life.

My back feels cold and I'm suddenly aware of my nakedness. I pull at the hospital gown to make sure everything is covered and adjust the sheet around my legs and bottom.

"Well… I was going on a business trip to Boca Raton. I took a taxi to the airport, picked up a paper, and drank a cup of coffee. A few pages into the paper, I started shaking, crying, couldn't think straight—I just froze. Couldn't get on the plane. Couldn't do anything. I must have sat there for an hour trying to get myself together. Then I found my way to the phone, called Sally and she brought me to you."

"What were you thinking?" he asked.

"Just a bunch of confusing stuff. How my life is a mess. Feeling all alone. Feeling trapped. A lot of crazy thoughts running around in my head."

"What happened before yesterday?"

"You mean Sunday… or Saturday?"

"Let's start with Saturday if you want."

I feel as if he's thrown back a black blanket from over my head. I want to forget Saturday—like it never happened. I tried to ignore it all day Sunday. Got up on Monday like it was any other workday, put on my conservative garb, and headed to the airport—the corporate manager ready to rock and roll.

He watches me hesitating and wondering what to say, but he says nothing. Just lets me stew in my thoughts.

I start speaking guardedly, searching for words, not wanting to tell him the whole story. But I bet Sally has already told him what happened. I can tell him the events, but can I tell him the real story? Especially since I don't understand the real story. Would I have gone through with it? Did some invisible hand reach down and save me? I began to tell him what happened…

It was like any other Saturday. Slept late. After commuting to New York all week, I'm always ready for a long sleep. I got up around ten, made some espresso, and ate some toast with strawberry jam.

Sally was working in the study when I came downstairs—probably on a script for one of this week's shows. After breakfast, I went to her office, leaned around the door and said 'hello,' but only got a grumble in response. So, I went to the living room to read. Got pretty absorbed in Oriana Fallaci's book, *A Man*.

About an hour later, Sally came out and said something. Startled, I looked up from the book. I said, "I'm sorry, I didn't understand you. I was absorbed in my book."

"Don't you ever listen to me?" she asked.

"Sorry. I just didn't understand."

"You sure didn't," she said, leaving the living room and back into her office. The slamming door shook the walls of the old house, sending her favorite fox-hunting scene crashing to the floor.

"I've never known how to deal with her tantrums, so I try to ignore them," I say to Dr. Bernstein.

"How did you feel?" he asks.

"Attacked. Unloved. Alone. Angry."

"Angry at whom?"

"At her, of course. Yet... Yet... I was also angry at myself for getting involved with her."

I rush ahead, continuing with the story before he can ask me to expand...

"I tried to read the book, but I couldn't focus on the quivering pages. I was shaking like a leaf. I threw down the book and left the room."

Dr. Bernstein interrupts. "How did you feel?" he asks.

"What do you mean, how did I feel? I just told you."

"Well, tell me again."

"Well, I felt angry, trapped... maybe guilty for getting into that situation."

"What situation?"

"Leaving my first wife and getting involved with her," I say in a low voice. "Can I go on with the story?"

"Sure," he says.

"Maybe I shouldn't have said that, because I can't remember what happened next. I don't know what I did after the book. I can't even remember what I had for lunch."

"What do you remember?"

"Just walking down toward the pond," I reply.

"Want to continue there?"

"OK... It was a cool day, so I went to the bedside table, got the Llama, an ammunition clip, put them in my jacket, and went out the back door and down the hill. I'd been to the pond before, but never past it. I headed straight for some swampy ground on the other side. I jumped from clod to clod to keep from getting my feet wet. It must have taken me five or ten minutes to work my way across the swamp and toward the woods."

"Go on."

"On the other side, I stopped to look back across the pond to the house. The place is about 100 years old, so the roof was starting to sag in the middle and the chimney leaned over like an old man with arthritis. The roof was so moldy I couldn't tell if the original color was green or not. The house looked peaceful, but, to me, it felt like a prison."

"Did Sally know you'd gone out?" he asks.

"Sally wasn't in sight. She must have still been working in the office. At least I was away from her moods and shouting."

"And then?"

"I turned and walked toward the woods," I say. "There were no paths, so I tried to work my way through blackberry bushes, wild roses, and poison ivy. Got my hands scratched and bloodied. I gave up and decided to sit down next to an old, gnarled oak tree."

"The ground was moist and soft… and so cold it made me shiver. Yet, I wasn't sure if the cold caused the shiver or something else."

"What else?" he asks.

"I felt nervous and shaky, but the smell of mildewed leaves made me think of hikes in the Blue Ridge, near where I grew up."

"Sounds peaceful."

"Sure, it was a tranquil scene, but my stomach was in knots… and felt like I was choking—like some invisible hand was grabbing my throat. I was thinking, 'how the hell did I get into this mess? Where can I go? I am in debt. Not one of my friends had the guts to call me after I got with Sally. My children won't even talk to me, for God's sake. Who can I talk to? Who gives a damn?'"

I'm talking faster now, trying to get to the end of the story.

"Then, a cold breeze shook the limbs of the big tree, sprinkling acorns all around me. A squirrel inched toward one of the acorns, but quickly ran away when he realized that I was a living person. How wrong he was."

"I reached into my jacket pocket and felt the 9 MM Llama I'd kept hidden in the bedside table. It had been close to my body for almost an hour, but the steel was cold. The serrated handle felt rough—hostile to my hand. Irritating. Unfriendly."

"I bought the Spanish automatic in Colorado to protect myself while camping alone in the mountains, but luckily, never had to use it. The Llama is like a Colt 45, only smaller. I got a sharpshooter medal in the Army with the 45 so I know how to shoot."

"From my other pocket, I pulled out the clip, fully stocked with eight new shells leftover from Colorado. I snapped it into place, pulled back the slide inserting the first round into the chamber."

I look at Dr. Bernstein, watching for a reaction. He stares, only stares.

No surprise, no concern. Like he's heard this story before. I rush to continue, almost like I'm telling a story about someone else.

"I put the pistol on my lap and looked around. There was a soft bed of leaves about ten steps in every direction. Another huge oak stood about 20 feet in front of me. I leaned my head back against my tree while my thoughts raced like a rat in a maze."

"I lifted the Llama and pointed it at the oak. I aimed at a burl and squeezed the trigger. Pow! My ears rang with the crack. A small hole appeared in the head-sized burl. A good clean shot."

"I looked at the tiny wisp of blue smoke wiggling from the barrel of the Llama. Oh crap, the Llama jammed! The slide is halfway back, not forward in the firing position and the shell casing wedged in the open chamber so tight that a second shot was impossible. I tried to pull the brass casing out with my fingers, but yikes! It was too hot to handle. For what seemed like ten minutes, I waited for it to cool. This damn, cheap Spanish pistol! "

"Even when it cooled, I couldn't get the casing out, so I opened my pocketknife to pry it loose. That worked, and I loaded another round. Then, I heard footsteps."

"'What are you doing?' Sally said, calmly."

"'I'm trying to fix this pistol,' I said.'"

"She eased the pistol from my hand, turned around, and heaved it into the pond. She paused, staring at me with intense, questioning eyes."

"'Come on. Let's have some coffee,' she said, taking my arm. And that was that."

"What do you mean?" Dr. Bernstein asks.

"The incident was over," I say.

"Really?"

"Yep."

"Tell me. How do you feel now?" Dr. Bernstein asks.

"Sort of washed out. Tired. Scared. Tiny. Insignificant. But I just want to sleep."

"Think you can rest quietly tonight?"

"Yeah, I think so."

"Good, then. I'll see you tomorrow."

"Sure," I say.

As the doctor leaves the room, I turn to look for another falling leaf outside the window.

# A CALMER ASSIGNMENT

The IBM corporate education group, located in temporary facilities on 42nd Street in Manhattan, had an elite team of experts aiming to create leading-edge manufacturing techniques across the company. The Manufacturing Technology Institute (MTI) provided month-long resident programs to engineers and managers from many sites across the world. After a short interview, Sam Korin, Manager of MTI appointed me as Senior Faculty Member. MTI was one of five such elements of the Corporate Technical Institute.

This was full circle, back to my earliest experience with education and training, It built on my technological and managerial experience. It also represented a significant break from all the turnarounds, new organizational development, and other high-stress jobs of the last 20 years.

Through good counseling and medications, I was feeling stable and productive. Knowing my professional background, some of my fellow instructors asked me to give guest lectures to their class groups. The learners gave us strongly favorable feedback on my work, which boosted my standing in the team and my own self-confidence.

The preparation and teaching work provided an opportunity to learn, reflect, and explore manufacturing systems in a thoughtful way. This was a pace unlike any other time in my career. Jake Ever, an expert in information systems, and Keith Gardiner, a recognized thought leader in manufacturing systems, and I became fast friends, while we formed creative new approaches to our course topics.

After completing my doctorate degree at Pace University in 1982, I also became an adjunct associate professor in the MBA program at the Pace School of Business, teaching courses in strategic management at their Wall Street campus. This was a comfortable role that required only one night a week of class time and relatively little outside preparation. My work at Pace complimented my course preparation at IBM.

These assignments provided a way to explore my interests while doing something important to the long-range interests of the company's people and its strategy. And—I am out of the conflict and line of fire at the company's central core. This would have felt "out of sight, out of mind," in my earlier career, but at this time, it felt refreshing.

About a year after my start at MTI, the whole operation, Corporate Technical Education, moved into a newly built, hi-tech education building in Thornwood, NY. The facility included a large auditorium, lodging facilities for attendees, workout rooms, classrooms equipped with the latest multimedia devices, a television control room to manage the extensive video transmission service, and two televised classrooms broadcasting to IBM locations around the country.

Whereas we used transparencies, flip charts, and old-fashioned paper handouts in our classes in our New York facilities, at Thornwood, we began to incorporate video and other audio-visual techniques. Video cameras in our special classrooms could zoom in on mechanical and electronic devices to record or show audiences the details of the technology about which we were teaching. Participants in advanced classrooms could give instructors detailed and immediate feedback from a touchpad on their table. We began to routinely incorporate short quizzes or surveys, so feedback was immediate and accurate, letting us know if students were understanding what we were trying to teach.

My colleagues and I were enthusiastic about the new facility and the opportunity to experiment with new ways of engaging with students. This was quite a contrast with my days of teaching in Compelo Tech where a piece of chalk and a few transparencies were the primary media.

Our instructional team worked in harmony with strong trust and respect. We discussed issues openly, spun new ideas every day, and enjoyed coffees and meals together. This was the salve I needed, a place to continue building my self-esteem and professionalism. Students liked my classes, and my colleagues praised my work.

The education department at Thornwood selected me to attend a week-long session at the Aspen Institute, a program with men and women from different professions and locations, including. Derek Bell, a noted Black American scholar, and his wife. Although rare for an IBM training event, I was able to take Sally.

We explored politics, Greek tragedies, social trends, and case studies, even chose parts and acted out *Antigone*, the famous Greek play. Sally is an intensive advocate for women's rights, a feminist. She is quick to detect even the smallest slights to the status of women. Sally challenged Derek Bell, an elegant spokesperson for civil rights for Black Americans, to consider that human rights for women might be a more important issue. The discussions put me in an awkward position, sometimes forcing me to decide whether to join my wife in her quest or join Derek Bell, whose arguments appealed to the truth of my legacy. Sally said I should have defended her more enthusiastically. This was becoming a theme. She often says I am not strong enough about feminism or other issues, while her stridency often embarrasses me.

Shortly after moving to Thornwood, Tony Tunisi, the Director of Corporate Technical Education, asked me to become Program Director of Technical Education Planning, responsible for developing strategies and curricula for the broad spectrum of education and training for engineers, scientists, information technologists, and other technical people. In addition, I would lead the unit that administered the satellite television studio and classes. Once again, I had been asked to start a new operation that had never existed before.

Often, when trainers plan new courses, they do a "needs analysis" by surveying potential learners or their leaders, asking "What kind of training do you need to help you be more effective in your work?" They typically use interviews, focus groups, and surveys. But the surveyed departments can only see only the training to help them now, not in the future. Their answers seldom reflect what they need to prepare them for the next technology or the next wave of new products.

By contrast, we review the latest company, product, and technology strategies and develop a comprehensive analysis of the needed skills and jobs required to produce future products, technologies, and services. This activity puts me once again at the forefront of leading-edge developments.

The job classification, "Program Director" is not as high a level in the corporate pay scales as my job classification before going to New Mexico. My current manager, of course, is not knowledgeable enough to explain why I was demoted when returning from New Mexico. And it is too late to fight that battle. I am happy enough to have found an interesting assignment, though not in the mainstream of the business. Professionally, this was a good option, an excellent platform to hone my academic and professional skills, while working with intellectual leaders from different fields. Our organization is respected across the industry for our innovative approaches to education and training and we are certainly at the leading edge of video delivery.

During my morning rounds one day, I head over to the video studio to see the classes going on that day and chat with my team members operating the advanced technology necessary for the classes.

As I step into the studio, Joe Birch, the lead fellow, says, "Hey Grant, they're ready to launch Challenger. Do you want to watch?"

"Sure. Let's put it on the big screen so anyone walking by in the hall can see through our big windows. Can we also project into the classrooms here and in the other locations?" I ask.

"We can do that," Joe answers. "Do you think the instructors will object?"

"Let's announce to the classes we're going to project the launch. I think everyone will appreciate it," I say.

In a few minutes, all our screens are focused on the rocket sitting on a launch pad at Kennedy Space Center. I went outside the studio to join other people who gathered in the hall to watch the launch.

Soon the Challenger blasts off, blowing out fumes like the snorts of an angry inverted bull.

We watch as the rocket ascends into the sky. But in just 73 seconds, the rocket disintegrates, emitting a furious multi-colored ball of smoke and gas with two cloud columns projecting into the sky above like the antennae of a massive insect.

Our eyes freeze. Our minds freeze. Our hearts freeze. None of us can speak, don't know what to say. Finally, someone whispers, "Oh my God," and we all turn to look at each other.

I suddenly remember everyone watching in our video classrooms has seen this tragedy, an event now forged into our memory. I step back into the studio to talk with our video team while considering if we need to say something to the assembled classes watching the video. We decide to trust each instructor to know how to work with his or her class group.

After a while, I return to my office to stare at the wall, trying to absorb what just happened. Soon other members of my team come in. Some had seen the event, others not. We talked about the astronauts: Michael J. Smith, Francis R. (Dick) Scobee, Ronald E. McNair, Ellison S. Onizuka, Sharon Christa McAuliffe, Gregory Jarvis, and Judith A. Resnik. Someone had a picture of the crew. They were suddenly part of our family.

# ESTHER

One of the most difficult leadership challenges occurred during my time at Thornwood. Here is the story…

I watched a tear roll softly down Esther's cheek as Tony Tunisi stepped to the podium, his well-groomed beard hardly betraying his taut expression.

"Good morning, everyone. I'm glad you could all make it and I know you have a busy day. But we have a few important announcements and thought we should come together to hear them.

"First of all, we're kicking off the 23rd class of Advanced Manufacturing Systems this week. Sam and his group have done a wonderful job in developing and delivering programs in advanced manufacturing. We're leading the world in this endeavor. Congratulations, Sam. I hope you have a great class group.

"Second, I want to announce that Joe Hartford has decided to retire. Joe has been with the company over 25 years and has built a great record of innovation and accomplishments. He established our first systems engineering program 12 years ago and built it to the premier program in the industry."

It's over. Joe is leaving, but with the usual honors afforded to long term employees. Is this justice?

I remembered six months ago, when this whole thing started.

"Are you OK? You've seemed a bit tense lately," I asked.

I'm not much of a morning person, but Esther and I decided we should meet early until we'd installed the new comprehensive education system in Thornwood, IBM's technical education center. Esther, with her department of professionals, was coordinating the project, installing the computers, network, software, and training everyone to use the system. It was a mind-boggling task requiring technical proficiency, smooth human relations, and, sometimes, guile.

I'd suggested the meetings when Esther and her department transferred to my group from another department, headed by Joe Hartford, one of my peers. Tony Tunisi, Director of Technical Education, our manager, felt Esther's activity fit better with my group than with Joe's. I welcomed the change, because the project looked challenging, and Esther and her team were highly regarded as professionals. Half of them had PhDs.

Joe Hartford, her previous manager, had been a key figure in the development of the company's software products. Tall, thin, and erect, with a military crew cut, Joe looked more like a Marine colonel than a corporate middle executive. Joe wasn't happy to see Esther's department transferred to me. He, too, liked the project and had worked with Esther before we all transferred to our center from New York a year ago. He took special interest in helping her move from her previous role as curriculum designer to Manager of Distance Education. In our meeting to discuss the transfer, Joe said, "Take good care of Esther. She has great potential as a manager, and she's a very special person."

"Oh, I'm OK, just a little nervous about our schedule," Esther replied.

Her intense blue eyes stood out in contrast to dark hair and skin. Esther was the essence of a corporate manager—confident, firm, creative, ambitious, and energetic. She came to work in a full wardrobe of navy blue and dark gray suits, heels to match, and silk blouses—the mark of a professional who was serious about her career and who knew how to impress the corporate hierarchy.

I watched her fidget in her chair. It wasn't unusual for her to be brimming with manic energy, bouncing from subject to subject in rapid fire sentences, but something wasn't right. Esther's agitation was increasing day to day, and I wasn't sure why.

"Let's talk about the schedule," Esther continued. "Yesterday, we released two modules with no difficulty. We ran a training session for two of the departments and the outlook looks good for the rest of the week."

"Then, why are you nervous?" I asked.

"Come on, Grant, you know me by now, always thinking something can go wrong."

"OK. I'll leave it alone. Get together tomorrow again? Let's talk then about how your people are doing," I commented.

"Sounds good. See you then," Esther offered, gathering up her papers.

Pondering her demeanor, I stared at the door after she left, then turned to other projects.

The next three day's meetings were routine, Esther's department was on top of the schedule and was enjoying good relations with user departments. I relaxed, knowing Esther had everything under control. I didn't have to worry about her project, so I focused my energy on other things.

The following Tuesday, Esther was visibly agitated.

"What's wrong?" I asked. "You're like a cat on a hot tin roof."

"It's nothing. Just me. Too much coffee this morning," she snapped, eyes flitting to me, the telephone, the miniature car on my credenza, the window, the door.

"Esther. What's going on?" I pressed.

"It's something I have to deal with. You can't help."

"Maybe I can. Tell me," I replied, trying to sound neutral—unthreatening. What is she worried about? Maybe she and her husband are having troubles. Who knows what goes on in people's private lives? I'd really like to know what's bugging her, but maybe she's right—I probably couldn't help.

"No, Grant. Really, it's my problem."

Exasperated, I said, "OK. I'm here. If I can help, let me know."

"Sure," she said, getting up to head out the door. "Have a good day."

On Wednesday morning, Debra, our department administrative manager, leaned into my office. "Helen Porter wants to see you as soon as possible. She says it's personal."

Dr. Helen Porter worked in Esther's department, carrying a major responsibility for developing advanced education programs. Helen had a PhD in Education, was assertive, bright, ambitious, and one of the few Black women with PhDs in the company.

At 10:00 am, Helen stepped into my office, glaring at me with fiery eyes.

"I just can't work with that woman anymore!" she blurted. "She's just too damn critical. Everything I do is wrong. She's trying to control every detail. What makes her think she's smart enough to run my part of the project? I didn't go through 20 years of school to be treated like a child."

An hour later in my office, I related the essence of the conversation to Esther.

"I couldn't figure out what Helen did to provoke you," I offered. "Didn't understand what the real issue was. Is she really behind schedule?"

"It's me," whispered Esther.

"What do you mean?" I asked. "You know, Esther, it's OK to keep your personal problems to yourself, but when they start to affect your work or your relationship with your people, then the problems become a work issue."

"It's been coming a long time. It's just gotten worse lately. I've been feeling edgy, tense, short-tempered, afraid. I hate to come to work in the morning," Esther said.

"What do you mean, 'afraid?'" I asked. "Are you afraid of failing?"

"No… No. That's not it at all. I'm just afraid."

"A… Afraid of what?" I pressed. What can she be afraid of? We work in a safe place. Our colleagues are friendly, congenial, even kind. We have some of the best working conditions in the world. Maybe she's just lost her self-confidence. Maybe she's got problems in her marriage and is afraid of losing her husband.

Esther sat silently. Glanced up at me, then back to the floor.

Finally, she said slowly. "I… I can't tell you."

"Why? Is it so personal? If so, you really don't have to tell me."

"It's business, it's personal, but I don't know how to deal with this. Can we talk later?"

"Sure, but are you going to be all right?" My God, what is going on? But what? Why can't she tell me? I thought she had confidence in me.

"It's Joe," she blurted, glancing at me.

"What do you mean, 'Joe?' Joe who?"

"Joe Hartford," she said.

"What about Joe?" I asked.

"He's been bothering me," Esther whispered. "He meets me every morning in the parking lot. He knows when I arrive and waits there for me."

She's talking a mile a minute now.

"And he calls me ten times a day to tell me how much he loves me. He tries to meet me in the cafeteria to eat lunch with me. I can't do anything without seeing his face. He's always there."

"My God, how long has this been going on?" I asked, hardly believing my ears.

Joe struck me as a somewhat formal guy who often talked about his wife and family. If anything, he seems overly preoccupied with propriety and company demeanor. This just didn't seem in character with the guy I knew. Yet, I really didn't know him well. We'd only been working together for two or three years, and he came from an entirely different division of the company.

"It… It started when we were still in New York," Esther continued.

"That's two years ago!" I said.

"Actually, more than that. It really began when Joe first recruited me from Government Systems Division. At first, I thought he was a kind, people-oriented manager who wanted to make sure his employees did well, but then it turned bizarre."

"Bizarre?"

"Yeah. He started leaving notes in my office. At first, they were innocent, like 'Happy Monday morning' or something like that. Then, when I went on a trip, he left a rose and a note that said, 'I missed you while you were gone.' Well, I thought he really values my work, although I'll admit the red rose threw me for a loop."

She continued, "But, later in the day, my worst fears were confirmed.

Joe came to my office with a big smile and asked me how I liked the rose, then he told me how lonely he was without me being around; he didn't miss my work, he missed me. Then there were the things..."

"The 'things?'"

"He started leaving gifts and mementoes in my desk drawers. An obscene statue of two people entangled together and stuff like that. He even left a note in my suitcase on top of my underwear after another one of my trips. After a while, I got too nervous to work," she said.

"My God!"

The more Esther told me, the worse it got. This was shocking—an unbelievable story. Yet, I knew Esther would never make up such a strange tale. What should we do? What's the solution to this?

"I was afraid to tell anyone. Joe is such a respected guy. I wasn't sure anyone would believe me," Esther said sadly, with teary eyes. "I was so happy when I was transferred to your group."

"I know. But it continued. He's still bothering you. We have to address this," I said.

"By the way, did you tell him how his actions were making you feel? That he was affecting your work?"

"Sure, but I don't think I was firm enough. I told him many times, but half-jokingly and with a smile."

"The next time he approaches you, I suggest you tell him in no uncertain terms."

"It'll be hard... he thinks we're still friends, but I'll do it. Grant, I feel better after talking about this, but I'm exhausted. Can we talk on Monday?"

"Sure, let's carve out some free time. I have a meeting at 9:00 am, but I'm going to cancel it. Want to meet at 8:00 as usual?"

* * *

Esther arrived in my office on Monday morning looking tired, red-eyed and carrying her briefcase and a duffel bag. We walked silently down the hall to the coffee machine together, put in our money, and drank the bitter fluid, hoping for a transfusion of energy.

She said quietly, "As usual, Joe was in the parking lot this morning. I told him I wanted him to leave me alone. He said he didn't know what I meant."

Back in the office, we evaluated our options, talking through how difficult this could get. Neither one of us knew of any other sexual harassment case in the company. Maybe this was a first. The thought scared us. How would top management deal with this? Nevertheless, we decided to talk to Tony Tunisi.

"Should we both go?" asked Esther.

"I should probably talk to him first," I said, not being a 100% sure of my answer. But he'll need to hear your story. Look, this might get rough. Once we begin this process, there's no backing up. And the going could get rough. People will want to know details, and they'll ask if you provoked Joe or cooperated with him."

"I know. But I'm ready," Esther said firmly. "Oh, by the way, look at this!" She dumped the contents of the duffle bag on my desk—notes, trinkets, a piece of jewelry, the statue, and a few other things.

"I don't think we have a choice. You can't go on working this way. We could transfer you to a different job or division, but then Joe would probably continue to harass someone else," I said. "I'll set up a time with Tony today. OK?"

Two hours later, I walked into Tony Tunisi's spacious office. I asked Tony's secretary to make sure we weren't interrupted and closed the door.

Tony was a PhD from MIT who'd developed a companywide reputation for his brilliant engineering mind.

"What's up?" he asked with a smile.

"Got something sensitive to talk about. I made sure you had the time and that we wouldn't be interrupted," I said grimly.

"Sounds serious."

"Could be."

Without preliminaries, while Tony listened in shocked disbelief, I explained how, after weeks of wondering and watching, Esther had finally explained what was bothering her. I related her story without, at first, revealing the identity of her harasser.

"She's a beautiful woman. I can see how someone would be attracted to her. Do you think she invited this?" he asked.

"No. She didn't provoke it."

"My God, that's terrible!" Tony exclaimed. "I'm surprised she's been able to work. Who… who the hell would do something like that?"

"Uh… Uh… You might not like this. It's Joe," I stuttered.

"Joe!"

"Yeah. Joe. Joe Hartford," I said softly.

"What! How can that be? That guy's as straight as an arrow. He's happily married. Has a grown daughter. Joe! I can't believe it. Are you sure Esther didn't start this?"

"I'm sure. You should talk to her to see for yourself."

"Yeah! Yeah! You betcha! I can't believe this. Joe! Could he be that stupid? To do this on the job?"

Both of us had known company employees who'd had affairs, but romance was not acceptable on the job or with people who reported to you.

By four 4:00 pm, I felt as if I'd worked a week. My mouth was the Sahara, my eyes felt like I'd been in a sandstorm, and the damn oxford cloth shirt was wearing a ridge in my neck. I was standing at the coffee machine, loosening my tie when Esther returned from her meeting with Tony. Her pace and manner seemed relaxed and her expression inscrutable

"How'd it go?" I asked, not knowing what to expect.

"Not bad, I think. Although I'm not so sure he believes me."

"Why? Did you show him the stuff?"

She smiled, "Yeah. In fact, he asked if he could keep it. I took pictures of the stuff and made a list of every item before I brought the bag down here. I didn't make a copy of the notes. Maybe I should've."

"It should be all right. Tony is a solid guy."

"He told me to tell you to call him right away."

Back in the office, I called Tony. He said he believed Esther's story but found it incredible that a guy like Joe would do the things she described. We chatted about how it's hard to tell what goes on in the inner recesses of a person's mind, then turned to what to do next. We decided to meet with Harry Burton, the Personnel Director, as the next step. Tony felt he himself should be the one to confront Joe, but he wanted to make sure he had the backing of Personnel and potentially upper management before proceeding.

The next morning, we were in Harry Burton's office. Harry had the build of a defensive guard for the New York Giants, but one who had long gone off his training diet. He still retained the requisite 280 pounds, but his muscles had long ago turned soft. On him, the corporate blue suit and striped tie resembled a waterbed with a blue and white cover. Harry was a career personnel man—he'd spent his whole career recruiting, counseling, designing benefit plans, and administering the company's personnel policies. He knew the ropes. He also knew Joe and Esther.

"My God, Joe Hartford! And Esther! Joe should know better than this. Two years! Why the hell did Esther put up with it so long? Are you sure she didn't encourage him?" Harry pressed.

Tony and I reiterated our confidence in Esther's story.

Harry went on. "Look, we've got to get Joe's side of this—and fast. He's a director, by God. We can't just dismiss him out of hand. And I'd better let corporate know about this."

Soon we were being drilled by a couple of Corporate Personnel's investigators.

Harry Rickles, short, with swept back hair, and a pockmarked face, scowled. "What is this woman like? Is she flirtatious?"

"No, she's a top-performing professional and a good manager," I replied. "Sure, she's good looking… but…" I answered.

"Is she ambitious?" he continued.

I answered again, "Well… like all of us, she wants to advance in the company, but I don't think she'd use flirtation as a way to move ahead."

What is this son of a bitch trying to do? Indict Esther? Does he know Joe? Why didn't he ask about Joe first?

My question was answered quickly. Harry shot back, "I know Joe Hartford, and I don't think he'd do something like this. He must have been provoked—or at least encouraged. And, if she hated this, why did she wait two years to say something?"

"She was scared," I said confidently.

"Scared of what? Joe's not a violent man," Harry scowled.

"Come on, Harry. Joe was once her boss," Tony said. "She was concerned about her career."

I wanted to ask why Corporate Personnel was defending the assailant rather than the victim, but I decided not to press that point.

I said, "I know it's hard to believe Joe did this, but we have notes and some pretty obscene statuettes as evidence."

Tony jumped in, "I've talked to Esther, and I'm confident she's telling the truth. Plus, she's scared to death. I don't know how she's been working as well as she has."

It seemed like we went over and over the story five or six times, almost as if Harry was trying to remember every detail. He took meticulous notes on a legal-sized yellow pad in handwriting I thought he'd never be able to read, all the time wearing a pained expression on his face. His colleague, a younger guy named Mark something, sat silently at the end of the conference table, like an apprentice watching the master.

"Go ahead and talk to Joe and let us know what happens. As far as I know, this is our first case involving someone at a director level."

Later, I sat at my desk, trying to concentrate on the day's mail, shuffling the papers over and over, looking at my watch, and waiting for the phone to ring. Damn, it's 4:20 pm. Tony's meeting with Joe started at 3:00. What can be taking so long? We didn't even talk about what the company might do with Joe. That means more meetings. More uncertainty. But Harry and the corporate personnel people wanted to get Joe's side of the story before deciding what to do.

Esther burst through the door. "Grant, I just can't do this! What if he gets fired? What if he gets angry? Will he ever leave me alone? What will people think? I don't want to be transferred. I like my job. He's a director—they'll never move him."

I tried to assure her everything would be all right. We talked quietly for a long time. The phone rang, and I whirled to the credenza. It was Tony. He said Joe had initially denied everything but demurred when Tony offered to show him the notes, the presents, and the mementoes. Yet, he acted surprised that Esther didn't like his affections. Eventually, Tony told him such actions were inappropriate toward an employee, even if she didn't overtly object. Finally, the conversation turned to what would be done next. Joe didn't want his wife to know, and he didn't want people in the company to know about the incident. Tony told him he could lose his job, but he wanted to hear Joe's side before deciding.

"What was his demeanor?" I asked.

"He was defiant in the beginning, then he got angry, but at the end he was sulking," Tony replied. "He's in a state of shock."

A week later, at the all-hands meeting in our auditorium, Tony stepped to the stage, leaned into the microphone, and, after a few other announcements, said, "Thanks for coming out on such short notice. I just wanted to announce that after a long and distinguished career in the company, Joe Hartford has decided to take early retirement to pursue a new path in a university. As of Monday, Joe will become Professor of Information Systems at Bowman State University. We'll miss him, but our loss is the University's gain. I'm sure many students will benefit from Joe's extensive knowledge of computers and software. We'll miss you, Joe."

No warning to others. No signal that Joe did something wrong. No lesson to other managers. A simple acceleration of Joe's time schedule. He always wanted to go teach. We just helped him do it faster. We saved his face. We saved the company's face. But what about Esther? I watched her staring aimlessly at the stage. What now? I wanted to read her mind.

I also wanted to read Joe's mind. Is he some sort of pervert? Or is this just some guy trying to cure the loneliness of his mid-life crisis? Something many of us felt but did not act upon. Whatever he is, I'm happy he's gone. And I am disappointed at our management's lack of courage.

# RETIREMENT

12 of us are seated around the walnut conference table where we had discussed strategy and curriculum for hours over the last two years. But this day is different. It's my last day at IBM, my retirement party. Some party. No one seems happy to see me go. On the other hand, that's not surprising because these are ten of my closest associates in the company, some of whom have been companions over my multiple jobs here at Thornwood and at other locations: Frank Contey, who could take one of my ideas and turn it into a working project, Mary Lou Michelini, once my assistant, now a highly proficient computer programmer, Don McCoy, my salty pragmatic advisor who knew all the nuances of managing difficult people, and Sally, my wife, who looks as if she would rather be somewhere else. Looking at the people around the table, I realize I am closer to most of them than to my own wife, who doesn't give a damn what my last 30 years at the corporation were like.

Pictures of IBM computers line the walls, the 650 MDDPM, the 1401, the 7070, the System 360, the Personal Computer. Each one occupies a node in my memory; stories wrapped in squared off angles of the company's expert branding team. Damn. I grew up with these things. Like an X-ray, their internal circuits reveal struggles, conflicts, incisions, and ultimate success. In the early days of the 650, Olin Lilly, a technician, was the only person in manufacturing who totally understood the machine's anatomy. What would he think about these latest monsters with millions of times as much computing power? What would he think of the company that once put its people first, to the one today struggling with market share and profitability?

This event symbolizes how the company has changed since I began my career. I remember the days when retirement was a big celebration at the company. Whole departments of 30 or more people were invited for a festive lunch in an upscale restaurant, sometimes including entertainment. The location's General Manager usually spoke to honor the retiree, and often brought a check. In addition, the company sponsored big annual luncheons with hundreds of people to honor all retirees of the year.

Like other such events today, the company allowed me to invite ten people, not including me and my wife to a lunch of poached salmon in one of our regular conference rooms with an ambiance of white boards, easel stands, overhead projector, and standard gray walls. There are many other people whom I would like to have thanked for all their support over the years. I should write each person a note, but I'm simply too tired of this place to do it.

IBM in 1987 is far from the company I joined in 1957. John Akers, IBM's current Chairman said IBM's goals are: to enhance customer relationships, to be the leader in products and services—excelling in quality and innovation, to grow with the industry; to be the most efficient, and to sustain profitability, which funds growth. How sad, how ordinary. IBM is now just another big, bureaucratic company, owing, I think, to the legacy of Frank Cary and to the US Justice Department's antitrust suit. The principle, "Respect for the Individual," so prominent in the early days is absent from Akers' list.

The company is going all out to reduce employees. I decided to forego a possible promotion to accept an early retirement option, also enhanced by IBM's program to provide faculty members to certain colleges and universities. This fall, I will join the University of Bridgeport as Associate Professor of Engineering and Associate Provost.

And another incident demonstrated another possible career path. One day, I received a call from an executive at ITT, another large corporation in New York City, asking me to help them audit one of their key business and technology strategies. I responded with interest but expressed doubt that IBM would approve such a project. Nevertheless, I showed Sam Korin, our manager, to find out if the company would approve. A few days later, he told me, to my surprise, the executives had no problem with the venture.

After spending several IBM vacation days with ITT over the next four weeks, we met at their headquarters to review my report. Everyone in the meeting praised the results and gave me big applause. Walking down Fifth Avenue toward Grand Central, I thought, "Damn, that felt good. That's what I should be doing all the time." It confirmed my sense of direction.

Now, at my retirement luncheon, Tony rises to address our small group. "Grant has done a great job… *blah… blah… blah.*"

Tony and I had worked well together. He was an authentic intellectual with strong personal and professional values. But he hated conflict and I often became his executer on a few tough projects. Toughness is not my strength, either, but my strong determination often boosts my courage. Tony wanted me to stay at the company and offered me a promotion in the planned organization change. But that option seemed like more of the same, not the change I needed.

When Tony finished, I stood to say my piece, looking in the eyes of each person around the table, telling a story about our work together. The company I loved is long gone. Politicians often say, I didn't leave my party, my party left me. That phrase accurately summarizes my feelings about IBM. I certainly changed over the 30 years, but still hold Thomas Watson, Jr's core values: respect for the individual, excellence in everything we do, top service to the customer. The company lost those along the way. I saw disrespect from Frank Cary. Saw the company sacrifice honesty for the sake of PR about the salary plan. Saw how they failed to recognize the exceptional success of Don Estridge's leadership of the PC program. The company was heading into difficult times, and it made me sad.

I return to my office to get two file boxes of my personal items, stopping to say a few personal words to each person, said with my tears and theirs.

I sit at my personal computer, which was filled with ideas and files accumulated over the past several years. In true IBM fashion, no one asked me for the files, although I offered to transfer them. I open the computer and type "Erase C:*.*," the instruction to erase the hard disk. I am getting the hell out of here.

# THE UNIVERSITY

We are gathered in the dining room of President Janet Greenwood's house on the campus of the University of Bridgeport, waiting for her to arrive at our staff meeting. Arriving here after being President of Longwood College in Virginia, she spent $100,000 renovating this historic house to suit her tastes.

Freshly starched tablecloths cover the table around which we are seated, six sterling silver candlesticks with new 12-inch pink candles sit in a precise row, three on each side of a vase of freshly cut flowers. Crystal wine and water glasses grace each place setting of fine china. There are three forks on the left side of my plate, and I am thinking, "Start from the outside. Salad, main course, dessert. A seven-course lunch. What the hell?"

Janet Greenwood finds her seat at the head of the table, followed closely into the room by the Black woman, who accompanied her from Virginia, bringing a tray of soup cups. I silently squirm in my seat seeing this woman in a subservient position. Has she always been Greenwood's maid? Who pays her? Greenwood does not introduce her, does not acknowledge her to our group.

After a few words to introduce the meeting, Greenwood distributes the agenda for our meeting of the top officers of the University. I sit across from Ed Eigel, the Provost to whom I report with the deans, CFO, and others at their respective places around the table. The first item on the agenda is the 1988 budget deficit.

Damn! Here we are, in the elegant setting, discussing how deep in the red we're going to be next year. This is crazy. Opening the discussion, Greenwood says all of us are going to experience a budget cut. Ed Eigel and I stare at each other. He knows, with my industrial experience, this must seem like an insane asylum.

Next, Greenwood explains how she intends to upgrade the university's obsolete information technology system, starting with the financial system. During the discussion, I express the need to maintain parallel systems to make sure all data are preserved and all transactions can be captured while the change is taking place. I suggest starting the IT conversion in other departments first might be a more prudent strategy.

Greenwood says, "That may be the way they do it in business, but that is not the way we do it in academia."

I wince.

\* \* \*

Janet Greenwood and I started at the university on the same day. The previous president, who hired me, retired. During my first visit to her office, it was comforting to see she and I had read the same books about organizational behavior, economics, and public affairs. But as time went on, I concluded that I must have reminded her of her ex-husband, if she had one. She wore hostility on her sleeve, not just for me, but also for other leaders.

I came to the university under an IBM program where the company would pay half my university salary for a period of two years, a good deal for the institution. UB appointed me Associate Provost and gave me a faculty position as tenured Associate Professor of Engineering Management. In addition, I was appointed Director of the Connecticut Technology Institute (CTI), an organization designed to promote small businesses in Connecticut, and to help students become more entrepreneurial.

The Institute (CTI) was similar to the function we started in the late seventies at the University of New Mexico. We had available grant funds, so I hired a small staff and set to work sponsoring seminars and other programs for small businesses around the state.

Our unit was also responsible for administering a federal grant for over $3,000,000 to erect an annex to the engineering building, thanks to Senator Lowell Weicker. Because of my low confidence in the university's accounting system, especially with Greenwood's ambitions for the financial information systems, I assigned one of my team members to independently keep account of all monetary transactions. Our unit was thriving despite the institution's larger problems.

Just before beginning my term at UB, Sally and I bought a small white house in the town of Bridgewater, reasonably good commuting distance from Bridgeport, the site of my university job. I immediately joined the local Democratic party committee, which helped me quickly integrate into the community. Our house was less than a mile from the local horse stable, so Sally was able to purchase a horse and join the Fairfield County Hounds, the fox hunting club, made up of members from the surrounding communities and from New York City. Almost every weekend, the club chased foxes or the scent thereof all around the hills and valleys of the farmlands.

Bill Stuart, a horse trader, chief selectman of the town government, president of the Democratic Committee, owner of the stables, was also the titular leader of the fox hunting club. Bill with his balding head, narrow mustache and 5'5" frame was the little king of the town, having his finger in everything going on.

Actually, Bridgewater was more akin to a village than a town, having one street with a country store, red brick town office, two churches, one of which must be Congregational according to New England tradition, and a variety of colonial houses. But, in Connecticut, a town is a form of government for a given geographical region. In this case, the Town of Bridgewater was the smallest such in Connecticut.

Moving to Bridgewater helped overcome my sense of isolation. The active political committee became a source of friends and colleagues. I knew how the local town-meeting governments worked. Public meetings and town meetings, often raucous, were how the community voted on the town government's budget and tax rate for the coming fiscal year. Bill Stuart, as First Selectman, asked me to be the moderator for several of the town meetings of over 100 local residents.

I also became the public address announcer for the annual country fair. I spoke over a super-loud public address system, describing contestants and winners of livestock competitions, sheepdog demonstrations, wagon pulls, and whatever came along. After a while, everyone in the small town knew me or my voice.

# HAWAII

Sally and I kept two homes, one in New York City and the other in Connecticut. Since New York was the center of Sally's career, that became her primary residence, whereas, after my retirement and migration into consulting, Connecticut was my hangout. Weekends and occasional nights became our together time.

Sally loved exotic vacations. One night, she suggested finding a horseback riding venture in Hawaii. Within a couple of days, she had scheduled the two of us for a guided tour of Molokai, Hawaii, had purchased the plane tickets, and announced we'd be leaving in two weeks.

Good grief, I thought. We're going to spend a week on horseback when I don't know anything about riding. The thought of sore muscles and runaway horses clouded my brain.

"This should be fun," Sally said. "We can see sights not accessible by foot or car. Isn't this exciting."

"Sure," I said, faking enthusiasm.

The next day found me at the local horse stable.

"I need some horseback riding lessons starting today," I said.

"How about at three this afternoon?" Joanna, the manager, said. "Brenda, one of our best instructors can work with you. Have you ever ridden before?"

"Not much, but we're going on a weeklong excursion in two weeks, and I have to learn by then."

Brenda and I started our daily lessons at three.

In our final lesson, I said to Brenda, "Let's talk about all the 'what-ifs.' If the horse bucks, runs away, bites—or whatever."

Brenda walked me through a series of emergency procedures: how to dismount if needed, how to control an unruly animal, how to deal with a runaway, how to detect danger. At the end of our time together, my confidence about horses was better, but not great.

Upon arriving in Honolulu, we looked for the small airline we'd booked to take us to Molokai, which was just ten miles wide and 38 miles long, Hawaii's fifth largest island. The attendant asked us to wait a few minutes and the pilot would be with us.

What? The pilot will be with us. What kind of airline is this?

"Good afternoon," says a voice heading toward us.

I look around to see a thirty-something fellow with a baseball hat and a young boy, probably around eight or ten.

"So, you're the people going to Molokai?" the man asks.

"Yes," Sally says, looking as puzzled as I feel.

"Well, we're going to fly you and show you some of the most beautiful sights in the world. Follow me."

Ugh, I thought. We're going to be flying with a 30-year-old pilot and a ten-year-old co-pilot.

Soon, we were tucked in the back seats of a four person Cessna and taxiing down the runway to fly the 60 miles of ocean to Molokai, an island with around 7,000 mostly native people.

"Thought I'd show you some of the sights on the way," the pilot says as he moves to a lower altitude flying next to cliffs bordering the ocean like monuments to the native gods of Hawaii.

Circling the island, he banks, taking us up a fjord-like valley covered by jungle foliage that is punctuated by a stream that seemed to fall 1,000 feet into the valley below. Wow, we could never have experienced this in a commercial airliner.

Turning to Sally, I asked, "Did you plan this?"

"No, it's a complete surprise. I thought we were getting a commercial flight as part of the travel package. This is fantastic."

* * *

Bright and early the next morning, we are in our riding clothes, jeans, and L.L. Bean shirts. Our horseback riding guide meets us in the lobby of the hotel. She's about four inches shorter than Sally, with hair she forgot to comb this morning, dressed in jeans and a blue flannel shirt. Similar to the pilot, she is not native.

"Hi, I'm Susan. I'll be your guide for the tour," she says.

"How many other people are there going to be?" I ask, expecting six or eight.

"Just you two," she says. "It will be just the three of us. We have some good horses for you."

I don't know whether to be scared or pleased. I could fade into a group, perhaps hiding my amateurish riding abilities, but now there is no place to hide.

Every day, we trek out to terrain like I've never seen along the cliffs overlooking the sea, which triggered my fears that the horse might not know better than jump into the sea, slowly riding across a vast plain with grass up to my stirrups, up and down narrow trails overlooking rushing mountain streams.

On the fourth day, I am feeling comfortable in the saddle on a horse that seems to recognize me in the mornings. The sun is low in the eastern sky, and we are on a relatively flat gravel road, with a bank on the left, and a rock wall on the right, high in the island landscape. I'm wondering who built the wall and why it is here in this place. Sally and Susan are a few yards in front of me, horses walking slowly while we enjoy the vistas of Hawaii, the big island across the water. I, too, am relaxed, absorbing the tranquil views.

Boom. Suddenly my horse kicks up his rear legs, throwing me forward. I dropped the reins, so wrap my arms around his neck, holding on for dear life, as we gallop about 20 miles an hour past Sally and Susan. My head is pounding against the horse's neck in cadence with his strides. There is no room to dismount because of the rock wall and bank. What should I do? The island's edge is ten miles away, will he finally stop there?

Remembering Brenda's lessons, I reach out, finally finding one of the reins, tugging on it until the horse finally decides to stop. He's panting, and I am panting harder.

Sally and Susan arrive a few minutes after.

"What happened?" asks Sally.

I take a few minutes to catch my breath. "I don't know. He just bucked suddenly."

"Probably a bee," says Susan. "Sometimes that happens."

*Thank goodness for Brenda*, I think.

We continued enjoying the scenery and tranquility of Molokai for the next three uneventful days. But the runaway horse will be my most compelling memory.

Strange, though. Sally seemed more concerned about my riding ability than my own safety. There were no comments like, "I'm glad you're OK," or "I was worried about you." Maybe I was just some amateur on a runaway horse.

* * *

Sally likes upscale places, upscale things, upscale events. She gave my mother in Virginia a beautiful Tiffany porcelain tea set, but Mom couldn't find a place safe enough to store it. No one would actually use such a thing for tea, would they?

The television industry is a dog-eat-dog culture, different from my everyday work world. Our relationship is, in many ways, the flip side of my relationship with Joyce. Joyce saw me as the striver, always focused on work, struggling to climb the corporate ladder, whereas she was domestic. Sally seems out to change the world, whereas I am working in a quiet backwater. And, clearly, she sees me as a person with lesser intellect. Her photographic memory is a reward and a curse. She can read a full-page script one time, then say it word-for-word to the camera. She also plays back my arguments word-for-word whenever we have a dispute or difference of opinion. Of course, I have no idea if those were the words I used or not.

When she comes on strong, I tend to close down, which, of course, infuriates her more. I've read that psychologists say silence is just another way of exercising intimidation. Perhaps. But, as before in my life, I don't know how to deal with her outbursts that seem to come out of the blue or are triggered by some thought about her father or some other guy.

Perhaps I need to be more sympathetic, more kind, more understanding. I talk to Dr. Bernstein about this, but he usually asks how I feel rather than offering ways for me to interact. So more and more I find solace alone in Connecticut, with quiet time to read and contemplate. I am in this strange suspension, not knowing where I'm heading.

There are no neighbors close to our rental house. Sally has some colleagues in New York, but the television people are not my type. When Joyce and I separated, there was not a single person in whom I could confide. Now, a few years later, that is still a problem. Sally and I talk, but mostly about her challenges or issues; seldom about my hopes, dreams—as if I have any. But I am stable, can work, can think straight, and can take care of myself. That is good news.

# STICKING A TOE
# IN POLITICS

As a result of my work in the community, the local Democratic committee asked me to run for the Connecticut House of Representatives in our sixty-ninth district, a district with a Republican incumbent. I was wavering, not having any experience with being a candidate, and wondering how much a campaign would cost. But Bill Stuart or one of his cronies had a reporter from a local newspaper surprise me with an interview. When the call came at my desk at the university, I gave vague answers to the reporter's questions, trying to avoid being pinned down. It didn't work. By the end of the interview, I had announced my candidacy for the 69th district and was off and running.

I quickly called Sally to tell her the results. She was not just supportive, but enthusiastic.

"This will take a lot of time," I said.

"That's OK. You can do it," she replied.

Janet Greenwood, however, was chagrined. She initially agreed to my candidacy and that my work at the university would be unencumbered. But, when actually having to confront the decision, she was not pleased. Yet, my competent staff at the Connecticut Technology Institute was strongly supportive and agreed we could carry out our programs as planned.

I formed a campaign team from members of the Democratic Committee and others from the community. Rick Boswell, a person I knew well, became my campaign manager and Bill Stuart became a team member. They were two people who knew the territory of our district. It was an uphill battle to unseat an incumbent in a Republican district, but we started working with wild abandon, asking for contributions, organizing fundraisers, and developing policy positions.

It was not easy to ask people for money, but I soon learned if a person gave you a contribution, even one dollar, you were probably also getting their vote. But I felt very much at ease developing policy positions and discussing issues with potential voters. Hearing what people had to say about their lives and concerns was important to me, and people reacted well to my interest in them.

Person-to-person campaigning was the way to get votes in the district. During the six months of the campaign, I knocked on over 2,000 doors, meeting over twice that number of people. The vast majority of people were friendly and interested in the issues. I was chased by only one dog and had only one person slam a door in my face; "I don't talk to liberals," he said. Strange reaction from an elderly man who clearly was on social security.

Along with other candidates, I was invited to Hartford to meet Governor William O'Neill. He asked me about the opinions I was hearing on the campaign trail and for my suggestions for his priorities. I expected a symbolic visit, but instead, had a good discussion of current Connecticut issues.

One of those issues was gun control. There was a bill being considered in the legislature that would require all gun owners to carry their permit anytime they traveled with a gun in their car. This seemed simple logic for me, but gun owners were resisting.

During a debate with Arthur O'Neill, my opponent, currently the representative from the 69th district and not a relative of the governor, he stated his strong opposition to the gun permit bill.

I said, "I think people should carry their permit and leave the gun locked in a safe." That drew a huge round of applause and laughter from the audience.

A coalition of unions in Waterbury asked me to address their Saturday afternoon meeting for the possibility they might endorse me. I stepped into a room of about 100 people drinking beer and smoking.

A guy twice my size with frazzled thin hair, and needing a shave, offered me his hand, a hand so thick my fingers hardly enclosed it.

"Glad to meet you. I'm the chair of this gang," he said.

The chair introduced me, and I stood looking at a sea of skeptical faces.

I gave a ten-minute stump speech, then held my breath. At least ten hands went up. Smiling, I motioned to one of the questioners.

"What do you think about the state of unions in the state?" he asks.

After I answered questions for about 30 minutes, the chair came up, asked for one more question, thanked me for coming, and walked with me to the door.

"We'll be discussing your responses and I'll let you know in a couple of days where we stand," he said, smiling.

Two days later a letter arrived telling me that the unions had endorsed my candidacy. Imagine that. An ex-IBM executive receiving a union endorsement. That might be one for the record books.

Governor Michael Dukakis ran for president, and Joe Lieberman for senate. Joe Lieberman and I shared the stage in several meetings in our district. Joe won his race against Lowell Weicker, the incumbent, but, in spite of hard work, I lost mine.

It's tough to lose, even if one expects it. I knew the chances of winning were slim, yet it seemed like a worthy cause. Losing did not trigger old insecurities. I felt self-confident all through the campaign, learned to speak with confidence, and how to organize a group of volunteers. I had the opportunity to talk about important issues with thousands of people, a rare occasion in one's life. We did OK.

Sally was a good supporter throughout the effort. She joined me at important events, occasionally speaking up to support my positions, giving positive advice several times.

But Rick Boswell and Bill Stuart dropped off the team during the last month of the campaign. "Why?" I asked, but neither would explain. Their timing was suspect because a week before their resignation, I publicly supported a bill to help protect women in domestic violence cases.

I continued my work at the University of Bridgeport after my election loss, but the future of the institution looked bleak. Budget deficits were deepening as were the divisions among the top leadership team. Although I held a tenured faculty position, I decided to resign at the end of my two-year term, giving me the space to move into full-time consulting.

# PRAGUE IN 1991

Bill Weimer, a colleague from IBM, and I started our company after having worked together in IBM corporate education. We developed a warm and collegial relationship while sharing an interest in good books, education, politics, and cultures. Bill spent three years in Brussels as his last assignment at IBM, and he seems to know every good restaurant there and in Paris. We both left IBM about the same time, then started a small company to consult in education, training, and international project management. We enjoyed some exciting projects in Italy and Czechoslovakia, the latter project soon after the iron curtain fell in 1989.

Through Bill Weimer's European contacts, we landed an assignment to teach a seminar on international project management at the Czech Technical University in Prague, Czechoslovakia, one of the oldest and well-known technical universities in all of Europe. Bill also asked me to teach a course in Verona, Italy on the way back from Prague.

We arrived in Prague just over a year after Russian troops left the country in July 1991. I had no idea what to expect on my first visit to an East European country. Surprisingly, we required no special visa to enter. Not only was that easy, but the immigration people at the airport greeted us with big smiles as if we were long-lost friends.

Sally, after learning about our project, decided to join me on the trip. We spent two nights in Paris on the way to Prague in an upscale hotel she chose. It was not the Ritz, but the room was decorated in modern European style and had an elegant bathroom. In Prague, the host university had arranged our accommodations in one of their facilities I assumed was a student dormitory.

Our taxi delivered us to the door of a classic building that could have been the original facility at the university's founding in 1707. It has ten-foot-high, arched windows forming the ground floor and two additional floors of rectangular windows topped by a facsimile of the architect's eyebrows.

We pick a door, step inside to see a man in a dark suit seated at a small desk. He looks up at us and heads to us with a big smile.

"You must be Dr. Tate. Welcome to our university," he says with almost no accent.

"Yes, and this is my wife," I reply.

"I'll show you your room," he says. "Let me help you with your bags."

We go up a flight of stairs and down a hall with endless doors. We stop at one. The man inserts a key and welcomes us inside.

We step in to see two cots covered with brown wool blankets, a sink like my mother had in the laundry room, a window with no drapes or shades, a tile floor with no rug of any kind, one overhead light, and a small door to a bathroom.

The man shows us how to turn on the light, then offers to show us the bathroom. I was relieved to see a normal toilet and small sink, not one of those French stand-up facilities with an open hole. A stand-up shower with no curtain stood in the corner.

He hands me the key, saying, "Have a nice stay here in Prague."

I place our bags on one of the cots, turn to Sally and say, "Do you see a place to hang our clothes?"

"This place is horrible! I'm not going to stay here," she says. "How can you allow them to treat us this way?"

"They've been under communist rule for years. I'm just thankful they have a place to put us up," I reply.

"This is a hell hole. I'm not going to stay here."

"I'm not going to insult our hosts by complaining about the facilities," I say.

"There you go again, unwilling to support my needs."

"It's only for three nights, we can survive this," I say.

"Well, you might, but I won't," she says, stepping out the door. "I'm looking for a telephone."

I find a hook, unpack my bag, hanging up my suit hoping the wrinkles will fall out during the night.

After 15 or 20 minutes, Sally is back.

"I'm leaving in the morning on an early plane," she says.

"Where are you going?" I ask.

"Back to New York. Where else?"

"Our workshop starts at 9:00 am, and I have to get a good night's sleep. Hope you have a good trip home," I say.

The next morning, I leave for our workshop in a near-by building, knowing they would have coffee and snacks waiting for us. In the midst of the room discussion, I had forgotten to look up Bill Weimer to confirm my arrival. Nevertheless, he greets me with a big smile when I step into the seminar room.

"The guy at the desk told me you two had arrived," Bill says.

"Yes, two arrived, one left," I say with a sly grin.

"What do you mean?" he asks.

"Sally couldn't take the room, so she's heading back to the States. After experiencing an upscale hotel in Paris, she couldn't deal with real life in Prague," I reply.

"Oh. So sorry."

"It's OK. We'll actually have more freedom now," I reply, affirming how relieved I feel. Bill and I can spend whatever time it takes conducting our seminar, hanging out with the participants, exploring the historic city, staying out late, getting to know people—all without me having to worry about pleasing Sally, attending to her tastes, enduring her critiques, adjusting to her schedules. And—I can sleep soundly each night, knowing our seminar is going well.

* * *

Sally's behavior reminded me of a similar situation in Nashville when I took Mom and Aunt Ruth there for a special vacation. Aunt Ruth, Dad's sister, has been one of my closest confidants ever since childhood—in many ways, closer than my own mother. She spent much of her life around Washington, DC, and she always gave me the benefits of her life experiences. During one of our discussions, she said, "I've always wanted to go to Nashville." Soon after, I scheduled a trip with Ruth and my mother to visit the Grand ole Opry and other sights in Nashville.

Fearing Sally might try to interfere, I told her, "This is a really special trip for Ruth, Mom, and me, so I've planned the agenda accordingly. You can join us if you want, but this trip is for them and their interests." Sally decided not to go.

On the morning after our first night in Nashville, Sally called me at the hotel saying she wanted to join us that night. She went to the Grand ole Opry with us, looking unhappy through the whole performance.

"What's wrong with her?" Ruth asked. "She looks so unhappy."

The next day we were on a tour bus and an unknown man across the aisle asked Sally if she was OK. She glared at him and said, "Leave me alone!"

That afternoon, she went to the airport and flew home.

* * *

We called our seminar, "International Project Management," but we have broad experience in education and business, so our participants are eager to drain us of everything we know. Our transparency charts only serve to start the discussions. The 24 people in the class are mostly male and range in age from 20 to sixty. There are a few university professors, but most are business people or potential entrepreneurs.

The university plies us with coffee and a variety of pastries, many like the Polish immigrants served in Endicott, years ago. They offer us sit-down lunches of beef or lamb, multiple vegetables, and rich desserts. I wonder where they are finding supplies for these elegant cuisines in these times.

At lunch, I am sitting next to Prof. Krajnik, a professor in the economics department, continuing our discussion from the seminar.

Curious, I ask him, "How did you teach economics during the communist years?"

"We used Samuelson," he answered, referring to a famous American text.

"What? How could you do that?" I asked.

"When they confiscated all our books, we hid one copy of Samuelson, broke it up into chapters, and distributed them to loyal faculty members in the department. When we needed certain chapters, we knew who had them. We never let the communist sympathizers in the university know we had them," he said.

He continued, "The communists issued their own version of the book with many of the important elements redacted. It was a joke. Their whole theory made no sense. But we kept teaching good economics and our students never knew we were not complying with communist doctrine."

The story seemed incredible to me, but I accepted it in good faith. This is but one example we heard of the Czech resilience during the communist years.

* * *

Bill and I spent our free time exploring the historic city. The Old Jewish Cemetery, too small to contain the corpses over the years, created an indelible image in my memory.

During our walks around the city, we stopped in a small shop where the young shopkeeper met us at the door. The shop was closed yesterday when we walked by the same spot.

"Why is your shop closed on Tuesday?" I asked curiously.

"I am teaching class," she replied.

"Oh. Are you teaching art at the university?"

"No. It's because I want to be famous."

I was puzzled.

"Do you want to be in films?" I asked. She was certainly pretty enough to be in the movies.

"No, famous like Ford or IBM."

"Oh. You want to be famous in business," I guessed, wondering if her meaning got lost in the translation of her thoughts into English.

"Yes! Famous in business all over the world. On Tuesday, I teach 23 assistants how to make marionettes. I want people in all countries to get pleasure from my art. For 14,000 crowns, about $400, I will take a picture of you, then two months later we can mail you a marionette of yourself with your own clothes on. These marionettes on the shelf, of course, are much cheaper."

Madame Vanda, owner of Fantasie Marionettes, was the first true entrepreneur I met in Prague. Private firms are just beginning to emerge in Czechoslovakia and the change is dramatic. Newly painted and decorated restaurants are catering to visitors from overseas and locals who can afford their fare. One called "Canadian Lobster" claims to have a daily air shipment of shrimp and lobster from the coast of Canada. New stores display a variety of western and Czechoslovakian goods. Czechs no longer wait in long lines to peer into those windows as was shown in American videos. They seem to take the windows for granted, although the average person cannot afford most of the goods. I saw a sports store with a trail bike listed for 38,000 crowns ($1,200). This is six months' salary for the average college professor in Prague.

More encouraging than expensive bicycles is the supply of books. Not only have a number of private bookstores opened, but one can purchase books from street vendors almost as frequently as in New York. There are vendors who peddle guidebooks and picture books to the tourists, others who cater to readers of Czech novels, those who specialize in magazines from all over the world, and, of course, smut peddlers who distribute Rambo paraphernalia and other western junk. All books are expensive to Czechs and seem to be four- or five-times American prices.

The influence of American firms can already be seen on the landscape. There are a number of trolley cars and other spaces in Prague emblazoned with Marlboro ads.

It's working, too. Czechs smoke. It took me days to again get used to so many people smoking. Also, one of the first signs to greet me on the way from the airport was a large model of a Pepsi can and McDonald's was just opening its new store at Nova Maestra. Its front was tastefully designed, and its golden arches were confined to the interior of the store. I did not go inside, but the facility seemed about three times the size of the average American McDonalds.

I felt embarrassed that American culture is more vividly represented by Rambo, cigarettes, soft drinks, and hamburgers than the more positive values from our country. Yet, there are other signs: Arthur Andersen Consulting and Coopers and Lybrand have established offices in downtown Prague, and they are advertising on billboards. Several Czechs expressed concern that big American corporations that brought offices to Prague have hired ex-communist party officials to represent them in the country. The typical Czech comment is "How can the companies be so stupid. Don't they investigate people before they hire them?" The credibility of such American firms is severely damaged in the minds of the Czechs we met.

The proliferation of people like the marionette lady is an encouraging sign. Entrepreneurs, wherever they are, seem to share a common desire to succeed. Through 40 years of a communist regime, their spirit was smoldering in the hearts of many Czechs. Madame Vanda said: "I don't do it for money. I like to see people get pleasure from my art. I want a lot of people to have my marionettes."

Czechs are rushing to find ways to start small businesses. One young engineer, a part-time teacher at the technical university, is starting a small software firm writing programs for use in small to large businesses. As the owner of the firm, he is working about 12 hours a day, six days a week, a typical schedule for a manager of a start-up in any country. "I never could have done this before 1989 and it scares me to think that I might not succeed. But I keep going because I believe we can have a good product."

These entrepreneurs are experiencing the exhilaration of starting a new business in an uncertain economic environment.

\* \* \*

Sally and I are nearing the end. I hate the thought of a second divorce, to have made such a bad decision. How can I face my family and friends? Yet, those who have seen Sally and I together will probably not be surprised.

Sally spends most of the time in her New York apartment while I am in our house in Bridgewater, CT. We are together most weekends when she comes to Connecticut to ride her horses and participate in the weekly fox hunting events. I've come to dread the possible conflict. We often go out to eat on Saturday nights but have grown to expect the inevitable conflict. I've told her how I feel, but she diminishes it as just another ill-informed argument, from a person with lesser intellect.

I am successfully fashioning a life of my own in Bridgewater, once again feeling confident about my abilities, having developed new friendships and a place in the community. My relationship with David, Lynn, and Laura remains tenuous, and Sally has been a deterrent to any family relationship. Mom tolerates her, but no one else wants to be in a room with her. They immediately detect her hostility. My cousin Sylvia's husband took me aside during a visit to their house, saying, "How the hell did you get in this mess? She is a real bitch." John, an expert in cattle and animal husbandry, minced no words. And that was in reaction to one of Sally's more civilized days.

I started therapy with Dr. Susan Randers in Danbury. Of all the therapists over the years, she was the best match, talking about reasons behind fractured relationships, feeling overwhelmed with responsibility, putting up with verbal abuse for too long, forgiving myself for not living up to my family ideals. Finally, about six months ago, we decided we'd met the goals, ending the sessions on a high, confident note.

Some months after our last session, I attended a community dance at the town hall. Rock music shook the walls, reminding me of my middle age of 50 plus. I sat. Listening, watching the young people dancing gleefully, thinking of having missed this whole era. A friend, Julie Donevan, walked over briskly, saying, "Come on, Grant, let's dance."

"I don't know how to dance that stuff, Julie."

"The hell you don't, get off your butt," she said, pulling me to the dance floor.

Yes, it was a hell of a dance, over several numbers.

At the end, Julie said, "It's time you get out of that mess and live your own life. I've seen your unhappiness. It doesn't have to be that way."

I filed for divorce from Sally the next week.

When we had our final conversation, she said, "I didn't know it was that bad."

"What?" I replied. "We've been talking about this for a year. Did you think I was faking it?"

# RECONSTRUCTING
## *A LIFE*

# WEIMER'S CALL

One day, I picked up the phone to hear Bill Weimer on the other end.

"I need your help. Can you come over?" Bill asked from Paris.

Less than a year after he and I began working together, Bill got an offer from EuroPace to go to Paris as CEO/Managing Director.

"You've got to take it, Bill," I said. "You love Europe, so follow your dream."

So Bill was off to Paris while I settled in for some local projects in the USA.

At the time of Bill's call, I was in my office in Bridgewater, Connecticut, working on a project for the Town of New Milford, having filed for divorce from Sally three months earlier.

"When do you want me?" I asked Bill.

"As soon as you can get here," Bill said.

"It'll take me a week to get ready," I replied.

Son David came up to help me pack my essential belongings in a storage module, and the following Monday evening TWA took me to Paris.

David and I had carefully packed things away, but damn, I left my Tony Lama cowboy boots sitting in the middle of the bedroom floor. Never mind, I'm outta there.

# MONTESSON

I had a flat in Montesson, a stone's throw from the Seine. It was the time for such a place, for I was licking the wounds of a failed relationship. On summer days with windows flung open to cool breezes from the garden, children babbling, birds chipping, I lay on my bed contemplating the Gothic patterns in the three-meter-high ceiling of my hidden villa. Swirling this way and that, the plaster artist seems to have anticipated my mood and the tides that surround my life.

It's a cold Samedi. The rain is sweeping across the valley so hard that the trees across the Seine are barely visible. No one expects such weather in June, so the apartment complex owners would never consider turning on the heat. Hot tea, my "writing" sweater, a toasted ham and cheese sandwich, and the heat from the oven have made the place bearable. This rain gave me a good excuse to play squirrel today—to stay home with my French book, word processor, and other reading materials. Next weekend, I will be in Amsterdam for a business meeting, so this is the time to get some reading and domestic chores done.

The kitchen in this apartment is ideal for writing and sipping tea. Although small, the table has adequate space for my portable computer and a placemat. From my chair, I can see the tree-lined back lawn of the old manor house. When they converted this old farmhouse into apartments, the builders retained the picturesque features: the old stone well, the rock silo that looks like the remnants of a castle tower, the six-foot wall that partially surrounds the property. Across the fence is a chicken yard where my alarm clock lives. He was quite confused by this dark weather because his first crow was about 8:30 this morning. It's a good thing that it was not a workday.

I am struggling with the French language through trying to communicate with people, listening to tapes and the TV, and solving the exercises in a workbook. My ear is getting tuned so that I can understand some things; I've learned to write numbers on checks, but the pronunciation is driving me crazy. I'm beginning to wonder if my southern heritage has doomed me to slow speech forever. I simply cannot say the sounds fast enough to get out a French sentence. The book said that it may take 20 to 30 tries. I've only tried about ten, so maybe all is not lost.

# THE VOICE

"Grant! Grant!" the voice said.

Last week, I was awakened in the night by a voice—a distinct, loud call of, "Grant!" I sat up in the bed thinking that someone was at the door, but no one was there. I simply noted the event as a dream and went back to sleep. In the morning, I could clearly remember the voice ringing in my head. How could it have been so vivid? Why was it calling me? Was it my father's voice?

For years, I have been searching for a mission—feeling that I had a purpose in life but having no idea what it was. I simply kept accumulating skills and education, thinking that someday my purpose in life would be clear. Yet, nothing happened. I did my 30 years in industry, had a family, held some responsible positions in the church and the community, worked in a university, and ran for a political office. Nothing seemed to be the "thing."

This time of solitude is like a soothing calm. I've never had time to myself like this. I've never had a place of my own. I can read and listen to music out loud without anyone thinking that they're being ignored. I bought two red towels yesterday without worrying if they match anything. There are socks drying in the bathroom until I decide to put them away. I have not known myself outside the context of someone else's life.

My professional life here is active and stimulating. The people at the office are bright and highly motivated. I got engaged with the job on my first day, so my contribution is visible. Some of my tasks are taking me to Germany, the Netherlands, and the U.K. where I am renewing old friendships and making new ones.

It is an exciting time to be here. There are big changes in the European Community and Eastern Europe. Czechoslovakia separated into Czech Republic (Bohemia) and Slovakia. Bill Weimer and I visited there less than a year ago, and we heard nothing of this. George Bush and Yeltsin signed an arms control treaty, also another surprise. Maybe the world is making progress. But the war in Bosnia with all its atrocities continues.

Amid the chaos, I am now in a tranquil place.

# ANCOLIEN

The RER commuter train is running on time this morning, taking me from my apartment in Montesson to the La Defense complex outside Paris. Stepping off the train, I can see in the southeast, the sun lighting up the Arc de Triomphe in all its glory. This line from La Defense to the Arc de Triomphe, is part of the Axe Historique that follows the course of the sun from its rising in the East to its setting in the West, also aligning other notable sites in Paris, such as the Louvre, the Tuileries Gardens, and other places I've been exploring since arriving many months ago. The EuroPace office skyscraper lies about 500 meters on the other side of the large median.

I stop midway at the coffee shop.

"Bon Jour, Monsieur," Marie says, placing a large cup of café au lait and a croissant on the tall table. After my first three stops here, she learned my routine, bringing me the same every morning.

"Merci, beaucoup," I say, smiling. Wow, I love this French coffee.

I enter EuroPace's conference room on the 23rd floor. From the window, we can see workers far below with picks and wheelbarrows beginning their day's work on the skyscraper next door. La Defense is several kilometers from Paris city-center because planners did not want towers to ruin the city's majestic skyline. So, they built a new commercial center here.

Soren, Yvonne, Lucinda, Mia, Helga, and a few others are already in the room waiting for our weekly status meeting to begin. Isabelle Kuhn, the financial controller, is a free spirit and music lover who slipped into accounting years ago to make a living. She is a good financial officer, but there is a musician inside screaming to get out. She sings a lot in the halls of EuroPace.

Bill Weimer and his wife Julie live in Paris and spend much of their time visiting museums, historic sites, and enjoying gourmet restaurants. We always joke about our "cultural conflict." I look for the restaurants with the ordinary people, Bill finds the elegant. I ride second class on the train, he rides first, willing to pay twice the price. I keep telling him how the most interesting people are in second class and in ordinary restaurants.

Soren Nipper is from Aarhus, a city in Denmark. His personal values reflect that upbringing. He works hard and knows how to be a good friend. Soren traditionally gets his head buzz cut once a year and spends the next 12 months with whatever grows out. Soren is an exceptionally skilled writer, creator, and distance education producer.

Denyse Saab has lived in France most of her adult life but was born in Egypt and raised in Lebanon. Denyse is one of the best editors of English text I've ever worked with. She is a talented and well-organized TV producer. Her warmth and compassion radiate like the summer sun.

* * *

EuroPace provides training and education via satellite television to organizations in most of the European Union's 15 countries. This work is similar to the project that Bill and I started at IBM, when we transmitted high-tech training via video to plants and labs around the USA.

As usual, on Monday, we compare notes on our weekend, quite an interesting exercise, since there are people from seven countries on the staff.

"How about you, Grant?" someone asks.

With a big grin, I say, "I spent the weekend in Amsterdam on the back of a beautiful Dutch woman's bicycle."

Everyone howls with laughter.

"Are you kidding? Tell us another one," Soren says.

"It's true. A few weeks ago, on that trip to one of our clients in Amsterdam, I met a wonderful woman who was a receptionist at the hotel. She's tall, has a gorgeous smile, and we had a great conversation. So…last week I called her and invited her to dinner in Amsterdam. The next day, we met in the morning and toured the city on her bicycle. And you know what? My butt is still sore from sitting on that damned bicycle rack."

More laughter.

Bill Weimer steps into the room to start the meeting. Bill still looks the corporate executive with expertly knotted striped tie, white down shirt and blue suit, while the rest of us look like a motley crew from downtown Paris, dresses in various patterns of red, blue, and yellow for some women, slacks for others, primarily open shirts for men including me.

"How are things coming along for the *Friday Magazine*?" Bill asks. *Friday Magazine* is our new weekly TV news update for scientists, engineers, and programmers around the EU.

"We've signed Derek Braebert as our host, we've lined up the guest speakers, and the scripts are mostly complete," I say. "We'll be ready to kick off on schedule in three weeks. We're doing a pilot with Derek on Friday.

English is his second language, so we're making sure the scripts have words he can pronounce."

Next, we review programs for the week, feedback from clients, and obstacles any team member is facing.

A few of us hang around after the meeting.

"What's her name?" asks Soren.

"Ancolien," I answer. "As you know, I'd sworn off dating for the last year, but meeting her changed my mind. She was so easy to talk to. I've been short on good conversation for a long time."

"How did you meet her?" Soren asks.

I told him the story of how we met on my trip to Amsterdam about a month ago…

I had stayed in a small, traditional Dutch hotel where she was working as the receptionist. While checking in, I made some crack about her cup of tea looking as if it had been there since morning. She laughed and said, "Actually, I don't like tea when it's too hot."

She gave me a key to the room with some vague instructions to go up the stairs, turn right, and down the hall. I dragged my bag up the steps, but not finding the room, I returned to the lobby for more instructions. She laughed and sent me for another search. That time, I found the room after exploring every corridor.

Later, I returned to the lobby, and she said, "Would you like some beer or wine? We have a small bar."

"That sounds delightful," I said, meeting her at the small counter of a bar. I sat on one of the tall stools, looking into her big cyan eyes, now getting a closer look at a tall, athletic, Dutch woman with a ready smile, a keen sense of humor, and speaking English with a slight accent.

"You sound like an American" she said. "What are you doing here?"

"I work for a company in Paris and am here on a business trip," I answered as she handed me a glass of chardonnay.

"How about you? I doubt if you are a native Amsterdammer."

"I'm from a small town up north, Uithuizen. I came here to study history and work," she says.

"I've never seen that part of the country, yet I have read about the boy with his finger in the dike," I say, grinning.

"When you see the dikes, you'll know a finger wouldn't stop a leak," she laughed. "My family's house is only a few kilometers from the dikes. And they are huge."

We compare notes on growing up in small towns—the Netherlands and the USA.

I notice her looking at my left hand. Ridges from the removed wedding band remain on my ring finger.

"Yes, we separated many months ago, but the ridges remain, along with a few other scars," I say. "The divorce is pending."

Then we keep talking for maybe an hour. She had to break away several times to greet other hotel guests but came back to talk. At the end, we felt comfortable enough to share phone numbers, and I called the next week to ask her out to dinner.

"That sounds good," Soren says. "Maybe she's someone special."

"Yes. I believe she is."

# BASTILLE DAY

I always wanted to be in France on Bastille Day. Today, I got my wish. The celebration started last night with bals (dances) in St. Germaine, Houle, the Bastille, La Defense, and other sections. My old bones didn't feel up to dancing in the street all night, so I planned to curl up with my French workbook for a quiet night at home.

That was a futile wish. The first big flash-boom came around 11 o'clock. There were about two seconds between the light and the sound, so that must be from one of the communities across the Seine to the north. My bedroom window faces that direction, and my third-floor balcony was the ideal platform to watch the fireworks show.

To my left, the skies over St. Germaine, about six kilometers away, were lit with blue and green. Another display, dead center from my window, was just across the river on the western border of St. Germaine. On the far right, people in the town of Maisons-Laffitte were shooting their fireworks from the highest hill; probably the one on which the chateau is located.

Although enthralled with these displays, I decided to check in the other direction for signs from La Defense or Paris. Sure enough, I could see the bursts from Paris—about 30 five kilometers away as the French crow flies; and also, a number of small towns between here and Paris were competing for the sky. As the last burst came at midnight, I could hear a rock band from the distant hills. The dancing had started. Good morning, Bastille Day.

Because of the activity, I slept through the rooster's 7:00 am call even though my clock radio was set. All I heard was the news that Steffi Graf won the Wimbledon Women's Tennis Tournament on July 4. What? That was ten days ago. The parade on the Champs Elysees is due to start at 10:00 am, so I rush to the bus stop.

A roar in the northern sky intensifies as I scamper toward the bus stop. Five large radar-watch planes pass directly overhead at low altitude. Shortly after, three sets of five fighter planes blast by—then more and more and more. I am under the air parade from the base just north of here. While I am counting over 50 planes, I almost miss the bus.

Surprisingly, on a holiday morning, my bus and train connections work, so there is hardly time to read the newspaper. I get off at Argentine stop because all Metro entrances and exits farther south will likely be blocked for security reasons.

Arriving at the street, I find it completely blocked to traffic and people. Yet, I work my way toward the Arche de Triomphe just in time to see a large group of army vehicles roar down the street. The people are ten or 12 deep along the street so it is a fight to see anything. The parade is supposed to take place between 10:00 am and 1:00 pm.

But now it's 11:30 am and things are suddenly quiet except for the polished policemen guarding the parade route. I wait. Ten minutes pass. Then 20. Finally, two jeeps, five huge army tanks, and three trucks rumble by shaking the entire city. Not very colorful, these brown tanks. Oh well, bands and costumed performers may be following.

I work my way through the crowd to the barriers that line the street, peer toward Place Concorde, supposedly the starting point of the march. Nothing but a line of policemen across the street—standing at attention. Another ten minutes. Then 20. No action. no fire trucks, no horses, no bands, no majorettes. People start to leave—many asking what happened to the parade.

The Champs-Élysées lay in ruins. The macadam looks more like a plowed field than the most famous Parisian boulevard. I imagine that two hours earlier, 45-ton tanks, battalions of soldiers, howitzers, missiles, and flags had traversed the city while jet aircraft turned flips overhead. Every year on Bastille Day, July14, France decides to tear up the city simply to show the world its military power. We have tanks, we have guns, we have missiles. We have soldiers, and they all speak French.

The tanks were gone, the planes quiet, the crowd dispersed. A great military giant had gone back to sleep.

I walk to Chez Dominique on the left bank and indulge in a crêpe and a bottle of cider while watching an older man fondle his young companion at the next table and seeing two men smoking Gauloises arguing over a parking place. The Bastille was stormed on July 14, 1789, but today, after a big parade, French life goes on.

# LOSING LEO

It's a quiet evening in Montesson. All the Bastille Day fireworks have been spent and the rain clouds have moved on toward eastern Europe. The sun is setting over the hill on the other side of the Seine a little sooner than yesterday. Birds are squawking from every tree to mark the first rays of sunshine in over a week. Summer is over and autumn is arriving.

My environment is so different from that of six months ago—another continent, a different job, new vistas opening. But some bad news arrived last night. My friend and colleague from IBM days, Leo Kilcoyne, died in a tragic car accident.

It's hard to imagine the US without Leo in it. Good, solid, steady Leo has been in my life since 1965—almost 30 years. I remember when he and I first met. Me, being one of the only IBM people to arrive from Endicott, I moved fast to claim an office in our temporary building in Boulder, before those Poughkeepsie and Kingston people arrived. I took my nameplate out of the briefcase and posted it on the door. A few days later, Leo walked by, saw the name, and stuck his head in.

"Hi, I'm Leo Kilcoyne. I guess we'll be working together."

"Yep, I've heard of you," I replied.

We chatted for a while, and I remember thinking that he was different from the other Kingston crowd I knew. He was warm, easy going, and seemed to care about the people he worked with. He was not the "ship it no matter what" type of manufacturing manager.

Through the years, my respect for Leo grew as we worked together. When the plant was falling apart, he knew how to hold the team together. When the vultures from headquarters arrived, he knew how to talk to them. He was stability in the storms.

Europe also reminds me of him. As far as I know, some laundry still has the underwear he left in Stuttgart and either forgot or didn't have the time to pick up. If I guess right, it was the latter. Leo always arrived at planes at the last minute. So, he probably thought that he would have plenty of time to stop by the laundry on the way to the airport. But, as usual, he was talking until it was too late.

We plotted strategy at many a plant manager's meetings over here in Europe. He and I developed more schemes and implemented them in one month than others had in years.

Sometimes, in our quiet moments, we talked of what it would be like after IBM—when both of us had retired. We imagined sitting on a park bench in Santa Fe, drinking wine and watching the people go by while reminding each other of stories from the past. By the time such a possibility could have become a reality, I hated IBM, but he seemed to keep enjoying it.

Maybe part of my estrangement from the company was there were so few managers like Leo—and I was no longer working directly with him. At the time, I wondered how I would feel about the stories in retrospect. I knew the most fun I had enjoyed at the company was during the time that he and I worked together. There were no others who could hold a light as far as management was concerned.

Last night, when I heard about Leo's passing, I grabbed some cheese, bread, and a bottle of wine and headed for the park bench out on the lawn here. It was a quiet night. No people were walking by, and Montesson is not Santa Fe, but in my memory, and in my soul, Leo and I had a bottle of wine together.

Friendship was integrated into our entire relationship. There was no forbidden territory. He touched us all. He helped mold our lives. He changed the world in thousands of little ways. Leo Kilcoyne—a good man; a man at peace with himself, God, and the world—a rare person in this time or any other. I will miss him profoundly.

# NEVER BIKE
# IN PARIS

My apartment is about two kilometers from the nearest grocery store, Carrefour. The train station is almost three kilometers. Frequent buses make shopping or commuting reasonably easy, but, in non-commuting hours, buses are less frequent. I need transportation, perhaps a bicycle

Veronique, a woman at the EuroPace office who is married to an unknown film producer, has been my mole into the culture—she seems to know where everything is, how to get tickets to every event, can interpret every grunt of local slang, and gets a big kick out of watching Americans trying to cope. Veronique reminds me of a San Francisco hippie, with long flowing brown hair, eyes staring out of charcoal makeup, flowered long skirts, and skin-tight tee shirts. Some of my colleagues call her, "Arty Veronique," because of her aversion to rules of behavior and off-color French language that even I can tell is different from other French natives in our group.

Veronique quickly identified the place for me to buy a second-hand bicycle called "Bicoune." It is located on Blvd Beaumarche, near the Bastille in downtown Paris. "Just ask for Ricardo," she said. "And he speaks English."

On Tuesday, I called Ricardo.

"Do you have any second-hand bicycles?" I asked.

"*Si*, uh, *oui*, uh yes. Can you come to the store?"

"Of course, I'll see you this afternoon."

We were scheduled to do a television shoot at a studio in the city starting just after lunch, so it seemed a good opportunity to visit the shop while I was downtown. So what if the studio was near the Eiffel tower and the shop was all the way across the city, near the Bastille—the subway, Metro, will make that easy.

On the way to the TV studio, I bought a racy straw hat, in the style of Tennessee Williams, from a small chapeau shop. The hat created quite a stir when I entered the TV studio—no question—I was not your typical Parisian.

At 4:00 pm, we finished the shoot and I was on my way to the Bastille, using the familiar Metro. When Ricardo saw my chapeau, he gave me a mocking grin and said, "Oh yes, you are the American!"

It took me about 45 minutes to select a three-speed Dutch model bike with a bell, a light, a small luggage rack, and a civilized seat—it was just my size.

Ricardo asked, "Do you want to try it out?"

"Sure," I said, excitedly. "Where?"

"Just go around the block."

"Around the block" in one of the busiest traffic areas in Paris and in the middle of rush hour seemed daunting. Nevertheless, I gave it a try. Luckily, I found a small cobblestone street that was barely wide enough for two cycles to pass, much less cars. But... I was able to stay upright, and the machine performed well.

Ricardo seemed pleased to hear me say, "I'll take it."

In a few minutes, I completed the transaction and asked, "Can I take the bike on the Metro?"

Ricardo got a shocked look on his face. "No, absolutely, no."

"Well, I have to travel to the suburbs," I said, with concern. "How do you suggest that I get there?"

"Well the RER may let you on."

The RER was the commuting train that I ride every day from the suburbs to work. It has only limited stops in downtown Paris. To get around Paris, one has to use the Metro—somewhat equivalent to the New York subways, only nicer. In metropolitan Paris, the Metro and the RER share some stops. Others are exclusively RER or Metro stops. I had to locate an RER stop that was not shared by the Metro.

The nearest RER stop was about two miles away, at a place called Chatelet—one of the biggest squares in Paris. It has about 20 Metro stops and only one or two entrances to the RER—but where the hell are they?

I headed to Chatelet with my new chapeau in one hand, my briefcase strapped to my back, pushing my new bicycle. Once in a while, the traffic would break and I would dash to the street, jump on the bike, and pedal like mad—hat in hand, briefcase on back. In about 20 minutes, I was in the vicinity of Chatelet. It was even larger than I remembered. I had a map, but it was no help—RER stops were not marked.

Oh, well, let's try a Metro stop. So, down the steps, I went. At the end of the steps was a ticket booth, behind which were three smirking Parisians. One shouted the equivalent of "Get that thing out of here!"

"C'est la RER?" I blurt.

"@#$%^&&**(%$#*&^%," the man shouts.

I shouted, "screw you," and retreated up the stairs.

Next, I spotted a policeman in a starched, official uniform. He had a pleasant face and had stopped at a street-side cafe for a cup of coffee. He gave me some directions and I finally found the right station. By then it was 6:45 pm.

I took the bike down the two long escalators to the ticket booths, waited until there was a big crowd around the ticket sellers, darted for the turnstiles, threw the bike, my briefcase, and my body over the turnstile, and, in my first stroke of good luck, arrived at the platform just as the right train pulled up. I put the bike on the train and settled down for the 30-minute ride to Sartrouville, close to my apartment.

The bike ride from the train station to my apartment seemed like heaven. The summer sun was low in the sky, the breeze cool, and the traffic sparse. The three kilometers rolled by in no time, and I was free of trains, metro stops, shouting ticket sellers, and honking horns.

Arriving at the apartment, I thought it was a nutty decision to buy a bike in the middle of Paris. There must be a bike shop in the village close by. But that damn Arty Veronique is probably laughing about the crazy American she sent on a wild goose chase.

# MAISONS-LAFITTE

Having wheels opened up the area for exploration. During my trek to the supermarket in the rain yesterday (Saturday), I located a good map of Montesson and surroundings. There is a lot to explore. Perhaps the "bike" should have been a Harley instead of a conservative three-speed Dutch bicycle. I set out down the dirt road alongside the rock wall that protects the manor house of my apartment. In about a half kilometer, the road met the Seine, so I turned right toward Sartrouville, the town with the railroad station, toward my destination, a bridge that leads across to Maisons-Lafitte. My map indicated that there was a lot of green space, parks, and a hippodrome, the French term for a horse racing park.

The dirt road along the Seine was full of mud holes after the rain, but I successfully avoided splashing the people whom I occasionally met strolling along the path. One group had built a fire of logs to roast bratwurst and other unrecognizable food.

The Seine is not a particularly clean river (in fact, it's just plain dirty); nevertheless, there were many sails and motorboats out there today. I follow a two-meter-high rock wall for about a mile. Standing on the pedals, I could see a verdant meadow with buildings in the background. This is the Institut Interdepartmental Theophile Roussell. To me, it sounded like a theological seminary, but my French friends told me that "Theophile" is simply a man's name. This bears more investigation.

At the end of the rock wall, the path merged into a paved road that seemed to be the back route to Sartrouville. On the left, there was a grassy area between the road and the Seine with lots of carefully landscaped suburban houses on the right. The motor bridge across the river was about three kilometers from the beginning of the paved area.

Across the bridge, I could see my destination: the village of Maisons-Lafitte. Crossing the bridge, I was greeted by a sign, "Maisons-Lafitte, Village of the Horses." Shortly thereafter another sign instructed drivers that horses have priority. Soon, I found out why. Maisons-Laffitte is the locale of one of the major horse museums in France and the scene of many horse shows and races. Soon, I met a trailer loaded with horses going in the opposite direction. This was closely followed by about five others. Damn! I probably missed a big event! By then it was about 7:00 pm—certainly too late for a horse show.

In another half mile, I found where the trailers came from: a monstrous "hippodrome" with racetracks, riding rings, and training areas. Obviously, I missed the show everyone was on their way out. Disappointed, I turned to the left and headed back to the main part of town through another neighborhood with manicured lawns.

At the center of town, a sign pointed the way to the "Chateau. "The narrow winding street finally led me to something right out of the picture books: the Chateau Lafitte. All the horsey set had gathered there to hear the award ceremony after the horse show.

The first prize seemed to be a two-horse trailer, the second a one-horse trailer. Hermes saddles apparently were reserved for honorable mentions. In a while, some distinguished-looking men arrived, stepped to the front of the crowd, and began speeches and awards. Riders in classic riding coats, form-fitting pants, and tall boots stood among the townspeople.

Of course, everything was in French. There was no one who could translate the show into English, but it must have been big!

I left the chateau on a large boulevard that seemed to go on for kilometers; but, after a short distance, The entire town was laid out like spokes of wheels. I decided to follow one of the "spoke" streets to explore the town. Each street was tree-lined with a plot of grass dividing the two directions. The street had no end in sight, so I again turned toward the center of town. There were posters all over the place. I stopped to read one of them. I just missed seeing one of the finals for the French Olympic Equestrian team preparing to compete in Barcelona 1992! That is what the horse show was all about.

Now, even more disappointed at having missed the event, it was time for a break.

By then it was about 9:00, pm and I was 30 minutes or more from home. There is a light on the bike, but a dim one. Nevertheless, the Thai/Chinese takeout looked to be my kind of place. Apparently, I was the first American to roll up on my bike all day; so the man behind the open counter gave me a big smile, said "*bon soir*," in a Chinese accent, then shifted to English.

He had a lot of "goodies" displayed inside a glass counter. I pointed out several of them and he explained that it would take a few minutes to cook them. Soon he returned with some of the most delicious Chinese miniature egg rolls and a variety of unidentifiable treats. Each morsel was wonderful.

With still about an hour of light left, I headed home—down the hill, across the bridge, along the river road, through the woods, and back home.

Maisons-Laffitte—a town to explore further, a horse center, a good restaurant, lots of wooded streets, a chateau to tour, a horse museum. Is there enough time in the summer to see all of it? After about two kilometers of pedaling, I came to the highway bridge to cross the river and return home.

Breathing the air of freedom was a new experience. A dream I never dared dream. This was Wynn's Field, my unexplored fantasy, the unexplored colors of an unimagined rainbow. No one said, "don't go into Wynn's Field," as my mother often said. No one said freedom is a sin. No one said wait for me, wait for me.

Biking is a path to freedom. When did I ever before have a day like this?

# SAD JANE

One of the outbuildings on the property where my flat was located was dedicated to a self-serve laundry for the renters. Like the main house, the place seems constructed to last centuries with a masterful brick exterior, concrete floors, and windows two meters high. A mildly fruity odor permeates the damp air, in spite of the extra-large clothes driers constantly turning against the back wall. Three foldable ironing boards sit askew around the oversized space, waiting for a resident to try their hand with the 220 volt European electric irons.

It's taken quite a few tries for me to get the hang of French appliances, but after a couple of weekend laundry days, my process is running smoothly. Making homemade biscuits, baking an apple pie, and ironing shirts seemed essential skills for adulthood during my childhood dreams. So, each week, I wash my clothes, dry them, and set about ironing my button-down shirts leftover from IBM.

This Saturday, I'm on my second shirt, getting ready to iron the sleeves and collar. A forty-something dark-skinned woman, who entered the room wearing a black hijab, goes to another ironing board ready to start her work. But, instead of ironing, she is watching me—staring at me. I wasn't sure what was going on because it was unusual to see someone dressed like her look so directly at me.

Nervously, I continue to iron, finish the shirt, hang it on a nearby hook and pick another from my laundry basket.

"Hello," the woman says, in surprisingly good English.

"Hello," I answer. "Do you need help?"

"No. Would you like for me to iron your shirts?" she asks.

I'm wondering if she thinks my ironing is terrible, but I say. "Oh. Thank you so much, but I can manage."

"Sorry to bother you, but I've never seen a man iron a shirt," she says with a smile.

"Thanks again," I say, smiling back.

We quietly continue our ironing, while I wonder what cultural rules she broke by asking me the question.

Although I met them early after I moved in, I seldom encountered Jane or her husband face to face. They lived in one of the apartments on the first floor of this Chateau. Their apartment faced the walkway to my unit.

Often, when I came home from work at 7:00 or 8:00 pm, I saw Jane staring at the TV set, smoking, sometimes with their son slumped in another chair—also staring. I assumed that the husband traveled a lot or kept late hours, probably to the dissatisfaction of the rest of his family. They don't seem happy.

Derek, about 12 years old, kicks around a soccer ball for hours; bouncing it against a big boulder on the far lawn or against the side of the building close to the driveway. There are children his age in the apartment complex, but they seem to ignore him. On some days, Jane or her husband join him for a few minutes, as if playing soccer is a duty of parenthood. I was tempted to go play with Derek, but he seemed uninterested in my attempts to engage him in conversation. It was not a language problem, he speaks with a beautiful British accent.

Last weekend Jane was washing laundry in our shared laundry room. I could no longer ignore her sadness.

"Hi, I'm Grant. I met you and your family when I moved in. I live upstairs," I said over the top of my laundry bag.

"Hello, I'm Jane. How long have you lived here?"

"Oh, since last June. How about you?"

"We've been here two years, and we're looking for a place to settle," she said.

"A lot of people here are doing that. This is a place of transients. Where did you come from?"

"Lebanon. We left after things got too bad to stay."

Over the next few minutes, I began to understand some of the reasons for the family gloom. Jane is English, her husband, Greek. Derek was born in Lebanon. The husband is a salesman and distributor of food products. Jane worked closely with Frank Reed, one of the Americans who was taken hostage in Beirut.

"No doubt you've heard of Frank Reed," she said. "I used to work with him—in education. When he was kidnapped, my job and spirit went away. When things got so bad, we decided to leave. So we've been looking for the right country ever since. I think we'll try England next. What do you think of the French?"

"Oh, I've had good experiences here," I replied.

"Well, I can't wait to leave. Everything is still in boxes, so it will be easy."

Jane described her life here: living in isolation, waiting for her husband to come home at nine o'clock, then fixing dinner, watching hours of French television and being bored by it, having nothing to do but wait for a call to drive to the train station to pick up her husband, feeling badly that she was not able to find a job in teaching or education, being sick, and spending a lot of time in the French medical system that she suspected was not nearly as good as the British.

"How is Derek doing in school?" I asked.

"He goes to the international school at St. Germain and is doing all right. He knows languages and writes well. When we go to England, he can go to a good school."

As I listened to the story of a family adrift, three lonely, unhappy people, their loneliness a consequence of being set adrift by war and political forces. Would England or any other place finally give these three people a home—and make them a family. Or—was the source of their remorse internal?

I put my clothes in the washer, inserted my token, and pushed the green start button.

"It's been good to meet you, Jane," I said.

"You, too." For the first time, she smiled.

But I noticed a black bruise under her left eye. I left the room wondering if her husband was right-handed.

# LEAVING PARIS

Now, after almost a year at EuroPace, the project is starting to wind down. About three months ago, I suggested we survey our clients, especially the big companies around Europe, to determine how many people attended our classes. The corporate situation had changed since EuroPace's origin three years ago. The companies who initially sponsored the organization had reorganized into smaller units, and the individuals who were original strong supporters had moved on to other posts or retired.

Soren and I divided the 15 countries we served and had our secretary plan two train trip itineraries. Soon we were off interviewing clients all over the continent. At the end, we met one cold January day at the Bull Inn, a historic pub in a village named Story Stratford near Milton Keynes in England, to compare notes, sitting by the fireplace, sipping ale. The results were plain; our viewership had declined to an unsustainable level. The content was still relevant, but companies were no longer sending their employees to the sessions. Soren and I returned to EuroPace to recommend we shut down the organization.

Three weeks later, I rented a small Renault van, loaded all my possessions, and headed to the Netherlands to pursue a consulting project with the Dutch Open University. Although entirely loaded, there was one small spot in the back of the van. Stopping at a good wine shop, I selected six bottles of good Sancerre and put them in the empty slot. I was ready to go.

# HELLO, NETHERLANDS

While at EuroPace, I started working with an international team developing a European Master of Business Administration program delivered via distance education, a project sponsored by the European Commission. The team consisted of representatives from distance teaching universities in The Netherlands, Ireland, Germany, U.K., and Spain.

I worked closest with the Dutch team on "Strategic Issues for Management in the European Context." When I finished my consulting assignment at EuroPace, Ger Jonkergouw, from the Dutch Open University said, "Why don't you come over to the Netherlands and work with us? You can complete the project here."

Staying in France would have required proficiency in the French language and culture, far beyond my ability to order coffee and croissants, whereas most Dutch business people speak English. While at IBM, I worked with both Dutch and French people. Clearly, for an American, working in the Netherlands is the best choice. Language is easy; culture is compatible.

Working at EuroPace was an exhilarating personal and professional year. Even though I was sad to leave, my next venture in the Netherlands seemed like a good opportunity.

On the day before leaving, eight of us broke open bottles of Champagne and shared lots of stories, laughs, and hugs.

I finally convinced the group that good old firm American hugs were preferable to the French custom of touching each cheek and kissing the air.

\* \* \*

Getting to the Netherlands requires me to drive through Paris, a frightening prospect. The great circle at the Arc de Triomphe is chilling. Someone said half of the cars in Paris have to be in motion because only half have a place to park in the city. On this Saturday morning, the roads are packed. Where can all these people be going?

Nevertheless, I successively navigate my way through Paris with little difficulty, although, admittedly, I circumnavigated one circle twice before being able to exit to my desired street. The French have this strange thing about the right of way, where the driver on the right always has the right of way. And, damn, do they take advantage of it.

Strange. No nervous pangs, no fright about unknown driving. Instead, excitement envelops me—a new adventure, a new country, new people to meet, new challenges in my job. Paris showed me I could live on my IBM pension even without consulting income; most of that went into the bank. Sure, I walked away from the marriage with Sally with no house ownership and little capital, but I am free to learn, work, and explore—to see new places and meet new people. Sally might still have my Tony Lama boots, but that is all.

Those old critical voices are gone, Joyce's, Sally's, my own. Instead, an echo of smiling new colleagues from many countries sharing stories, accomplishing things together, building trust.

Rolling down the window, I breathe the damp, cool French air rushing in at 120 kilometers an hour. I am free.

# MEERSSEN

I am in the small town of Meerssen, hoping to find an apartment. The community's cultural hub is the pub where locals meet each night to watch European Football and have some Limburger beers, of which there are 143 brands within a short radius. You can always tell when the crowd has gathered by the volume of bicycles parked outside. Most of the bikes are parked as if the rider jumped off while the thing was still rolling—there is no order. They must drink quietly, however, because there was hardly a sound as I walked by on my way from the train station to the hotel at about 8:00 pm. Apparently, the Dutch team has not scored.

When I arrived at the Hotel Koningin Gerberga, Mr. Verstappen was eating his dinner while watching a large TV screen in the living room that doubles as a lobby. He never stopped chewing as he stood up and handed me the key to number three.

"You know where it is?" he said, knowing full well that, after three visits, I knew the place well. After all, how can you get lost in a hotel of ten rooms?

"Sure," I said. "How have you been?"

"Very well. It's good to see you," he said, still talking through his food.

The last time I was here, he treated me to a home-cooked meal. Although I chose one of the lightest items on the menu, he kept bringing more good Dutch cooking. This place is like home—but with service! The Verstappen's grandchildren and the cat also help liven up the place.

Tomorrow I will explore the area. This "Limburg" region, at the edge of Belgium and Germany, is blessed with rolling hills, excellent food, and warm hospitality. Nearby Maastricht is the oldest city in the Netherlands and is trying to become an international center for culture and education. The European Community "Maastricht Treaty," signed in 1991, just last year, put the small city on the international map. Meerssen is only about eight kilometers from the center of Maastricht.

The Dutch Open University is located in Heerlen, about 20 kilometers in the other direction. Trains between Maastricht and Heerlen link all the small towns in between (such as Meerssen) every 30 minutes. So, my task for tomorrow is to see if it is possible to find a small apartment, at a reasonable price, available immediately, close to a rail line, and where I will not need a car. My friend and colleague, Ger Jonkergouw lives in Valkenburg, one of those stops, so being close to him would give more opportunities for work and friendship.

Many European countries have an "Open University" where people from all over the country may sign up for undergraduate or graduate college-level courses. Students receive a package that contains study guides, textbooks, self-administered tests, computer-aided instruction, and videotapes. The universities offer normal college curricula, including engineering, liberal arts, science, and a variety of other subjects.

A student can get a bachelor's or master's degree without ever attending a class. However, there are "study centers" at various points around the country to provide library, computer support, and tutorial help. Some courses require students to take a final exam at a study center.

It is easy to enroll. A person may sign up for one course or for a full degree program. Entrance requirements are liberal—almost anyone can take courses. And the cost to students is relatively affordable for most people.

Most countries do not have a community college system like the United States, so distance education universities offer adults a path to increase their education. Changing career paths as an adult is much more difficult in Europe than in the United States. Salaries are often pegged to a person's age or time in the career. So, if a forty-year-old accountant wants to become a programmer, possible employers might surmise the new programmer would have to be paid like a forty-year-old, not like a junior programmer.

I am working with the Dutch Open University to help them develop an MBA course in "Strategic Issues for European Management." It is designed to help graduate business students understand the new European Community and to apply that knowledge to help their companies be successful in the European market.

The projects included three video modules: A panel of businesspeople discussing strategic issues in Europe, a program of interviews with officials from the European Commission, and a case study with MEXX, a Dutch fashion company that markets clothes all over the world. Also, I wrote a module for the coursebook called, *Organization Structures for the New Europe*. This was a 100-page text of new approaches to international business organization.

I also have other projects outside of the Open University, such as teaching technology management to students at a school called the European Institute of Technology, located in Verona and Florence, Italy. I was there for a week last December, another week in early March, and will return for another in June.

A third project will begin next week. In that one, Soren Nipper, with whom I worked at EuroPace, and I will be preparing a strategic analysis of the European Association of Distance Teaching Universities.

The projects use a great deal of my background, are technically complex, and involve working with people from several countries. I am able to work at my apartment, but I go to the Open University or other places as required. For instance, yesterday we had a series of meetings in Brussels, and on Friday we will go to Amsterdam to meet some directors and videographers to help us produce video elements to support our program.

It's surprising how quickly the Dutch integrated me into their team. They had some visibility of my work at EuroPace, but my orientation here has been easy. Of course, by this stage, I had over 20 years' experience knowing and working with people from many countries and cultures in Europe, Asia, India, and Latin America. I've always been curious to learn about other people, how they live, how they think, how they work, what they believe, what is important to them.

During the many airline trips to places all over the world, I tried to meet strangers. Some of them later became friends. When encountering a stranger on a plane or in a restaurant, my inner voice said, "You have this one chance in a lifetime to meet this person. If you say nothing, the opportunity is lost, never to appear again."

As a result of that voice, I've met hundreds of interesting people, such as Debra from Paris, who eventually ran away to a tropical island to be with a ship captain, and Julia, who was head of an international scientific organization. There have been some sad ones, also, such as the young opera singer returning home to the USA from Milan struggling to decide whether to tell her husband she had fallen in love with her maestro.

The singer was but one example illustrating that people respond warmly to a person interested in their story, someone who will listen sympathetically—something that might be missing in their life.

I wish I had tried to find a sympathetic listener when I needed one.

# VALKENBURG

The next day, I rented a bungalow located at the edge of Valkenburg, a nearby town.

There is an open field just next door bordered by a country road that extends to a farm. Tourists rent these bungalows during the summer season to walk in the hills, drink beer in the cafes, dance in the pavilions, soak in the hot springs, and gamble in the casinos. The little town is full of good restaurants and hotels. The highest-rated restaurant in the country is at the Hotel Juliana, just a few blocks from my new abode. At this time of year, only the locals are here during the week. But, last weekend, the town was full of cruising teenagers, German tourists, and others seeking a good time.

The bungalow is a typical rustic tourist cabin with cathedral ceiling, brick walls, ceramic tile floor, and room to sleep six. There are two bedrooms and a sleeping loft. The bath is typically Dutch-—an open shower with nothing to keep the shower water from splashing over the entire room. The kitchen is a small alcove with a gas cooktop and a small refrigerator whose door is warped to the degree that one must kick it to make the door close completely. The motion has become a habit already—slam—kick!

The entrance has a delightful cathedral ceiling with a ladder to the loft. My stereo, purchased in France, is already filling the space with synthesizer and Bonnie Raitt music. From the dining room table, I can see the patio where spring birds dart among the landscaped trees looking for worms or pieces of bread that I threw out there. There are nuthatches, blackbirds, lots of pigeons (who wake me up in the morning with their cooing sounds), and a variety of others. There are many ravens in the fields, but they seem to be searching for big prizes, like corn. They don't bother with my bread.

Valkenburg is an historic village of about 7,000 people in the Limburg Province, the southeastern region of the Netherlands, close to Belgium and Germany. A small river, the Geul, runs through the village, water propelled by adjacent hills. Ruins of a castle dating back to 1672 overlook a village center marked by traditional Dutch bakeries, restaurants, gambling casinos, and a variety of other shops. Restaurants are plentiful, extending their dining spaces into the streets. On a typical weekend or Dutch holiday, festive tourists crowd the streets, gambling their guilders in clever machines designed to take their money, and drinking the famous Limburg beer. Locals told me that a beer-fest weekend in Valkenburg is a coming-of-age event in Dutch boys' lives.

So close to Germany, the village was occupied by the Nazi's for over four years. It's said the Dutch resistance lived in the complex network of caves, left behind by miners, under the village. American troops liberated the place in 1944. One corner building downtown still shows the scars where an American tank cut too short and knocked off a corner of the masonry. Other buildings still show pockmarks of bullet holes almost 50 years later. Memories of World War II are still prominent in Dutch family stories.

Valkenburg's train station is the oldest in the country and offers convenient connections to Maastricht, the nearby city of 150,000, with its subsequent connections to Amsterdam, Brussels, Aachen, and other locations around Europe. Living in the village seemed like a good bet if I could put up with the weekend crowds.

1992 was a big year in Europe. In February the various countries signed the Maastricht Treaty, forming the European Union. It seems like a big event to me, the European countries finally getting together in one big unit with a government, potentially one currency, and many unintended consequences they certainly don't anticipate. The Dutch summer of 1992 was approaching, bringing with it higher rent for the short-term apartment secured after my arrival here at Valkenburg aan de Geul. Soon it will be time to look for a new place.

\* \* \*

Yesterday morning was my time to settle some basic items of living. First, there was a bank account. The bank manager started the conversation by saying I could not have checks unless there was a regular salary going into my account. Needless to say, we had a few words about that and he finally agreed that I could be an exception.

Next was the PTT, the public agency that administers the post office and the telephone service. My objective was to get a phone as soon as possible. I first went to the window where people buy stamps and asked about getting a telephone installed. The man told me to get the form from the rack "over there," fill it out and bring it back to him. In the rack, there were a hundred different forms, all in Dutch. I finally located one that said, "*nieuwe telefoon*," took it to a desk and tried to read the multiple questions. I could tell where to put my name, address, etc., but then the questions got very obscure. I took the form over to the tourist office just down the street where a young woman helped me with a smile. Upon returning to the PTT, I gave the form to a woman at the stamp window who checked it over, making a few corrections.

"How will I know when they will install the phone?" I asked.

"They will call you," she said, dryly.

"Where? I don't have a telephone." I said.

"Oh. They will come to see you."

Let's hope they do.

In the afternoon, I ventured over to the Dutch Open University to meet the people with whom I'll be working for the next three months. It was a cold day here—around 45 degrees Fahrenheit, but clear and windy. Heerlen is about 13 kilometers away and, as with every place in Holland, has a good bicycle path.

Naturally, I decided to try it by bicycle. It was a lousy decision! The first few kilometers were uphill, and the wind was blowing in my face so strongly that I had to pedal even while going downhill. After an hour and a half of riding, I arrived in my colleague's office smelling like a wet rabbit. At least the wind was at my back on my way back home to Valkenburg and I was able to make it in less than half the time. Lucky thing, since my legs felt like rubber.

After the first few days in Valkenburg, I miss France and the French. Living conditions are easier here in many ways, most of the people speak English, and I already know a lot of people. Yet, the passion and intensity of the French people made every day there a rich experience, an adventure. Take the day train operators went on strike.

I got on the RER at Sartrouville at my regular time for the ten-minute ride to my La Defense office, knowing there was a small possibility of a strike. But at La Defense, the train kept going, stopping nowhere in Paris, finally stopping at Boissy Saint-Leger, the end of the line southeast of Paris. The station was jam-packed with anxious, confused people milling around wondering what to do next. I too, milled around, looking for a telephone while feeling thankful for the franc coins in my pocket.

There were long lines at telephones, coffee stands, and information kiosks, so I found a comfortable spot, sat down, started reading some papers from my briefcase wondering if my colleagues were concerned about what happened to me. Yet, I suppose most people in the area know about the strike and would not be surprised the train stranded thousands of people. So this is France.

After an hour or so, the trains started running and I, along with hundreds of people, returned to our tasks for the day.

To the French, this was just another day. Confused, yes, but no one seemed particularly agitated or angry. This is the way it is. I wondered how Americans would have reacted. I have a strange affection for the French with all their quirks, passions, and history. They taught me something every day.

Hemingway called Paris "A Moveable Feast." Let's see if it is moveable to Valkenburg.

# SOREN

The following weekend, Soren Nipper, my friend and co-worker from Paris, visited me in Valkenburg. We spent two days exploring Maastricht at night and the countryside at day. On Sunday, we biked out across the hills, photographing castles, watching Dutch children playing with spring lambs in a huge field, passing old traditional farmhouses, and sampling Dutch and Belgian beer in small village cafes. There is a famous beer in the region called "Gulpener." We stopped in the town of Gulpen where we tasted the real stuff. After the pressure of helping to close EuroPace over the last several months, it was good to have a weekend to relax and act like a couple of teenagers.

# IN THE SHADOW
# OF THE CASTLE

My current apartment becomes very expensive in the summer because it is designed for summer vacationers. So, I am looking for a more permanent place. That means yet another change of address. Let's hope that the next one will be a bit more permanent.

But how do I find an apartment? My Dutch friends told me to register with the Dutch Housing Authority at the village government building. But, once registered, a person typically had to wait two years. I looked all over for a place in one of the large farmhouses that are found in the small villages around here, but friends explained that people with lots of money buy them for renovation and privacy.

One weekday, I decided to hit the streets to find a place. Besides, it was a good day to explore, with clear skies and the scent of fresh water flowing in the small river.

A window full of pastries caught my eye, so I found an outside seat, ordered a *rijstevlaai* (a rice flan), a cup of strong Dutch coffee, and watched the people walking by. Continuing my walk, I spied a construction worker standing in a door front to a three-story building of brown arenaceous marl stone, typical of the region.

Approaching the man, I greeted him in my sparse Dutch, quickly shifting to English, and said, "Are you building something new?"

"Ja," he replied. "Nieuwe appartement."

"Owner? Eigenaar?" I ask, hoping he understands.

"Boven," he answers, pointing up the stairs.

"OK if I see?" I say, pointing to my chest and then up the stairs.

"Ja," he replies, stepping aside so I can enter.

I go up two flights to the third floor to meet the owner who greets me with a smile. After short introductions in English, he tells me the apartment is in the final stages of renovation and will be ready in two weeks. He leads me on a tour of a living room, kitchen, two bedrooms, a rooftop patio looking up at the ancient castle ruins, and a large unfinished bathroom.

"The shower will go in this space," he says.

I smile and say, "Looks perfect for a large bathtub."

"You're right, let me think about that."

When I moved in a few weeks later, there was the tub, which became a wonderful way to relax after a hard day's work.

One of the bedrooms is nice sized, the other quite small, but large enough to turn into an office. The bath is almost as large as the large bedroom, with a place for a clothes washer. It is covered with beautiful gray tile and has lots of light. The "main room" includes space for a kitchen, living room, and dining area. Double doors lead out to a terrace here that faces a steep hill on which sits the ruins of the 15th-century castle. The whole building has been completely renovated so the apartment has new white, textured wallpaper and will have gray wall-to-wall carpet throughout. The main disadvantage of the place is its location in the tourist section whose streets are jammed with walking people in the summer—especially on weekends.

I was fortunate to find a nice, two-bedroom apartment right here in Valkenburg. It is unlike anything that I ever imagined considering—on the third floor (something like a loft) over a shop on one of the walking streets in downtown Valkenburg, with a rare Mexican restaurant just down the street.

# CRAZY WEDDING

Cort Johns, a friend who is an American professor and teaches at the University of Maastricht has been trying for several weeks to marry his German girlfriend who works in Switzerland. First, he went to the town hall in Valkenburg to check out the procedures. They told him, "no problem, just fill out these papers." He filled out the papers, then showed up at the town hall the following Friday with girlfriend Corolla who drove over from Switzerland, and her parents from Germany. The official at the town hall said, "Oh, everyone knows that there is a two-week waiting period."

Frustrated, everyone returned home to wait out the two weeks. The second try was scheduled at Kasteel Oost (Oost Castle), last Saturday at 11:00 am. This time, I decided to accept Cort's invitation to witness the event. So, on Saturday, Ancolien, who had come down from Amsterdam, and I dressed up, bought some flowers, and headed over to Kasteel Oost on our bicycles. We arrived at 10:50 am, walked up the many steps to the entrance, and were led into a stately room by a man at the castle.

By that time, the ceremony was already over, and everyone was standing around talking. Cort and his bride were occupied with the official who had conducted the ceremony, so Ancolien and I started introducing ourselves to the bride's family. They spoke little English, but fortunately, like most Dutch people, Ancolien speaks some German. Soon Cort and Corolla spotted us, and we showered them with hugs and flowers. They were surprised because I had indicated previously that we probably would not be able to attend.

"Come join us for lunch," Cort said, enthusiastically.

"Oh, we will not disturb your plans. It could be a problem to add two more places," I said.

"That's no problem at all."

"Where is the lunch? We're on bicycles."

"We have no plans. I thought that we would go to the Hotel Juliana."

"Well, we can ride our bikes and meet you there," I said.

"Oh, that would be wonderful. Would you mind making reservations for nine in my name?" smiled Cort.

"Of course not. We'll see you there."

The Hotel Juliana, one of the highest-rated restaurants in the Netherlands, is a memorable place to have lunch. Ancolien and I laughed all the way about a "professor" who had no plans for his wedding lunch.

When we arrived at the hotel, the receptionist told us that they did not serve lunch on Saturday. When the rest of the party arrived, we decided to check out Kasteel Wittem—about 16 kilometers from Valkenburg. We parked our bikes, jumped into the back of Uncle Walter's VW, and started looking for Wittem Castle.

We had a wonderful lunch outside, next to a stream with black swans swimming. We drank Champagne in elegant glasses, ate and talked until 5:30 in the afternoon. Four of the nine people spoke both German and some English, so there were enough interpreters to make the conversation flow. Besides with enough Champagne, all languages become easy. When we left the castle, the mother of the bride took our hands and thanked us for coming. Her warmth and hospitality transcended all language and national boundaries.

The bike paths around Valkenburg lead to castles, streams, spacious farms, and historic, mining caves. Many of the buildings are constructed of marlstone in which early miners obtained building materials, thus resulting in a massive network of underground passages.

During the weekend, I asked Ancolien if she'd like to come live with me in Valkenburg. That would mean leaving a job she hates at a database company in Amsterdam. She majored in history and administration at high school and university but has not finished her degree and is wondering about the next step.

We talked at length about the age gap of 30 years between us. I'm 57, she is 28. It seems daunting, especially when we look at the implications for the future. And, of course, there is the cultural difference, Dutch and American. Yet, both of us grew up in small towns and she's more like me than someone from New York or Chicago. We're of the same mind on values, philosophy, and how we spend our time. Unlike my past relationships, she understands my work, knows what drives me, and helps me make critical decisions. If she sees me going quiet or disengaging during a discussion, she encourages me to express my feelings, quite a change from my past relationships. I, too, love hearing about her since of exploration, her interest in learning, and observing her comfort in interacting with people from other countries and cultures. She is wise beyond her years.

Shortly after moving into the new apartment, I sent Ancolien three postcards.

The first said, "Come with me and we can see the world together."

The second, a week later said, "Come with me and you can finish your degrees in the United States."

The third said, "Come with me and I'll love you forever."

Two weeks later, I rented a small van, drove to Amsterdam, loaded it with Ancolien and her belongings, and returned to Valkenburg to begin a new era.

"This is a long way from Orange, Virginia," rings in my brain when in a new place or when beginning a radically different experience. Sometimes, my inner reaction says this is not your place, this is not your culture. But, this small town, this country, feels comfortable. My year in Paris was the most stress-free year of my adult life. This is freedom—freedom to work at things I love, freedom to travel, freedom to learn, freedom to meet new people, freedom to explore, freedom to create. And freedom from corporations, cars, and petty managers.

* * *

Soon after Ancolien arrived, we went shopping in Maastricht, purchasing a futon, chairs, and other items—a symbol of our commitment to our relationship. Both of us were happy to see we shared modern tastes in decorating. We dined outside for occasional lunches and dinners, with almost daily coffee breaks at the local cafes. Visitors from the castle above wave at us when we're eating dinner on the patio. Every weekend, we join Dutch women to stock up on bread from one of the three bakeries nearby.

We've turned one of the bedrooms into an office with a workspace for each of us. It looks as if concentrating on distance education and educational technology will give us good business opportunities, so we decided to form a Dutch BV, a small business corporation to pursue the market ideas. Ancolien knows how to handle all the administration, set up accounting, obtain bank accounts, and lay the business foundation, including registering the business with the local Chamber of Commerce, the responsible agency.

There was one important remaining obstacle: I needed a work permit and visa to remain in the country.

My Dutch colleagues laughed at me when they learned I was trying to get a work permit by starting a company and hiring myself; thus, giving myself a work permit. But that is exactly what Ancolien and I set out to do. She spent a morning in the university library and found two provisions in the Netherlands-United States Tax Treaty that allowed Americans to receive permission to start businesses in the Netherlands. A few days later, we went to the Immigration Office with our papers.

The Dutch immigration officer, his over six-foot stature indicating he was probably a bureaucrat from the Hague or Amsterdam area, looked down at me and said, "Mr. Tate, your visa expires in 60 days, what are you going to do?"

"Well, sir, we're starting a company that is going to hire me, a person with much needed educational and technical skills in this country."

He laughed as if to indicate that was an absurd idea.

At that point, Ancolien put two documents on the desk and shifted into Dutch language.

After reading them over, he retrieved some forms from the drawer, made some entries, and asked me to sign at the bottom. I passed them by Ancolien for approval and then signed. I had my work permit and visa. The agreement allowed us to do business in the country, and because of the new treaty, in all the countries of the European Union. And, as a Dutch company, we could bid on and perform work for the new European Commission.

* * *

My weekly newsletters kept my friends in the USA, and my mother, up to date on my life and travels, but I remained estranged from David, Lynn, and Laura, due to Joyce's efforts to keep us apart and incommunicado. I should have worked harder to reestablish our relationships but working through my own issues of exhaustion and self-esteem took most of my energy. Coming to Europe has been the path to recovery and I cherish Bill Weimer's phone call that initiated the new adventure.

# LIFE IN THE NETHERLANDS

People here often ask me what I miss about America. I usually reply with, "wide open spaces and a dishwasher." The Netherlands is a beautiful country—especially this time of the year when the flowers are in bloom, and everyone is showing off their gardens. Tulips are not the only flowers featured; all the flowers are beautiful. Every bit of space here has some useful purpose. Even the trees are planted in a grid so that you can sight a row of trees from every angle. So, you can see the relevance of my "wide open spaces" comment.

Small cafes can be found in every town, including the small villages. This time of the year, they feature tables outside where people sit to enjoy beer or coffee in the sunshine. This makes bicycling from village to village a special pleasure. Each small town highlights its own local beer, some are strong, containing six percent or more alcohol. You have to watch that stuff because it can make bicycling a bit hazardous. Many of the beers come in several grades of strength and color. So you can choose your poison within the same brand. Even for someone like me who is no great beer lover, it is a real adventure to try the different types.

This European adventure has proven to me that friendship and kindness are universal. My friends here share my worry about the violence in the world as indicated by news from such places as Bosnia, Texas, and South Africa—and we all share the frustration of wanting to do something, but finding no recourse but to wring our hands.

# FLORENCE

Standing by Michelangelo's statue of David, I realized that, like the Grand Canyon, no photograph can capture the magnificence of the work. Every detail is perfect, his face, his eyes, limbs, belly. Yet, his hands seem large and out of proportion. I wonder why.

This is only one of the thousands of masterpieces here. Florence is one big museum, but one has to taste the ice cream. I stood watching a man prepare my cone of vanilla and chocolate gelato. He gently molded the scoop into the perfect shape before he handed me the cone. "This is not ice cream," he said. "It is a work of art." And he was right. And it tasted almost as good as it looked. Someone told me that, per capita, Italians eat more pounds of ice cream per year than pasta. I don't doubt it, based on the number of people strolling on the streets with cones in their hands.

Julie and Bill Weimer were in town when I arrived. Bill is the finest gastronome I know. His objective in life is to eat in all of the best restaurants in the world—and he knows how to pick them. So, on Friday and Saturday, the three of us toured museums, ate in good restaurants, and compared good times. My only complaint was having to wear a tie to the restaurants Bill selected. Maybe someday he will be able to put some culture into this old cowboy. It was good to have time with Bill and Julie before they returned to the US in April.

On Sunday, Bill and Julie flew back to Paris, and I rented a small motorcycle to explore the hills outside of Florence. Bright sunshine lit up the city in hues of yellow and orange as I joined hordes of young people on their bikes competing for space on the crowded streets. Each terra-cotta tile of the roofs was visible and displayed its own shape and personality. Stopping for lunch, in contrast to Bill's gourmet eating, I sat on a terrace overlooking the city and ate pizza.

A fellow named Clayton Day moved the European Technology Institute from Verona, its previous location, to Florence last year. Clayton has successfully recruited participants from all over Europe. He draws English-speaking instructors from wherever he can find them to teach graduate-level courses on topics not usually covered in European universities. I fly to Florence several times a year to present my topics, usually regarding managing hi-tech organizations.

The students, too, are from all over: Slovakia, the Czech Republic, Germany, England, Croatia, Pakistan, Nepal, Scotland, Ireland. Bill Weimer spent the previous week with them teaching the principles of managing technical people. My week followed with case studies in which the students put the principles into practice. In spite of language barriers, the students performed like champions! We discussed a case that was designed to illustrate the need for sensitivity to race and ethnic differences. I had a young Black woman from Africa and a German engineer play the key roles. I was a bit anxious about the outcome, but the two did a fabulous job and the case was more successful than I hoped for.

After the formal classes were over, I met privately with each student to discuss their progress and anything else on their mind. Some of the challenges they face are formidable. For instance, the student from Croatia is struggling with whether to return to a war-torn country or seek his career somewhere else. By the time I left Florence, he had received word that he had landed a job in Holland.

\* \* \*

The morning sun ripples across the Arno as Ancolien and I head for Gino's Bakery for our morning cappuccino and pastry. Even at this hour, Saturday tourists crowd the Piazza de Pitti, stopping to look into the small shops typical of the Italian economy.

I picked up Ancolien at the airport yesterday, after a tiresome morning teaching. I was thrilled to see her wearing a broad smile, standing almost a whole head taller than the mostly Italian passengers. This is another chance for us to explore this place, so rich in art and history, together.

In spite of the crowds here, the autumn air smells fresh and clear, reminding me of Palo Alto, CA on a good day. It's cool enough for a jacket and it's a place to wear my straw hat purchased during my famous bicycle acquisition day in Paris. Ancolien wears a yellow, flowered dress, punctuated by a wide-brimmed yellow hat, its silk ribbon flowing in the breeze. We are smiling and chatting our way down the street, anticipating the taste of authentic Italian coffee.

A woman with two young children approaches us from the street.

The young boy and girl press next to us, holding out their hands. The woman moves in rapidly, muttering something in Italian mixed with another unrecognizable language. When I look down at one of the children, the woman grabs my coat with both hands, pulling me toward her. Her eyes pierce mine as she speaks again, even louder.

I struggle to pull away, but to no avail—her fingers sink into my coat. The next instant, Ancolien steps over, giving the woman a push that flings her almost into the street. "Leave us alone!" Ancolien says loudly, glaring at the woman. The woman responds with some strange, angry words and a quivering fist.

"Wow!" I say smiling. "I'm going to stick with you."

"She was trying to pick your pocket," Ancolien replies.

"Yes, I know. I was surprised at how aggressive she was."

"She's probably desperate, but she's teaching her children how to beg and steal. Sad," Ancolien says.

This was an example of Ancolien's strength and quick decision-making. Yes, she's lived in Amsterdam and perhaps had experience in dealing with difficult people. I, too, have experienced different situations in Paris and New York. But Ancolien's decisiveness and protective instincts feel different from previous relationships and it's comforting to me. This is a small incident in the broad scope of things, but it touched something deep. Someone cares enough to want to protect me. I feel less alone.

We perked up after our coffee. Gino's Bakery has an American name but was more elegant than any American bakery in my experience. They served our cappuccino in finely crafted cups and the pastries we picked from a meters-long glass display cabinet elicited instant saliva in my mouth.

We make our way along the Piazza del Pitti toward the Pitti Palace and our primary objective, Giardino di Boboli, the Boboli Gardens, noting several street-side restaurants as possibilities for late lunch or dinner.

We enter the gardens from Pitti Square, soon entering the grassy amphitheater with a wide pea-gravel walkway in the middle. Trees fill the hillside in front of us, but there is an inviting walkway leading to statues at the top of the hill. We head toward it. Near the top of the hill, we turn toward a beautiful waterway, dreaming of a place to relax by the water on a cool, dry sunny day.

The statues, the landscaping, the history, and the art are all beyond my wildest dreams, but my eyes are on Ancolien. We have established a special bond, a closeness I've seldom experienced. We are from different countries, but I am at home with her. Home is home now, not a den of conflict. She is teaching me how to recognize my feelings and express them. We are sharing our hopes, our fears, our similarities, our differences. She is from a small town. I am from a small town. Each of us is free to be our own person. That is a special gift.

The Ponte Vecchio bridge across the Arno glows in the light of the bright Tuscan sun, just after the winter solstice. Shops along the bridge cast long shadows although the clock towers have just struck 11. The air smells of river water, incense, cooked peppers, and asiago cheese.

A small group of tourists, probably American, judging by their wash-and-wear clothing, makes its way along the bridge, intermittently stopping hither and yon to finger the collectibles offered by the bridge vendors.

A flock of pigeons circles overhead in the cloudless sky, trying to get their bearings before heading home for their morning feed. Young children, holding waffle cones of gelato, giggle and run among the tourists, as if playing hide and seek in the crowd.

I stop by a window of glistening jewelry, silver, gold, rubies, emeralds, pens, bracelets, all handmade by Florentine craftspeople. A woman with dark eyes and full red lips invites us to enter. I stand in front of the display of emerald rings. She stands behind the glass.

I point out a gold band with a small emerald setting.

"Would you like to try it on?" the clerk asks Ancolien.

Ancolien is hesitant. "Ahh…"

"Yes," I say. And the clerk gently slides it on Ancolien's finger. A perfect fit.

"How do you like it?" I ask.

"It's beautiful," Ancolien replies.

"We'll take it," I say to the clerk.

"But… it's an engagement ring," Ancolien says.

I smile, looking into her eyes. "Yes, it is. Yes, it is."

We grasp each other's hand and embrace.

# HAPPY DUTCH WEDDING

Ancolien and I are seated at a massive walnut conference table in the historic town hall of Appingedam, Netherlands, a town formed 1,000 years ago, on the North Sea. We drove here this morning from Uithuizen, Ancolien's hometown about 25 kilometers away.

We spent yesterday with a professional photographer who followed us around the countryside taking pictures of us on dikes, under huge modern windmills, and in various poses around the countryside. Today, we continue that with pictures in this quaint seaside port near where Ancolien's parents grew up.

In the town hall, built in the 16 century, Ancolien's mother, father, two sisters and a brother, their spouses, and a Dutch judge look at us from their places around the table. The robed judge, with blond hair and a round, but chiseled classic Dutch face, opens a large book, reminding me of the family Bible in which my grandmother kept family data, turns a few pages, looks at each of us around the table, and prepares to start the wedding ceremony.

Ancolien's father and I have watched quite a few soccer games together in the family living room. I clapped and cheered when he did, trying to make up for my ignorance of European football and the Dutch language. He understands and speaks a few words of English, but I suspect he'd rather stay in his own comfortable world. He's been cordial to me, although he certainly regards me as a foreigner.

Her mother smiles, eyes darting from person to person, and I wonder what she is thinking. Her sister moved to Canada many years ago, 6,000 miles away in distance and connection. She's been concerned that Ancolien will follow the same path.

Everyone else is watching raptly with big grins. Hilde, within two years of Ancolien's age, is like the sister I never had. She has a boisterous laugh and a pragmatic, positive outlook on life. Sister, Harma, is not confident of her English, and I hope to get to know her better. Klassiert, her brother and youngest of Ancolien's siblings, likes to joke around, so we share laughs together.

I feel comfortable with them and with their spouses. My family is notably absent. Mom and my children know Ancolien from our visits to the US, but all need to know her better. Yet, because of Ancolien's warmth and encouragement, I am more confident than ever, she will be welcomed into our family.

The judge asks for our attention and starts the ceremony. She says each phrase in both Dutch and English, out of respect for me and for Ancolien's father. In a few minutes, Ancolien and I say, "I do," and we are officially married. Everyone cheers.

After the photographer takes dozens of family pictures, we go to a nearby restaurant for a big lunch together where we toast each other and enjoy roast beef, fish, noodles, vegetables, and homemade bread. After the toasts, I speak in Dutch, giving my thanks and commitment to Ancolien and the family.

When I called my mother a few days later to tell her we were married in a town hall built over 450 earlier than this year, 1996, she quipped, "I thought people were still living in caves then," adding "You had to travel the world to find the right woman. This time you got it right."

# OUR NEW COMPANY

After almost a year in our Valkenburg apartment, Ancolien found us another apartment in Aalbeek, a small gathering of rural houses on a high hill about two kilometers outside Valkenburg. The new flat is in an old brick farmhouse built around an interior courtyard, which had been converted to four relatively spacious living spaces.

There is a farm selling apples and other vegetables across Aalbeekerweg, the street in front. There are orchards in the fields beyond and lots of walking trails occasioned by badger holes. Our neighbors are friendly, but, like most of the Dutch, value their privacy.

Paul and Monique Daemen, our landlords, have three young boys and a huge Irish Wolfhound that likes to run with Ancolien and me as we explore the farm roads nearby. The farmers across the country open their paths and dirt roads to walking and biking as long as no one enters the fields. Even so, Ancolien and I tasted a few of the local apples that grow on finely pruned trees hardly higher than a Dutch boy's head (it's tall), but with yields so thick, one can hardly touch a limb or leaf without touching an apple. We've been sure the farmer wouldn't miss his two pieces of fruit. Because of the plentiful crop, we've been able to buy a whole bag of apples from the guy across the street for just over two guilders—about one dollar.

Just up the road, a farmer has a field full of healthy-looking sheep. A couple of the lambs love to play games, including jumping on the back of one of the old rams, then standing there to wait for his reaction. His face seems to say, look at these silly teenagers. Don't they have anything better to do?

A larger village called Hulsberg, about a kilometer down the hill toward Valkenburg—easy biking distance—has a village square, a grocery store, a post office, a bakery, a florist, a few other small shops, and, another feature we like: a Chinese Restaurant.

Within a week, once again, we converted one of our bedrooms into an office with two workstations to begin our work together. Ancolien became the head of administration and I the head of strategy and content for the new company, Bridgewater Research Group, NL, BV. We aim to use my expertise in strategy, educational technology, and distance education to do consulting projects around the European Union. Because our company is a Dutch BV, we became qualified to bid on projects with the European Commission and other country governments, as well as commercial organizations.

Early in my time in Europe, Soren Nipper, my friend and colleague from Denmark, and I collaborated in a wide-ranging study of the open universities across Europe. The study examined how each delivered its programs and how each was applying educational technology. The project was sponsored by the European Association of Distance Teaching Universities, headed by Nicholas Fox, and required us to interview important leaders in each of the countries. By the time we presented the report, we had an intimate knowledge of the state of distance education, had met leaders in the field, and established ourselves as knowledgeable experts.

The many open universities across Europe provided adult learners the opportunity to expand their knowledge and degrees, but they were delivering most courses in the early nineties, by way of text, CDs, and occasionally, face-to-face. Few had experience with video transmission, computer-based delivery, or other multimedia techniques. When I left IBM in 1987, we were on the leading edge of video production and delivery of training programs. And EuroPace, similarly, led the way to new techniques of distance education. So, there is a relatively small community of experienced experts across the world who can actually apply and implement technology-based distance education. That is the unique position our small company established in Europe.

After starting the Dutch company, we successfully landed important study projects for the European Commission (EC). We were winning over half of the projects on which we bid, unusually high for this kind of work. As a result, other experts in the field of distance education and education technology were eager to work with us. And most EC work required collaboration from at least one or two of the 15 countries of the European Union.

We conducted a series of research projects for the EC, *Telematics for Education and Training* (TET). Telematics was the term used to describe a combination of telecommunications and computer technologies. Each of these required organizing a team of researchers across the globe because the studies aimed to find out the status of educational technology in designated countries. We recruited important team members in each target country who helped us understand the local economic, technological, and educational environment.

For instance, Bill Weimer, now in the USA, helped us report on *Telematics for Education and Training in the United States*. We had other experts as we studied Canada, Australia, and the Netherlands. We published large reports to the European Commission on each of the countries.

Periodically, the European Commission in their "framework" programs requested research proposals in different technology segments, from organizations in the European Union (EU). When hundreds of proposals arrived, the EC assembled teams of experts to review and rank the proposals. I became one of the experts in the fields of information technology, manufacturing technology, and educational technology. We experts from all over the EU met in Brussels to select the projects to receive funding. This gave our small company an opportunity to meet other experts, build our reputation, and keep up with leading-edge technology development.

We eventually won a $300,000 EC project to help universities in Central and Eastern European countries (not yet in the EU) establish distance education systems in their respective countries.

When we received the contract papers, we were surprised to see the EC required us to have, in the bank, an escrow fund of a third of the total contract value, over $100,000. Ancolien and I thought our local branch of ABN/AMRO, an international Dutch bank, would be happy to provide us a loan for the escrow value, since we had a certified European Commission contract in hand. But, no! Our local bank president said he would be happy to keep our money if we gave him the $100,000. What the hell? What can we do?

After sweating for a couple of days, I decided to use my Stanford University connections to find a way out of the problem. My Stanford U. alumni record listed a senior vice president of ABN/AMRO located in Amsterdam. When I told him my dilemma over the telephone, he said, "Give me three days."

On the second day, he called me back and said, "Call Mr. Deckers at our Valkenburg branch. He'll be happy to help you."

"Thank you, sir, we deeply appreciate your help," I replied.

Mr. Deckers laid out the red carpet at the bank the next day. We had our loan processed within the next hour. Our colleague, Soren Nipper led the project for us, successfully setting up new approaches to higher education delivery in several Eastern countries.

We were working with the Central and Eastern countries after the fall of the "Iron Curtain" and the Berlin Wall. Many of the newly freed country leaders were eager to join the EU, but EU officials were concerned that managers in the East had been too indoctrinated in communist thinking. Therefore, the Eastern countries should find new methods of executive development. The EC commissioned one of their units, the European Training Foundation to develop those methods and write a manual for the process. I was appointed as one representative to a team of 15 experts to write the manual. My chapter, "Technology in the Service of Learning" was published as part of the book, *Management Development for the New Europe*.

As Operations Manager of our company, Ancolien handled all administration, accounting, contract administration, and translation. We paid associates in several different countries, which required electronic currency transfers and country fees. We continually prepared complex proposals requiring accurate cost estimates and maintained strict budget control of multiple projects and flawless tax accounting. Our success as a small business operating in a complex international environment depended on her competence and expertise.

Ger Jonkergouw, with whom I worked on projects with the Dutch Open University, became a good friend and trusted colleague. Ger, a philosopher, sociologist, artist, scientist, and writer was a creative, leading-edge thinker—a true renaissance man. He and I collaborated on many projects and idea development. Ger used painting as a way to open up new ideas for organizations that were creating strategic plans. He presented his ideas in many organizations around Europe.

We landed a project to study Japan but had no person fluent in Japanese to help us lead the project. We needed someone who understood the culture, was knowledgeable in technology and education, was a competent researcher, and could write in English. That was a big order. We bid on this project, thinking it was a long-shot bid. How wrong I was. Our success with the other projects must have swayed the EC evaluators. Our proposal expressed confidence we could find Japanese researchers. Yet, that was much more difficult than I expected,

A Japanese graduate student at Iowa State University initially joined our team but disappeared after he learned the scope of the project. After that, I asked my colleagues in Brussels to help me find someone. One contact suggested Mari Hyodo, daughter of the Japanese ambassador to Belgium and NATO.

I met Mari at the Belga Queen restaurant in Brussels. The restaurant was more upscale than my usual choice but finding a competent researcher for this project was exceptionally important.

I saw, turning the corner, a Japanese woman with a flowing navy blue tunic coming toward me.

"Are you Grant?" she said, stepping toward me, smiling.

"Yes. You must be Mari. I am so happy to meet you," I said.

She offered her hand and I clasped it gently.

"Thanks for coming. We have a reservation. Are you hungry?" I asked.

"Sure. This looks like a nice place," she said.

She spoke English with a slight British accent. No one, hearing only her voice, would ever detect her nationality.

The maître de showed us to the table while we continue talking, easily and fluently.

I learned Mari spoke five languages, had lived in seven countries, including the USA, was an accomplished pianist, and loved to read.

I explained the project to her, indicating it would take online, telephone, and possibly face-to-face research. She readily agreed, telling me she would be leaving for Tokyo in a couple of weeks to stay several months.

I explained how we communicate via email and telephone and our simple project progress report consisting of three numbers each week. On a scale of one to five, where five is best, tell us your number for each of the following: 1.) What is your confidence we will finish the project on time? 2.) What is your confidence you will be proud of our work? And 3.) What is your confidence we can stay within our budget? We also agreed to a weekly telephone chat.

At the end of the lunch, I was thankful to have met Mari, a competent, talented new researcher, and felt a big sigh of relief to have found a way to staff the project. I was fortunate to have located Mari.

We had another breakthrough that has helped us in these early stages, a beta version of a Japanese-English translation computer application. With it, we were able to translate documents and websites into acceptable English. From these results, we were able to list some specific questions for Mari to answer. Mari returned to Tokyo, conducted her study, and wrote an outstanding paper for inclusion in our final report.

We developed a solid reputation in our field in Europe and were engaged in significant, leading-edge work. Ancolien established a solid business foundation for the business, and we had an exceptionally good working relationship.

# *CLOSING* THE CIRCLE

# TO THE USA

In the summer of 1995, Ancolien and I took a month to explore the United States, a country she had never seen. We visited Mom for a few days in Virginia, assembled backpacking equipment, rented a car, and headed west. A long auto trip was a new experience for Ancolien, whose idea of a long excursion was a fifty-kilometer bicycle ride. Yes, her family in the northern Netherlands had a car, but they never ventured far. We stowed the camping gear in the trunk, leaving plenty of room on the back seat for Ancolien to nap during our 400-500 mile, early morning drives.

We avoided big cities but sampled small towns cafes, McDonald's, barbeque, morning coffee with bagels, and chicken-fried steak. We breathed the fresh air high in the Rockies, spent three days riding undisciplined horses on a dude ranch in Estes Park, CO, rented an adobe house for a couple of weeks in a Santa Fe barrio, and danced Texas Two-Step on the rooftop patio of the La Fonda Hotel. At every opportunity, we met ordinary Americans, every one of which was curious to talk to a person from another country. "Where're you from, honey?" became a common question.

While in New Mexico, we visited several Native American Pueblos, looking for a black ceramic pottery wedding vase, a specialty of certain artists in the region, as a wedding gift to daughter, Laura, whose wedding we were planning to attend on our return to the East Coast. Searching for a vase gave us the opportunity to visit several pueblos and meet Native artists. Ancolien was quick to establish rapport with several Native women at the pueblos. One woman invited us into her home to show us pictures of her family and grandchildren. We talked at length, each of us sharing stories of growing up in our different environments and countries.

Driving back to Virginia, we talked about what our life might be like in the United States; and where, in the vast country, might be the best place to settle. Mom and my children were on the East Coast, but my heart was still in the West because of my time in Colorado and New Mexico.

Our business was another thing to consider. We needed to be closer to the technology developments in the United States. What would be the best place from a business point of view? We decided against suburbs of big cities, preferring instead small college cities, close to good transportation because we wanted to maintain good ties with Europe. The East Coast quickly became the top choice. And I remembered my promise to Ancolien that she could finish her degree in the United States.

The following year, returning to visit Mom, we saw an announcement of some open houses on display at Lake Monticello, close to Charlottesville, VA, home of the University of Virginia, my alma mater. One of the houses excited us, the right size, the right layout, the right price. We worked out a plan with the builder and his realtor who were displaying the house. He would build us a house like the one on display on a lot we would choose later.

Ancolien and I described the kind of location and parcel we preferred and returned to the Netherlands. A couple of weeks later, a cassette arrived from the realtor with videos of three plots of land that would fit our chosen house. We picked one of the lots and building began.

Nine months later, Ancolien and I returned to the USA and moved into our new house. I was in the final stages of completing the Japanese project, preparing the report and presenting it to the European Commission. That meant spending the next few months continuing writing in the new location and, later, returning to Brussels to deliver and present the reports. Ancolien quickly enrolled in the local community college to continue her education. Her English Language qualification test demonstrated that her language training in the Netherlands had provided excellent preparation for her studies.

Completing the Japanese project was an ideal concentration for our first six months. Our researcher, Mari, accumulated all the data needed for the report and it was left for me to compile it into a coherent report. The office in our new house provided a quiet, well-equipped venue for the work.

The project also kept me in touch with my counterparts in Europe. But once I completed the project, American culture hit me in the face. I'd been away for five years, only occasionally visiting the USA. Everything was different from Europe and from the country I left five years ago. Yes, Ancolien and I watched Jay Leno and CNN International in Europe, but TV is not reality.

Kids on the street used slang that was foreign to my ears. No one had a cellphone five years ago; now everyone has one. European English had become my vocabulary. What are these people talking about? The cafes where Ancolien and I sat by the river sipping local beer or having coffee were left behind, replaced by McDonald's and other fast food places on every street.

In Europe, people in distance education and education technology knew of me and my work. In the US, no one knew or cared. Whereas the

European countries were advocating cooperation, the American culture is dog eat dog. If you want to be known, hire a branding expert.

Ancolien asked, "It hasn't been easy for you, has it?"

"You can probably see me struggling," I answered.

Ancolien had a clear purpose, to get her university degrees. I left my purpose behind in Europe. Now, I must create a new one.

At the professional level, I joined the Virginia Piedmont Technology Council and the Charlottesville Venture Group, local organizations focused on entrepreneurship and economic development, developed some good, trusted colleagues, acquired some free-lance consulting projects, while also raising my profile in the professional community. Although I engaged in some workforce development projects, my main focus became leadership and management in scientific and technical companies, my core skill set.

Our team in Europe had studied educational technology in the United States, publishing a report, *Telematics for Education and Training in the United States*. The report demonstrated the fragmentation of the American education and technology sectors, compared with the more centralized European system. I contacted a couple of entrepreneurial companies offering new approaches to educational technology, but ultimately decided they were not for me. And they, interestingly enough, saw little value in my international experiences.

An attendee at a local Chamber of Commerce meeting summarized the American attitude: "We have the best telecommunications system in the world," he said.

"Have you ever been to Finland?" I asked.

The other guy responded with a blank stare.

# JEROME

American politics had become another mystery, but I decided to try understanding it, especially since the state and local systems vary across the country. My town of Bridgewater, in Connecticut, used the town hall method to approve budgets and other important issues, but I had little knowledge about Virginia's local government system. So, I decided to seek out the local political committee as a way to start connecting with the community.

Jerome Booker and I arrived almost simultaneously at the parking lot where the local Democratic Committee was to meet.

"Man, your truck is dirtier than my van!" I said, offering my hand.

Jerome laughed. "You're right," he said. "I'm scheduled to clean it up next year. Where're you from? I never saw you before."

"I just moved here from overseas and am looking for a way to get involved," I said.

"Good. I spent a lot of time in Germany while in the Air Force. So glad to have you join us."

I learned Jerome was once a County Supervisor, and still a prominent leader in the county. He had been one of the highest-ranking non-commissioned officers in the Air Force and been a Supervisor in Fluvanna County for 16 years. He knew everyone. He knew the ropes. We spent a lot of time after the meeting discussing issues facing the county and who was involved.

As the months rolled on, for the second time in my life, I became an apprentice to a Black man, the first, to Haywood Johnson learning how to install stoves and lay flooring, second to Jerome Booker learning local politics. Working sometimes at his dining table, sometimes at mine, Jerome and I telephoned voters to win their support, ask for contributions, to convince people to take our side on issues. Jerome seemed to know everyone in the county, both Black and White. Before starting our phone calling, we'd go down the list of names, commenting about what we knew about each person.

Jerome said, "Ed Jones is always concerned about the county budget and the impact on his taxes. Mary Baldwin has three children and has complained about how the third-grade teacher treated her daughter."

Those notes made each call personal. "Hi Ed, I saw last month's budget meeting. What did you think about the capital improvement plan?"

"You must always ask for the person's vote—their commitment," Jerome said. "Most people will stick to a commitment they say out loud."

Jerome never attended a class on political science but acquired wisdom about local politics by the school of hard knocks.

His lessons translated directly to other activities in my life. "The first rule of politics is 'Know the vote before you get to the meeting.' This principle is important in business, non-profit, and civic work. When your group faces a critical decision, contact each person before the meeting to help persuade them to vote your way."

It never occurred to me that some people might think it odd for us to feel so comfortable in each other's homes. Being with Jerome brought me back to my childhood culture, back to the basics, back to breakfasts of eggs, bacon, and biscuits, back to living rooms of family pictures, back to simple family conversations, back to laughing and inside jokes. We could hear each other. We could see each other. We could talk about difficult issues, learning together.

I once asked Jerome how he dealt with the prejudice he encountered.

"I just ignore it," he said. "If you know you're right and doing the right thing for the people, you keep on working."

"Are you serious?" I asked. "It must have been hurtful sometimes."

"No. I am serious. I work with everyone. If someone is prejudiced, it's their problem."

Jerome never allowed himself to become a victim, no matter how many challenges he faced. He just worked hard to overcome obstacles and get things done for the people, such as getting the County to install a comprehensive water system for residences in the Fork Union area. He worked for all the people.

My work with Jerome and the political scene helped me feel more at home in the community, developing new friends, connecting at a personal level, and understanding current issues.

# THE LIGHT

The light is on.

Last night, when I left the workshop, I checked to make sure it was off. I remember pulling the cord and tripping over a tool box while feeling my way to the door while cursing the dark.

But tonight, it's on again. Perhaps the result of a visit by Sheila, the real estate agent who is selling Mom's house. Except for Mom and I, only Sheila has a key to the house. Mom certainly wasn't here; she's safely sleeping at the Orange Nursing Home where she moved last month.

It's strange that Sheila would be here in the basement workshop where Dad, brother Warren and I spent so many hours before he died 15 years ago. This was the classroom, the art gallery, the tool shop, the sanctuary.

We three built every workbench, set up every tool, installed every electrical connection including the single bulb hanging from the ceiling and it's a little pull cord stretching to the frame of the entry door, thinking we'd someday install a real switch. But reaching for the cord became part of our daily routine. Whoever got to the workshop first would turn the light on. Last one turned it off.

I can't imagine Sheila being here, pulling the cord. But the light is on.

I pull the cord. Remembering the familiar motion from my childhood. The workshop turns dark again. This time, I'm sure the light is out.

I called Sheila, who said she's been upstairs, but not in the workshop. She can't explain the light.

A week later, I step into the empty house. The furniture was sold last week, and Saturday's garage sale disposed of miscellaneous items. The place echoes with my footsteps, no Lawrence Welk on the TV, no piano in the den, none of Mom's paperweights, no collection of wooden horses Dad accumulated.

I open the door to the basement, proceed down the creaking stairs, turn the corner to the workshop. I freeze at the first rays of light on the floor

In the workshop I look around. The hammer is still where I left it at last visit, sawdust lays undisturbed on the table saw. Nails, screws, safety goggles, dust mask and who knows what covers the workbench. Everything is as I left it.

But the light shines brightly.

# MOM
# DRIFTING AWAY

"She's breathing quietly now," Warren, my brother, says.

"Yes, but still a bit labored," I answer.

We are here on a vigil at the Village Nursing Home in Fork Union, Virginia. Mom is in the final stages of her battle with dementia. Warren flew in from Texas three days ago when the final stages began. He's ten years younger than I, and has always been a calming, steady rock. He's father to four children, two of his own, two acquired with marriage to his second wife, Judy. And he is one of the best dads I've ever known. Family is his top priority, a trait I admire, but never been able to emulate. My drive, which Mom called ambition, has always crept to the top, even though my conscience told me it was wrong. That choice sure hasn't rewarded me with exceptional happiness or accomplishments. Quite the opposite. It's often driven me into the ditch. Nevertheless, I keep digging.

Mom's dementia obscured time and memory—hers and mine. I try to remember the good times, the times we enjoyed dinner, trips, games, laughter. A young geriatric doctor told Warren and me what to expect after we first saw the signs four years ago, the strange dreams, occasional erratic behavior, out of context stories from the past. That conversation triggered us to prepare contingency plans to move Mom from our family home on South Almond St. to the Orange Nursing Home, then eventually to the Village Home in Fork Union, to be within easy driving distance of me.

It was as if I was trying to catch Mom's hand as she was drifting out to sea. She seemed farther away with each week, becoming gradually less coherent. Sometimes she recognized me, other times stared at my face only seeing a stranger. Mom is only 20 years older than me. Is this me in 20 years? And every day visiting the nursing home seemed harder.

Aunt Ruth, who often felt closer to me than Mom, encouraged me, even pressured me to go every day. Ruth said, "She needs to see you."

But I sat with Mom during every visit, trying to talk to her, feeding her, holding her hand, with almost no response. I wanted to cry every day, but no tear would come. I just froze to keep from melting.

The nursing home was modest to say the least—not highly rated, but some staff members poured their hearts out to the residents and relatives.

One of the staff, Dorothy White, got through to Mom on a wavelength I could not duplicate. Dorothy, a woman from the local Black American community, sang traditional hymns in a soft voice matched by a smile that could melt icebergs. Instead of dreading the ten-mile drive to Fork Union, I looked forward to Dorothy's song of the day.

\* \* \*

Dorothy has been in and out of Mom's room on this last day, helping us work through our feelings. We think Mom has been suffering, but we don't know. Did she feel any pain? What was she feeling? Did she know what was going on? Is it good or bad that her life is ending?

In a while, a few last labored breaths end. Warren and I stand there, not knowing what to say. Dorothy comes to the door and one of us tells her the news, as if she didn't already know. Dorothy hugs us both. We continue to stand by the bed.

A short while later, Mr. Phillip Carter, the minister who serves the nursing home, and his wife, Mrs. Helen Carter, join us in the room and hold Warren and me close. Warm hugs from people who love us. Phillip is the pastor of a Black American Church in Fluvanna County, Helen works tirelessly to help people in need around the countryside, driving people to the Doctor's office for cancer treatment, advising on child care, and being a friend.

We talk quietly and the Carter's offer a prayer as we all hold hands. Warren and I are not alone, love surrounds us.

Dementia destroys the memory of its immediate victim, but it also destroys the memory about the person in the minds of the loved ones. How do family members recall all the good times before the downward slide began when every minute of recent times has been a struggle?

\* \* \*

Warren and I prepared a display of pictures and mementoes from Mom's younger days to help us remember the dedicated young woman who cared so much for her family. A person who preferred a quiet life but stepped up with courage to every challenge she faced. From the personal diaries from ages 15 and 16 she left us, we discovered a vivacious young woman, though growing up in a dispersed, rural area, had an early life rich in close relationships with family and friends, active in church and social events. A young person who loved dancing. Those diaries helped Warren and me recover our real mother.

# A NEW CENTURY

As we approach a new century, this country seems obsessed with news. In Europe, we watched CNN International, read the International Herald Tribune, and read the Economist, but never were we bombarded as in the US. Everyone seems glued to the news about Clinton's impeachment after having an interlude with an intern in the White House. More significantly for us, the European Union finally announced its single currency, the Euro, in January. A single currency across all the countries in which we operated would have saved us significant time and fees when we were doing projects in Europe.

We are in the middle of an era called the "dot-com" boom and internet companies are popping up all over town as people exploit new online businesses and e-commerce, where one can buy and sell goods and services online, without a physical storefront.

Last year, a local startup company that published a magazine, *Working Weekly*, asked me to write a column and, after a few months of that, hired me as director of strategic planning. Gail Bentley, an ambitious freethinker had no reservations about spending her investors' money, set out to grow a famous company. Gail had many flaws as a business person, but she knew how to hire talented people. I worked closely with two of them, Jennifer Till and Kathleen Shannon, developing new strategies and approaches to a wild marketplace.

Kathleen was an outstanding strategist with strong marketing and visual arts skills. Jennifer had a deep sensitivity to people and their relationship to their jobs, having run a small manufacturing plant in Pennsylvania.

After several months in our jobs, the company was headed for disaster, primarily because of Gail's naive, narcissistic approach to management. I tried several times to guide Gail's path through good decision making, but each decision she made was putting the company in more danger. Eventually, I submitted a list of seven recommendations to her that I hoped would save the company. When she rejected them all, I resigned.

Within the next several weeks, Kathleen, Jennifer and I decided to start a new consulting company to kick off in a few months, just after the start of the new year, the new century. I was thrilled to have this new partnership with two people with backgrounds quite different from mine. We were great strategists and problem solvers together. We soon agreed on a mission and set of values.

Our Mission: We aim to help leaders develop organizations that provide fulfilling job opportunities for their people, to help people feel a sense of purpose and satisfaction in their daily work by giving them the knowledge, skill, information sources, and systems to do their jobs better, and to develop new, creative solutions and approaches to organizational issues.

Our core Values and Beliefs: To conduct our work with honesty, integrity, fairness and a sense of purpose.

1. To follow our own leadership philosophy (as taught) in all dealings. If it is not acceptable to us, it should not be acceptable to our clients.
2. To provide the best in quality and service, while delivering a professional product at a competitive cost.
3. To show respect at all times for the individual, whether he or she is on the staff, a customer, or a supplier.
4. To do our work always with a sense of fun and optimism that will instill a "can-do" attitude in our associates and our clients.
5. To be good citizens of the community in which we live and work by contributing to thoughtful economic development, a safe and healthy environment, and harmony in the community.
6. We believe that profit is the reward for good leadership performance.

When I left corporate life about 12 years ago, I never wanted to see another top executive. Yet, helping people feel more fulfilled in their jobs has always been my primary goal in working life. That means working with CEOs and other business leaders, the people who set the rules of working life and determine the physical and organizational environment in which people work.

My primary conflicts with corporate executives were the result of our differences in the way people should be treated. Treating people badly to gain more profit was in conflict with my deeply held values. Now, setting out on this new venture with trusted partners, we will work with leaders who share our values and work for the good of their employees. We will do good work together. And, we will have fun.

\* \* \*

Ancolien enrolled in the local community college soon after our move to Virginia, majoring in biology, ultimately aiming for a degree in Occupational Therapy (OT). Ancolien was captivated by that career choice after many conversations with an OT who lived in our apartment complex in the Netherlands. She obtained her certification as an Emergency Medical Technician and joined the local rescue squad as a volunteer, even becoming qualified to drive the ambulance. Ancolien obtained her associate degree and has transferred to the University of Virginia to major in Psychology. After UVA, she will select a graduate school to obtain her OT degree.

We have seen much of the world together, and Ancolien is getting her degrees in the USA, two of my three promises to her. We have found our paths and given each other the greatest gift of all: the love, support, and freedom to be ourselves.

# RETURN TO NEW MEXICO

The morning sun lights up the sandstone cliff, highlighting dark pock-marks, the entrances to ancient Tewa people's winter homes at the Puye Cliffs. Ancolien and I are the only ones here at this hour, although some of the nearby Santa Clara Pueblo's current residents might say the spirits of the native people who lived here over four centuries ago surround us as a new century dawns.

It seemed fitting to visit Santa Clara Pueblo on this first day of a new century, returning to the place we bought a black pottery wedding gift for daughter Laura's wedding five years ago in 1995, and marks my return to the state where I heard news of Dad's death almost 20 years ago.

The Tewas who lived here carved living spaces into the side of the mesa, providing shelter from the intense sun and winter storms. They also con-structed summer dwellings on top of the mesa over 200 feet up the mesa's vertical face. They embedded foot and hand steps into the soft rock, so they could climb to the homes and fields at the top.

But those steps were built in a pattern that strangers or attackers could not easily decipher. A climber needed to know the pattern, or they might get stuck on the side of the wall. Only Tewas "in the know," could find a path to the top. I wonder if these people were the forerunners of corporate leaders. One must be "in the know" to find your way to the top. A misstep could strand you on the side of the mesa. Stuck, with no way up and no way down. Step out of the mold and you will fall to the bottom.

I failed to analyze the pattern. I got stuck in a job for five years, broke out of the mold by going to the University of New Mexico, then fell back to a lower level and encountered another set of patterns. Why did I get stuck? I could not answer that question, and no one was willing to tell me the answer.

When I jumped off the pattern and went to the University of New Mexico, I found another path, with a promising new village at the top, but was unwilling to make the family, financial, and social compromises necessary to follow my dream.

Perhaps I did not want it strongly enough. I had the technical, busi-ness, and intellectual skills, but something was missing. Did I actually want to climb higher on the corporate mesa? I had seen Ted Papes' corporate life close up and wasn't sure I aspired to live that way.

My disillusionment with corporate life might have started when I saw first-hand what that top executive life was like, what the people were like. Did I want to be a person like that? That issue coincided with my concern that the company had moved away from one of its core principles, Respect for the Individual. The company lost that value in the days of Frank Cary. At that time, he and other executives became preoccupied with protecting IBM against the US Justice Department's antitrust suit. Those were the years the company lost its focus on its people. And at my level, I was trying to stay true to my values and the company's, in spite of the actions and pressures of upper management.

After retiring in 1987, several of my colleagues who had also retired, initially said, "Our retirement is like dropping a stone in the sea, creating only a small ripple with no effect on the ocean." But when the steep decline in IBM profitability became public in the following year, we revised our comment to: "Look what happened, they really needed us."

Outside analysts said the company got behind in technology and lost contact with its customers, but underneath it all was the loss of its inner core. Yes, companies have no soul, but good ones have strong core principles around which the culture endures. IBM had lost its values. That was visible to me while contemplating the decision to take the company's retirement package.

I had at least two viable opportunities to leave the company, the first after completing the Sorensen Program at Stanford University, the second when finishing my sabbatical at the University of New Mexico. I failed to take a new road in each case for similar reasons. I was unwilling to take the risk to the family finances and the family relationships. Yet, a question remains. If I had a partner at the time who understood the options and encouraged me to follow my dream, would I have made the turn? The answer is unambiguously yes in the New Mexico case, and no in the Stanford case because IBM had invested a lot in me to go to Stanford, and I felt a moral responsibility to return to the company.

Indeed. The company invested in me not only in Stanford, but also in many other ways. My masters and doctorate degrees came as a result of IBM's generous education packages. And numerous other programs sought to make me a better leader. The company subsidized my excursions to Stanford and the University of New Mexico. There was a lot to love about the company. In my early career, someone from the Personnel Department told me that many people died shortly after retirement, seemingly because the company was their life, their purpose, their being. I never saw statistical proof of that, but it is plausible.

I feel that loss now. Not because I retired from the company, but because I felt we lost our core values. In the later years, I suffered from cultural dissonance, out of tune with my culture, the company's culture. That is the reason I could not find the path to climb.

How should we measure our own success? The corporate world has a simple answer to that: how high you climb, your pictures in the corporate archives, your listing in the annual report. But what if we measure success by how much we help people? Measured by that ruler, a much different picture of my career appears. In my IBM career, I had 15 management jobs, but only two of those existed before I arrived. 13 jobs were devoted to starting new organizations or changing organizations. We trained hundreds of people to get them launched in new career paths, introduced new products such as the personal computer that helped people at home and at work. I personally counseled hundreds of people over my years.

\* \* \*

I wonder what my life would be like now if I stayed at the University of New Mexico. For sure, I would never have met Ancolien, nor Sally for that matter. Would Joyce have actually returned to Connecticut without me? And could I have regained my relationship with the children with me in the West and them in the East? Would I have settled into an academic and consulting career, or even jumped into the wild New Mexican politics?

How many roads not taken have been in my path?

Human lives are backwards. Wisdom should come at an early age, when choices are abundant and opportunities abound. We need wisdom to make early decisions, not late when the choices are only part of murky memories. How do we detect and understand the stream of culture and tradition that sweeps us along restricting our choices, dictating right and wrong, like an electron whose path is predetermined when propelled through a magnetic field?

I didn't know enough, understand enough to avoid the magnetic field. I had good parents, a loving home, a family that loved me. That set a high bar, a bar I wanted to reach. I did not want to disappoint them. How could I possibly fail to live up to those standards?

It is up to each person to determine their own path, to understand their own values, to set their own goals, to overcome obstacles, to reach out for help and perspective when we need it. At every turning point, counsel from other wise people could have shown a bright light on the decisions, illuminating new alternatives, highlighting unexplored consequences.

My downward spiral stopped when I began reaching out to others for friendship and help, opening up to my feelings and vulnerabilities, and forgiving myself and others for not meeting the false standards I had set. Moving to a new country forced me to learn new rules, new cultures, new people, and helped tune my internal and external senses to what was happening around me.

Defining oneself is a lifetime quest. "Who am I?" does not have one answer, but has a different, evolving answer each day as one learns and develops. Sometimes that evolution is slow, other times, rapid. The slowest are the times when we are drifting, visionless. The rapid are the times when we are exploring, turning every encounter into a learning experience. Ultimately, finding oneself requires deep relationships with others, talking, sharing, having substantive discussions, and learning together.

Every day brings new experiences, new exposures, each of which can be a turning point, depending on the kind of decisions we make at each intersection. Those decisions may seem unimportant at the time but might have profound impact on ourselves and the people around us. Each person makes thousands of decisions every day, most are small automatic choices. Choosing what socks to wear is unlikely to change a person's life, but other decisions could put us on a significantly different path. Learning to tell the difference is an important skill.

We can learn to recognize decisions to accept or reject a new opportunity as important turning points, but other incidents may not be so clear. Meeting a stranger in an airport or a hotel, for instance. Random events open new doors, shedding new light on a person's direction. Every new experience or encounter contains the possibility for growth and learning. Attitude is important. Do we recognize new encounters as opportunities or threats? Do we face them with fear or enthusiasm? A "possibilities" attitude leads to growth.

The number of opportunities we experience depends on the number of interactions and experiences we create. Traveling, reading new books, attending concerts, and other activities increase our encounters with other people. Courage and curiosity can turn those encounters into rich new opportunities.

Yet, our choices have consequences. Other people are involved. Deciding to move or take a new job affects not just the immediate family, but also friends and family in the present location and those in the new location. Some of those people may be losing important relationships while others are gaining them. Analyzing those impacts is a complex task, but a task often not considered in depth when making a decision. How do we know who will be hurt and who will gain? Talking to people affected can provide, at least, a partial answer, but the unintended consequences or long term effects often cannot be known.

* * *

As the author, John Reese, said, "In the end we're all alone and no one's coming to save you." But before the end, being alone is a choice. Reaching out to develop warm, trusting relationships with others is the solution for bad choices, loneliness, and cultural dissonance.

* * *

"I'm going to climb the ladder to get a closer look," Ancolien says.

"Help yourself. You know how much I hate heights. But be careful, that ladder is about 50 feet high," I reply.

Watching her climb reminds me how much I admire her courage, determination, and sense of exploration, and how quickly the native women warmed up to her when we first visited here. Although she and I come from different countries, we both grew up in small towns and share the same culture. We are comfortable, we are free.

Last night, New Year's Eve, we enjoyed a Mariachi band, a luscious meal, and margaritas at the Rancho de Chimayo Restaurant, then walked across the road to enjoy the adobe fireplace in our room until the new year arrived. As far as we could tell, the world's computers did not fail as predicted by all the scary scenarios of the Y2K media frenzy.

"This place is a long way from the Netherlands," I said as we watched the burning logs. "How does that feel after three years in this country?"

"We've been together for seven years now. Wherever you and I are, that's home. Yes, I miss the Netherlands. It will always be home in some way. But we are together," she answered.

# EPILOGUE

*"What's it all about Alfie*
*Is it just for the moment we live*
*What's it all about*
*When you sort it out, Alfie*
*Are we meant to take more than we give*
*Or are we meant to be kind?"*
—Hal David / Burt F. Bacharach

I was fortunate to have experienced the birth and life span of the computer revolution. Although much of this book expresses my criticism and doubts about the IBM company and some of its leaders, in my time, it was a great company led by some giants of the industry, principled people who cared about their employees. The ethical and interpersonal values of the early IBM were consistent with my own principles. In the early company, trust, honesty, and personal accountability pervaded the culture. If someone made a commitment, one could depend on that commitment being fulfilled. That culture was the foundation of the company's enduring strengths. It was comfortable to believe in the company and where it was going. I later became disillusioned when it seemed the company was deviating away from that path. It was unsettling to finally realize, as Al Zettlemoyer said, the corporation has no soul.

I was just a small-town naive kid when first stepping in the door of IBM, never having experienced civic and organizational culture outside small town Virginia. The person who returned to the USA in 1997 after five years in Europe was quite different, living in a totally different world, different business environment, different culture, different family. Although facing personal difficulties along the way, I emerged a stronger, more resilient person with close friends and family.

Every era brings its own challenges, its own complexities. We face them with wisdom and emotions shaped by our own unique history, making decisions important and trivial that will determine our future and that of those around us.

The Personal Computer rocked IBM's world in 1981. Yet the company's executive leaders were blind to its implications. With personal computers, individuals and business users no longer had to depend on huge central computers for data processing and support. Small businesses could afford to have data processing in their own locations. Information technology was soon to be available to the masses. While thousands of workers worked every day to build electro-mechanical typewriters, PCs were rapidly becoming the word processors of choice. Yes, "a collection of electronic devices was replacing all that mechanical junk."

In 1965, Gordon E. Moore speculated that the number of transistors on a microchip doubles about every two years, and the cost of computers is cut in half. In the early 70s, I was part of a five-person task force tasked with looking at the impact of that phenomenon on the IBM company. After a couple of months study, we anticipated the day when we could get a whole computer on one or several microchips. We concluded that IBM should reexamine its strategies from top to bottom, to not just follow the trend, but to lead it. Small computers, distributed widely, would be the future marketplace.

When our small team presented the results to a gathering of top executives at one of their strategy sessions, they looked on silently as we spoke showing our projected trend charts. We fielded a few benign questions but could not interpret the group's reactions. When we finished, we were asked to wait outside the conference room for a while.

We waited. And waited.

Finally, the door opened and Spike Beitzel, a senior VP, stepped out, his white hair now atop a blazing red face.

"Are you guys crazy?" he said. "You spent two months studying this, and this is what you came up with? You think semiconductors are going to replace our computer line? What is wrong with you?"

With that, he pivoted, went back into the meeting room closing the door behind him. Aghast, we looked at each other in silence. What the hell? Are we going to be fired?

But nothing happened. We went back to our regular jobs and never heard about the incident again.

The personal computer fulfilled our prediction. But the PC was built on an Intel microchip and on an operating system provided by Microsoft that was then a 32-person company, because IBM did not have the insight or the capability to design and build what small computers needed to succeed or what the new marketplace for information technology required.

As a consequence, IBM began massive layoffs in the late eighties and early nineties. Company leaders always said full employment was a practice, not a policy. During my entire 30 years, there was never a layoff. So, it was a massive shock to long term employees who were laid off or terminated. To them, the IBM belief "respect for the individual" represented hypocritical words. The once hallowed manufacturing plants became hollowed out structures as one by one were being closed down. IBM was becoming a service company, no green walls, no parquet floors, no rough toilet paper, no lines of computers waiting to be tested, no massive retraining to prepare for new technology.

As I look back over the experiences outlined in this book, it's important to realize even small choices can have huge consequences. It pays to slow down, take time to think about consequences on ourselves and others. We will never be able to know all the consequences, but slow deliberate decisions beat snap decisions every time.

Learning from the wisdom of others also helps with those decisions. Self-sufficiency may be important, but it is also destructive if carried too far. Working, living and learning together makes us stronger. Collective wisdom is exponentially stronger than singular wisdom.

Accessing collective wisdom means being open to others, building trust, engaging in crucial conversations, sharing emotions, and being vulnerable. That requires a new kind of self-confidence, a self-confidence wrapped in humility and a willingness to learn. I have learned the skills involved are not learned easily, instead requiring deliberate practice to build new behavioral muscles.

Those skills are particularly important with respect to our partners, spouses or business partners. Choosing the right partner or spouse is certainly the first step but learning and growing together is an essential commitment. All of us change and evolve over time. Those changes can bring two people closer or create insurmountable differences. Joyce and I were evolving in different directions and at different velocities. I was in a fast moving exceedingly complex world of technology and corporate growth while she was fulfilling the traditional role of wife and mother. I dipped a toe into her world on weekends but did not give her the benefit of understanding my life and conflicts. Training and education were survival tools in my corporate role, not a list of initials after my name.

This book has been a study in self-awareness, but it is only a beginning. Finding oneself is a lifetime process, one that requires commitment, openness, and a willingness to learn. Every experience is a learning opportunity: explore, practice. and continually learn.

The organizational turnaround of Sterling Forest, and the accelerated startup of the manufacturing plant in Boulder perhaps deserve their own books. Also, the stories from my last 20 years running a small consulting company could provide many lessons for practitioners. At least one of these will make it to my bucket list. Watch this spot.

# ABOUT THE AUTHOR: GRANT TATE

Grant Tate is a servant leader, transformational coach, and business consultant who helps people learn how to thrive in our chaotic world. He challenges leaders and emerging professionals to answer the questions: Who am I? What am I called to do now? Who am I going to work with to get it done? Grant uses his writing and his role as CEO of Bridge Business Transformations as vehicles to develop strong relationships with clients and friends.

Grant lives in Charlottesville, VA with his wife, Ancolien. His children Laura, Lynn, and David live in the American Northeast and West.

CPSIA information can be obtained
at www.ICGtesting.com
Printed in the USA
LVHW081208150422
716295LV00005B/326